NEW MEXICO
TRAVEL ✦ SMART®

W9-CCF-420

Jemez Mountains

NEW MEXICO

TRAVEL ✦ SMART®

Daniel Gibson

John Muir Publications
Santa Fe, New Mexico

Dedication

This book is dedicated to my father, David E. Gibson III, who first awakened in me an appreciation for the beauty and value of literature.

John Muir Publications, P.O. Box 613, Santa Fe, New Mexico 87504

Printed in the United States of America.
First edition. First printing March 1999.

ISSN 1522-1016
ISBN 1-56261-423-1

Editors: Sarah Baldwin, Elizabeth Wolf
Graphics Editor: Tom Gaukel
Production: Rebecca Cook
Design: Linda Braun, Janine Lehmann
Cover Design: Janine Lehmann
Typesetting: Melissa Tandysh
Map style development: American Custom Maps—Albuquerque, NM
Map illustration: Laura Perfetti
Printing: Publishers Press
Front cover photos: *small*—© Unicorn Stock Photos/Charles E. Schmidt (New
                      Mexico State Capitol Building in Santa Fe)
                      large—© John MacLean Photography (Chaco Canyon National
                      Historic Park)
Back cover photo: © Leo de Wys, Inc./Steve Vidler (Route 66 Diner in
                      Albuquerque)

Distributed to the book trade by
Publishers Group West
Berkeley, California

HOW TO USE THIS BOOK

The *New Mexcio Travel•Smart* guidebook is organized in 16 destination chapters, each covering the best sights and activities, restaurants, and lodging available in that specific destination. Thanks to thorough research and experience, the author is able to bring you only the best options, saving you time and money in your travels. The chapters are presented in geographic sequence so you can follow an easy route from one to the next. If you were to visit each destination in chapter order, you'd enjoy a complete tour of the best of New Mexico.

Each chapter contains:

- User-friendly maps of the area, showing all recommended sights, restaurants, and accommodations.
- "A Perfect Day" description—how the author would spend his time if he had just one day in that destination.
- Sightseeing highlights, each rated by degree of importance: ★★★ Don't miss; ★★ Try hard to see; ★ See if you have time; and No stars—Worth knowing about.
- Selected restaurant, lodging, and camping recommendations to suit a variety of budgets.
- Helpful hints, fitness and recreation ideas, insights, and random tidbits of information to enhance your trip.

The Importance of Planning. Developing an itinerary is the best way to get the most satisfaction from your travels, and this guidebook makes it easy. First, read through the book and choose the places you'd most like to visit. Then, study the color map on the inside cover flap and the mileage chart in the appendix to determine which you can realistically see in the time you have available and at the travel pace you prefer. Using the Planning Map (pages 10–11), map out your route. Finally, use the lodging recommendations to determine your accommodations.

Some Suggested Itineraries. To get you started, six itineraries of varying lengths and based on specific interests follow. Mix and match according to your interests and time constraints, or follow a given itinerary from start to finish. The possibilities are endless. *Happy travels!*

SUGGESTED ITINERARIES

With the *New Mexico Travel•Smart* guidebook you can plan a trip of any length—a one-day excursion, a getaway weekend, or a three-week vacation—around any special interest. To get you started, the following pages contain six suggested itineraries geared toward a variety of interests. For more information, refer to the chapters listed—chapter names are bolded and chapter numbers appear inside black bullets. You can follow a suggested itinerary in its entirety, or shorten, lengthen, or combine parts of each, depending on your starting and ending points.

Discuss alternative routes and schedules with your travel companions—it's a great way to have fun, even before you leave home. And remember: don't hesitate to change your itinerary once you're on the road. Careful study and planning ahead of time will help you make informed decisions as you go, but spontaneity is the extra ingredient that will make your trip memorable.

© Daniel B. Gibson

White Sands National Monument

Best of New Mexico Tour

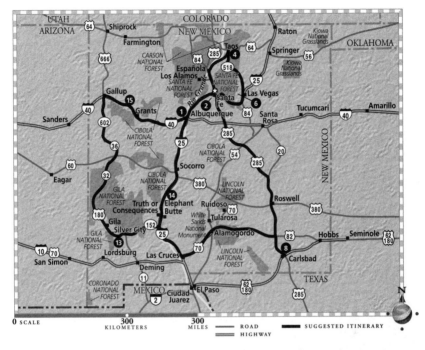

Here are some highlights of the Land of Enchantment, from its historic sites and cultural gems to its astounding natural beauty.

❶ **Albuquerque** (Old Town, Indian Pueblo Cultural Center, Sandia Tramway, Petroglyph National Monument, Rio Grande Nature Center)

❷ **Santa Fe** (Plaza, O'Keeffe Museum, Museum of Fine Arts, Canyon Road, St. Francis Cathedral, Pecos National Monument, Opera)

❹ **Taos** (Martinez Hacienda, Millicent Rogers Museum, San Francisco de Asis, Taos Ski Valley, Rio Grande Gorge Bridge)

❻ **Las Vegas Area** (Fort Union, Historic Districts, mountain villages)

❽ **Southeast Corner** (Carlsbad Caverns, Living Desert State Park, Sitting Bull Falls, Rattlesnake Springs)

⓭ **Gila Country** (Silver City, cliff dwellings, City of Rocks, Catwalk)

⓮ **Middle Rio Grande Valley** (Bosque del Apache, Socorro historic districts, Elephant Butte, ghost towns)

⓯ **Gallup and Grants Area** (Sky City, Chaco Canyon, Zuni Pueblo)

Time needed: 2–3 weeks

Art Lovers' Tour

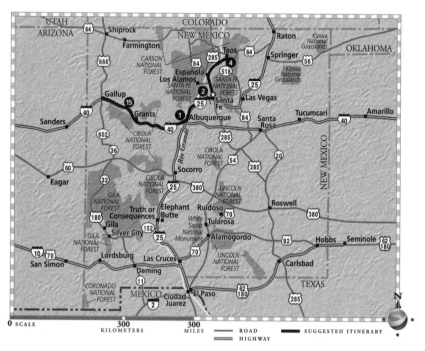

The state's art offerings range from outstanding museums and galleries to Pueblo Indian studios and pawn shops. Check out some of the options.

❶ Albuquerque (Museum of Albuquerque, UNM Museum of Fine Arts, galleries)

❷ Santa Fe (Museum of Fine Arts, O'Keeffe Museum, Institute of American Indian Arts & Culture, Museum of International Folk Art, Wheelright Museum, Museum of Indian Arts, Canyon Road and Plaza area galleries, SITE Santa Fe, Indian Market, Spanish Market)

❹ Taos (Millicent Rogers Museum, Harwood Foundation, galleries, D. H. Lawrence Ranch, Blumenschein Home, Taos Pueblo studios)

⓯ Gallup and Grants Area (downtown pawn shops and galleries, pueblos, Navajo reservation trading posts)
Possible one-day additions: Southeast Corner (Roswell Museum); Las Cruces and the Lower Valley (New Mexico State University Art Gallery); Gila Country (Silver City)

Time needed: 10 days

Hispanic and Indian Cultures Tour

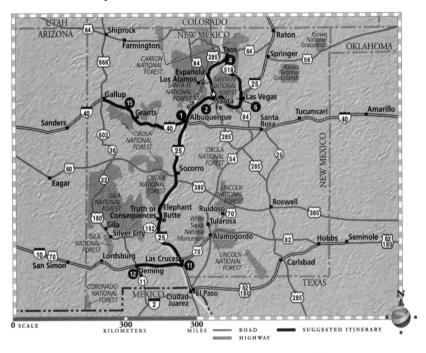

This tour provides insight into both the historic roots and the contemporary centers of Indian and Hispanic culture in New Mexico.

❶ **Albuquerque** (Old Town, Petroglyph National Monument, Indian Pueblo Cultural Center, Albuquerque Museum)

❷ **Santa Fe** (Plaza, St. Francis Cathedral, Museum of International Folk Art, Palace of the Governors, Museum of Indian Arts and Culture, Wheelwright Museum, Las Golondrinas, Pecos National Monument)

❹ **Taos** (Taos Pueblo, Martinez Hacienda, Millicent Rogers Museum, San Francisco de Asis)

❻ **Las Vegas Area** (Fort Union, historic districts, mountain villages)

⓫ **Las Cruces and the Lower Rio Grande Valley** (Mesilla, farm towns)

⓬ **Borderlands** (Pancho Villa State Park)

⓯ **Gallup and Grants Area** (Acoma Pueblo, Zuni Pueblo, El Morro National Monument, Chaco Canyon)

Time needed: 2 weeks

Nature Lovers' Tour

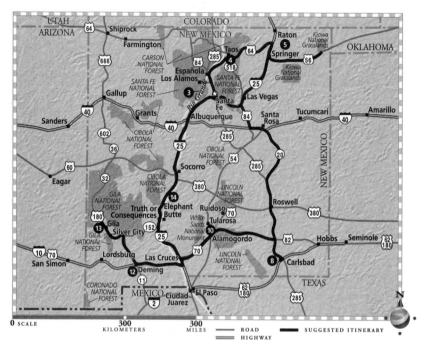

Take a trip focusing on New Mexico's surprisingly diverse and captivating natural attributes, from snow-capped mountain to searing deserts, from caverns and canyons to marshlands covered with snow geese and cranes.

- ❸ **Jemez Area** (Bandelier National Monument, Valle Grande)
- ❹ **Taos** (Rio Grande rafting, Taos Ski Valley, Wheeler Wilderness)
- ❺ **Northeast Corner** (Capulin Volcano National Monument, Mills Canyon, Johnson Mesa, Kiowa National Grasslands, Sugarite Park)
- ❽ **Southeast Corner** (Carlsbad Caverns, Sitting Bull Falls, Living Desert State Park, Dripping Springs)
- ❿ **Alamogordo and the Tularosa Basin** (White Sands, Dog Canyon, Valley of Fires)
- ⓬ **Borderlands** (Rock Hound State Park, Florida Mountains, Red Rock)
- ⓭ **Gila Country** (Gila Wilderness, Catwalk, hot springs, birding)
- ⓮ **Middle Rio Grande Valley** (Bosque del Apache, San Mateos)

Time needed: 2 weeks

Outdoor Recreation Tour

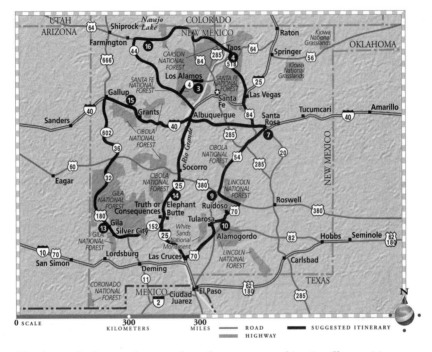

For those who love to do more than observe nature, this trip offers exciting outdoor adventures, from world-class skiing to quiet trout-stream fishing.

- **❸ Jemez Area** (Bandelier National Monument, skiing, hot springs)
- **❹ Taos** (Taos Ski Valley, white-water outings, fishing, hiking, biking)
- **❼ East Central Plains** (Santa Rosa lakes, Manzano Mountains State Park, Ute Lake, Gordon wildlife area, hunting)
- **❾ Ruidoso Area** (skiing, hunting, fishing, hiking)
- **❿ Alamogordo and the Tularosa Basin** (White Sands, hiking, Dog Canyon, Valley of Fires, Three Rivers)
- **⓭ Gila Country** (Gila Wilderness, Catwalk, City of Rocks State Park)
- **⓮ Middle Rio Grande Valley** (Elephant Butte fishing and water sports, Bosque del Apache hiking and birding, Apache Kid Wilderness)
- **⓯ Gallup and Grants Area** (El Malpais, Chaco Canyon, Zuni Mountains)
- **⓰ Northwest Corner** (Navajo Lake, Jicarilla reservation, Chama area fishing and cross-country skiing, Humphries refuge)

Time needed: 2 weeks

Family Fun Tour

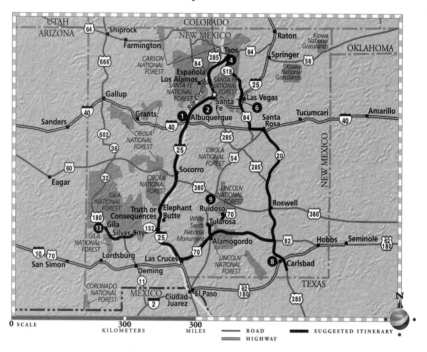

Have the little ones along? No problemo. Here's a list that will entertain and wear out even a hyperactive 10-year-old boy.

- ❶ **Albuquerque** (Rio Grande Zoo, Albuquerque Aquarium, Children's Museum, Sandia Tramway, Museum of Natural History, Indian Pueblo Cultural Center, Rattlesnake Museum, The Beach, Tinkertown)
- ❷ **Santa Fe** (Palace of the Governors, Las Golondrinas, Santa Fe Children's Museum, Santa Fe Southern Railroad, hiking or skiing)
- ❹ **Taos** (Rio Grande Gorge Bridge, Kit Carson Home, Martinez Hacienda, skiing or rafting)
- ❻ **Las Vegas Area** (Fort Union, Las Vegas wildlife refuge, fishing)
- ❽ **Southeast Corner** (Carlsbad Caverns and other caves, Living Desert State Park, Sitting Bull Falls, go-carts)
- ❾ **Ruidoso Area** (skiing, fishing, riding, Lincoln, Sunspot)
- ⓭ **Gila Country** (Gila Cliff Dwellings, Catwalk, Piños Altos)

Time needed: 2 weeks

USING THE PLANNING MAP

A major aspect of itinerary planning is determining your mode of transportation and the route you will follow as you travel from destination to destination. The Planning Map on the following pages will allow you to do just that.

First, read through the destination chapters carefully and note the sights that interest you. Then, photocopy the Planning Map so you can try out several different routes that will take you to these destinations. (The mileage chart in the appendix will help you to calculate your travel distances.) Decide where you will be starting your tour of New Mexico. Will you fly into Albuquerque, or will you start from somewhere else? Will you be driving from place to place or using some other mode of transportation? The answers to these questions will form the basis for your travel route design.

Once you have a firm idea of where your travels will take you, copy your route onto the Planning Map. You won't have to worry about where your map is, and the information you need on each destination will always be close at hand.

Very Large Array radio telescope, plains of San Augustin

Planning Map: New Mexico

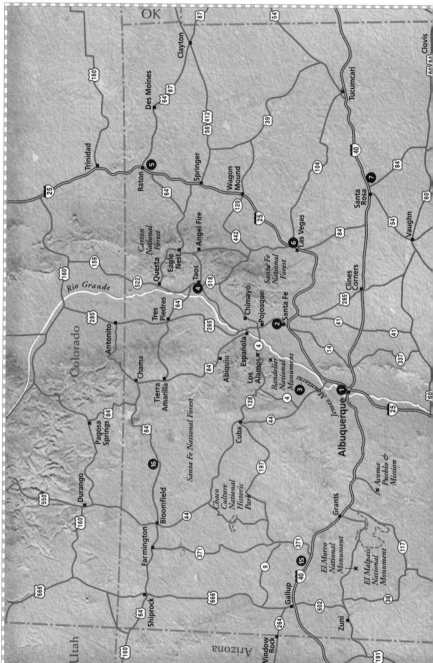

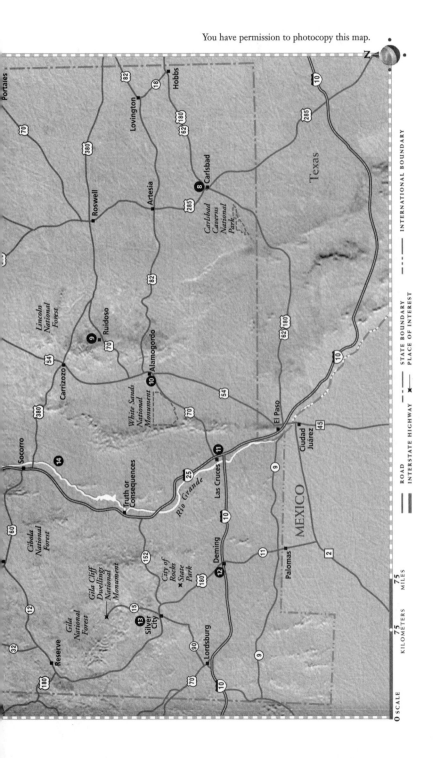

WHY VISIT NEW MEXICO?

New Mexico has been mesmerizing visitors for eons, so much so that is has been called "the Land of Enchantment." Indians came thousands of years ago and stayed. The Spanish arrived expecting to find immense wealth in the form of gold—instead they found dirt, but they too stayed. Travelers speeding across America on I-40 through New Mexico return years later to live here. People come to visit a friend and never leave. Such stories are common here. What is it about this place that casts such a spell?

Most people are seduced first by the state's beauty: huge vistas of mesas, plains, and sky backed by distant blue mountain ranges; green river valleys flanked by rock and earthen deserts; immense thunderheads pouring out veils of rain. This dramatic landscape serves as a backdrop for beauty on a smaller scale—a Pueblo potter delicately smoothing the elastic wall of a pot, a roadside stand displaying brilliant red chile ristras, a mantle of snow draping an adobe wall.

Though these images never lose their charm, the next stage of enchantment comes when you realize that New Mexico's allure extends beyond its postcard appeal to its history and the many ancient cultures that still survive and even thrive here. The bowl of steaming posole has a story to tell; the mariachi band tuning its guitars harkens back to the state's connections with old Mexico; the roaring river saw Hispanic colonists in oxen carts rumble torturously along its banks and Anglo miners pluck mineral wealth from its flanks. That cowboy sipping beer in a bar isn't a marketing ploy, and those colorful pueblo dancers don't exist merely to entertain tourists—they are part of a cultural continuum of many centuries.

Existing side by side with these old ways are jetports, Los Alamos National Laboratory, cutting-edge art galleries, world-class restaurants, modern shopping malls, and frame houses being thrown up as fast as the construction workers' nail guns will shoot. This contrast of the ancient and the modern makes for a lively and unpredictable environment. One can't help feeling that something amazing, wild, and wonderful might be around the next bend in New Mexico. The possibilities seem endless and the promise of discovery assured. In the end, it is a state of mind, not matter, that makes New Mexico so irresistible.

I welcome your arrival and hope this book will help you find what you are looking for. As the Navajos say, "Walk in beauty."

LAY OF THE LAND

The fifth-largest state in the Union, New Mexico has a wildly complex geography. Its convoluted face is crinkled by massive fault lines, upthrust ranges, dropped basins, and volcanic intrusions, and marked by canyons, mesas, buttes, spires, stone arches, and bridges. The land is rarely level. Combine these dramatic landforms with one of the world's clearest and driest atmospheres, enabling views of mountain ranges 120 miles away, and you have a place where the land is preeminent, a powerful and defining force of life in the region.

Most first-time visitors to New Mexico come expecting to find nothing but desert. To be sure, there *are* deserts here: The Chihuahuan Desert, in the state's southeastern and south-central areas, extends up the Rio Grande Valley as far as Socorro, and a piece of the Sonoran Desert is found in the far southwestern corner. But while parts of the state are indeed very dry, and its few major rivers—the Rio Grande, Pecos, Gila, San Juan, and Conchas—are not voluminous, deserts are only part of the landscape.

The state's most prominent landscape feature is probably the broad valley carved by the Rio Grande. This north-south waterway, coursing through the center of the state, has been a travel corridor for ages, a natural gateway from northern Mexico to the underbelly of the Rockies and North America. Its dependable water and moderate climate first attracted Pueblo peoples and then Hispanic colonists. Today it harbors the state's major population centers. Another prominent feature of the state is the Continental Divide, which runs parallel to and west of the Rio Grande from the Colorado line into Mexico. The divide directs streams and rivers to either the Pacific or the Atlantic Ocean.

New Mexico's northern realm is split by finger ranges of the Rocky Mountains, including the Sangre de Cristos—with peaks topping 13,000 feet—and the volcanic highlands of the Jemez. The mountains contain vast pine and quaking-aspen forests and a profusion of streams and small rivers. Ranges running predominately north-south continue through central New Mexico, where they are met by the jumbled mass of mountains in the Gila (HEE-la) country and the Sacramento and Guadalupe Ranges. Along New Mexico's eastern edge are extensive grasslands, where the fringe of the Great Plains sweeps up to mesas and plateaus fronting the major mountain ranges.

The state's northwestern sector is characterized by landforms of the Colorado Plateau, which dominates the Four Corners area. Here you find basins bisected by sheer canyons and plateaus of colorful layers of exposed sedimentary rock. Much of this rock lay on sea floors hundreds of millions of years ago, when the region lay at sea level near the equator. Other plateaus derive from wind-driven dunes here when the region was part of a huge desert. Widespread erosion of these sediments began about 10 million years ago, when the Colorado Plateau was uplifted by continental drift forces.

FLORA AND FAUNA

New Mexico sits at the geographic crossroads of North America. Within its vast expanse merge the Great Plains of the Midwest, the Rocky Mountains and Basin and Range provinces of the north, and the Chihuahuan Desert and a patch of the Sonoran Desert of the south. These distinct ecosystems occur in terrain that runs from 2,842 feet to more than 13,000 feet, which makes for a great diversity of plants and animals, from cactus and rattlesnakes to tundra flowers and black bear. With six of western North America's seven life zones— lower Sonoran, upper Sonoran, transition, mixed coniferous, subalpine, and alpine—New Mexico is home to 145 species of mammals, 92 species of reptiles, 26 species of amphibians, 120 species of fish, and 485 species of birds.

The geography of the state tends to isolate species from each other, with plants and animals marooned on mountain chains separated by desert and canyon lowlands. Temperatures can vary tremendously in areas only miles apart, often because of sun exposure. For this reason, many indigenous plants and animals are adapted to very specific local conditions. For instance, at White Sands National Monument a number of reptiles have evolved into almost all-white species, while their kin at nearby Valley of Fires display black coloration that matches their surroundings.

While New Mexico has been pounded by sheep and cattle grazing, hunting, logging, mining, and other extractive industries for centuries, many parts are still wild places where plants and animals flourish. In fact, except for the extirpation of the grizzly bear and the Mexican wolf (and the latter may be on the way to recovery through a re-introduction program just over the Arizona border), all major native mammals are still here. Many species of plants and animals, however, are endangered—from the rare Gila trout to the Southwest willow flycatcher. A growing appreciation for the region's rich plant and animal heritage may come just in time to stave off its loss.

HISTORY AND CULTURES

New Mexico carries the oldest seeds of civilization in the United States: well over a century before George Washington was chopping down his fabled cherry tree, Spanish colonists and their American-born descendants were strolling through the gates of the Palace of the Governors in Santa Fe. And even further back, while much of North America was under the glaciers of the last ice age some 11,000 years ago, Paleolithic hunter-gathers occupied portions of New Mexico, where the perpetual snows were limited to the high mountains.

Over time, these people, called Paleo-Indians, acquired the secrets of agriculture from Mexican Indian cultures, allowing them to settle into semi-permanent villages, beginning around 500 B.C. Known as the Basketmakers, they lived in pit houses—subterranean pockets carved into the earth and covered with logs and dirt—concentrated in the San Juan River drainage of the Four Corners area.

From around A.D. 500 to 700, this culture made substantial advances, moving into above-ground living quarters, expanding territory and trade networks, and refining their arts and religious rituals. Archaeologists label these people the "Pueblo I" culture, but they are also known as the Anasazi, which is actually a Navajo word for "ancient enemies." (The term "Anasazi" is falling out of favor but is used in this book because of its still-common usage.) Meanwhile, in southern New Mexico a parallel culture, the Mogollon (moe-guh-YONE), emerged.

The period from 900 to 1170 saw the Anasazi culture peak at New Mexico's Chaco Canyon and then mysteriously vanish, along with that of the Mogollons. Why? No one knows for sure, though an extended drought, resource consumption, and the arrival of nomadic, warring people—including the Navajo and Apache—all probably played a role. However, the modern Pueblo Indians of New Mexico, as well as the Hopi of Arizona, have long claimed to be descendants of the Anasazi, whom they prefer to call simply "ancestors." Archaeologists now support this theory.

Between 1200 and 1500 new villages with populations in the thousands began to pop up along the Rio Grande drainage and its tributaries between Taos and present-day Socorro, and from Zuni to

Pecos. Life was good for these Pueblo people, but a tidal shift was about to break over them: *La Encuentra* ("the Encounter"), also known as "Contact."

In 1540 people stood on the rooftops of Zuni Pueblo in west-central New Mexico watching Francisco Vasquez de Coronado lead 300 Spanish soldiers and 800 Mexican Indians and friars toward them in the first major European expedition into what is now the United States. The Zunis resisted his entry, and the pueblo was stormed and taken by the Spanish, setting the tone for an oft-violent relationship. Coronado came seeking gold and other riches comparable to those found in Mexico by earlier conquistadors, but instead he found farming communities with a highly evolved cultural and religious life. Disappointed, Spain and Mexico temporarily turned their backs on the region.

But in 1598 Don Juan de Oñate, a band of Mexican settlers, and Franciscan friars returned to the Rio Grande Valley, lured by its potential for agriculture and for converts to the "One Religion." Near present-day Española, they established the first European colony in what is now the United States: San Gabriel (see Abiquiu scenic route, pages 65–66). The Spanish crown's recognition of the Puebloans as people with souls was a double-edged sword. While other European colonists along the eastern seaboard simply labeled Indians as heathens unworthy of conversion and slaughtered them, here the Pueblo people were allowed to retain their ancestral homes and livelihoods while the priests tried to convert them. Because of this they are one of the few Native peoples never displaced from their lands, and they display a remarkably intact culture. But that's getting ahead of our story.

By the mid- to late 1600s, Hispanic settlements dotted the Rio Grande Valley, and the Pueblo people were reeling under accidentally introduced diseases and the combined oppression of Spanish secular and religious authorities. In 1680 they staged one of only two successful Native revolts ever undertaken on the continent and drove the foreigners out of the area. However, in 1692 Don Diego de Vargas returned—this time for good. The two cultures settled into a relationship that varied—depending on the individuals, political climate, and other circumstances—from extremely close to wary, with a great deal of cross-cultural exchange: from food to language to genes.

Today it's difficult even to imagine the isolation of those early communities. The trade link to Mexico, the Camino Real de Adentro ("Royal Road of the Interior" see Chapter 14 on the Middle Rio Grande Valley) remained the province's tenuous link to civilization, but Spanish authorities had little interest in or resources for its outpost in North America. Hispanic population crept upward; an 1821 census counted only 5,000 people in some 31 villages scattered along the Rio Grande corridor. Meanwhile, French and American trappers *were* interested in the area's bountiful wildlife and their numbers grew. At first they were arrested, but gradually were accepted and even intermarried.

When Mexico broke free of Spain in 1821, New Mexico fell under the authority of Mexico—which also had little interest in its northernmost land. However, Mexican officials did allow American entrepreneurs in Missouri—the closest U.S. lands—to launch wagon trade over a rough track called the Santa Fe Trail. Its trickle of trade became a torrent and proved to be the United States' foot in the Southwest's door. In 1846, at the outbreak of the Mexican-American War, U.S. troops under General Philip Kearny traveled the trail, occupying New Mexico. In 1848 it became part of a U.S. territory that also encompassed Arizona and portions of Utah and Nevada.

Up until this period, non-Indian occupation of most of New Mexico and the Southwest, other than a few missions in southern Arizona, was quite limited because of the fierce resistance of the nomadic Comanche, Ute, Paiute, Apache, and Navajo peoples. The U.S. cavalry, however, broke them in two bitter decades of warfare, and the next wave of change swept over the region, driven in part by a powerful engine—the Iron Horse. The arrival of the rails allowed for ranching, industrial-scale mining, and massive timber harvesting. This flurry of commercial activity led to the founding of many towns during the end of the nineteenth century.

The next chapter is still being written. Much of New Mexico coasted along in slumber until World War II, though it was enlivened by the arrival of artists and early tourists in the 1920s and 1930s in the north-central portion of the state. However, it was the 1940s that ignited an economic spark that still smolders today. Following the establishment of immense U.S. military bases here, small towns such as Albuquerque exploded into cities.

The 1980s and '90s have seen tremendous growth as a result of increased tourism, retirees and telecommuters seeking a home in the sun, and several high-tech corporations moving here. But, even with all the changes, the state's Indian, Hispanic, and Anglo pioneer cultures remain vibrant, subtly informing and transforming new arrivals. The ancient continues to inform the present.

Note: Throughout this book I make many references to "prehistoric" sites and cultures. This rather Eurocentric term simply means all time prior to contact between the Indians and Europeans.

THE ARTS

New Mexico is one of the nation's outstanding art centers—perhaps even the greatest, some might argue, particularly in traditional and indigenous fields. The Pueblo Indians' artistic record goes back thousands of years. The earliest surviving works are the petroglyphs (images pecked into rock) and pictographs (images painted on rock) found across the Southwest, some more than 3,000 years old. Modern Pueblo artisans are noted for their abilities in pottery and jewelry, as well as almost all contemporary arts. They are perhaps the preeminent potters on earth today—no small feat. The Navajos became some of the world's finest weavers and silversmiths in the eighteenth century and continue to produce beautiful silver jewelry, rugs, and tapestries today, as well as some micaceous pottery and notable folk art. Every August in Santa Fe, hundreds of Native artists and craftspeople display their work on and around the Plaza at Indian Market, the largest of its kind in the country.

The Hispanic settlers of New Mexico, cut off from their Mexican roots, had to learn to create almost everything they needed from scratch; they continue to be skilled wood-carvers, tin workers, weavers, furniture makers, and creators of all manner of religious art. Many are also working today in contemporary arts. Though it is not quite as big a deal as Indian Market, Spanish Market, held the last weekend in July in Santa Fe, celebrates Spanish Colonial arts as well as more contemporary work by Hispanic artists of northern New Mexico.

In addition to traditional Indian and Hispanic arts, New Mexico is known for its more recent influx of Anglo artists. Early in the twentieth century, Santa Fe and Taos were "discovered" by eastern seaboard artists fascinated and inspired by the still-flourishing artistic and cultural traditions of its Indian and Hispanic people. These newcomers settled in and spread word to their friends. Most prominent among the "arrivistes" was art patron Mable Dodge Luhan, who brought writer D.H. Lawrence to her home in Taos. Other prominent guests included photographers Ansel Adams and Paul Strand.

Luhan wasn't the only game in town, though. Standard Oil heiress Millicent Rogers became a major benefactor to Hispanic artists, and

Mary Cabot Wheelwright settled in Santa Fe, where she established a remarkable museum based on the work of her friend, Navajo medicine man Hosteen Klah. Wheelwright also owned a beautiful farm near Velarde where painter Georgia O'Keeffe first stayed in New Mexico. O'Keeffe's work continues to popularize northern New Mexico; in 1997 the only museum devoted to her work opened in Santa Fe and immediately became a major attraction. Writer Mary Austin was another prominent Santa Fe resident, who—along with a handful of other writers, poets, and outstanding painters such as Fremont Ellis, John Sloan, Will Shuster, Gerald Cassidy, and Randall Davey—put the small town on the art-world map.

Today people travel to New Mexico from all over the world, drawn by its rich artistic legacy. The making and selling of art has become a mainstay of the state's economy and social fabric. Santa Fe, Taos, Albuquerque, and Gallup are all significant art centers. But many other large towns—particularly Silver City, Española, Las Vegas, Truth or Consequences, and Roswell—lots of small towns, and most Indian pueblos also have surprisingly active arts communities. In Madrid, someone is working on a potter's wheel. In Trampas, a santero is sharpening his whittling knife. In White Oaks, a saddle maker puts away his leather punch. And at Zuni, a silversmith carefully pours liquid silver into his jewelry mold.

CUISINE

New Mexico's cuisine is varied, echoing its mix of cultures. In addition to basic ranch food, heavy on the beef and potatoes, you can find Pueblo Indian food, which mixes both modern American influences like hamburgers and bologna sandwiches with traditional Pueblo and Hispanic elements. Navajo favorites include mutton dishes and frybread. In Santa Fe, Albuquerque, and Taos, you can sample nouvelle cuisine—or New Rancher, Nuevo Southwestern, or whatever they're calling it this month.

In other words, no single culinary style defines the state's cuisine. That said, the food that originated with the melding of the Pueblo Indians and the Hispanic colonists is undoubtedly the most famous. Long called "Mexican food" by outsiders, it is really *New* Mexican, as anyone who has eaten in both places knows. Mexican and New Mexican food do share certain basic ingredients, such as beans and tortillas. They also both feature certain dishes—such as *enchiladas* (tortillas stuffed with meat or cheese, covered in chile and cheese and then baked), *posole* (hominy with meat and chile), and *carne adovada* (pork chunks slow-baked with thick red chile).

But New Mexican food is distinct in a number of ways, mostly in its heavy emphasis on chile, used here extensively and imaginatively. The state has festivals (see Chapter 11, Las Cruces and the Lower Rio Grande Valley) and even a magazine (*Chile Pepper*, based in Albuquerque) devoted to the subject. When you eat out, don't be surprised if your server asks you, "Red or green?" The question refers to red or green chile. They are distinct in taste, look, and tongue-burning quotient, but no hard rules apply to the latter characteristic. By the way, milk is a good antidote for "flame face."

OUTDOOR ACTIVITIES

The geographical, topographical, and climatic variations of the state lend themselves to diverse outdoor activities. Save ocean sports, it's hard to think of a single form of outdoor recreation that's not enjoyed here.

What are the best activities? That would depend on whom you talk to. A skier might extol the feathery powder and plunging ridgelines of Taos Ski Valley or rave about a cross-country trail in the Jemez. A golfer might recall the extremely long drive he hit at The Lodge at Cloudcroft. A hiker might rhapsodize about her ascent of the Truchas Peaks, Whitewater Baldy, or mellower outings. A climber might recall summiting the Organ spires near Las Cruces or looking down on Albuquerque from Sandia Crest. Visions of the wave that flipped the raft in Powerline Falls along the Rio Grande Box might haunt a boater.

You can find trophy trout waters in the San Juan; plains that call out for a fast gallop on a horse; and immense lakes where you can rip huge turns on water skis. Exploring the backcountry on horseback, digging for semiprecious stones, camping out under a pitch-black sky studded with stars, stumbling on an 800-year-old Indian ruin—the list of possible outdoor adventures is almost endless.

Dozens of state parks, a handful of national parks and monuments, national forests, and Bureau of Land Management holdings offer a wealth of outdoor recreation opportunities. Have fun and tread lightly. Further details on these and many other activities are found in the Fitness and Recreation sections of each destination chapter in this book.

PLANNING YOUR TRIP

Knowing when to visit a place is as important as knowing what to see and do once you've arrived. With that in mind, this chapter provides suggestions on timing your trip as well as basic information on weather, local dining and lodging options, budget, and transportation. Because reading about a place before visiting it can enrich your experience, this chapter also includes a discussion of some recommended nonfiction about and fiction set in the area.

WHEN TO GO

When you decide to visit New Mexico depends on what you want to see and do. Many well-known festivals and events—such as Indian Market, Spanish Market, and the Santa Fe Opera—happen during the summer (see the Calendar of Events in the appendix for more information). However, this is prime tourist season, so if you want to avoid crowds, plan a trip during other months. Another highly popular event, the Kodak Albuquerque International Balloon Fiesta, is in October, when the sun shines warmly, the sky assumes a deep turquoise glow, and the world seems to hold its breath awaiting the first winter snow. Around Christmas the air is crisp, the tourists are manageable, and the streets of Albuquerque and Santa Fe are lit with luminarias (also called farolitos, depending on where you are). If you are seeking skiing or other snow activities, prime time falls between early February and Easter.

Consider the state's climate when planning your trip. In general, the further north and the higher in elevation you travel, the cooler and wetter it gets. At 7,000 feet Santa Fe averages 14 inches of moisture a year, the nearby mountains twice that. Most moisture comes in brief, intense summer thunderstorms and occasional winter snowfalls—sustained rain is rare. Snowfall ranges from less than 2 inches a year in the Lower Rio Grande Valley to 300 inches in the highest northern mountains. January and May are the driest months, on average.

Winter, to most people's surprise, can be quite rough and lengthy in New Mexico, especially north of I-40. In Santa Fe, for instance, it can snow as early as September and as late as May. On the other hand, because of the general lack of humidity, high summer temperatures in much of the state are not as uncomfortable as might be expected. However, the areas along the southern border can be brutally hot from late May through mid-September. During any season throughout the state, temperatures usually range 25 degrees or more from night to day; mornings can be chilly even in summer, so dress in layers. And remember, because of the state's high elevation, sunlight is extremely strong here—don't forget sunscreen!

CAMPING, LODGING, AND DINING

In order to appreciate New Mexico fully, it helps to get close to the land, pick up some dust, and maybe wash it off in a river or lake. A steady diet of this will give you a fresh appreciation for a hot shower, a well-prepared meal, and a clean bed. New Mexico offers a range of lodging options, from deluxe hotels and elegant bed-and-breakfasts to simple motels and rustic campgrounds. If you plan to visit in the summer, over Christmas, during spring break, or for major city festivals, reserve accommodations far in advance, even for campgrounds, which can fill up quickly, with alternatives often far away.

You'll find an abundance of excellent dining options in Santa Fe and Albuquerque, and a good range of possibilities in Taos. In addition to the expected New Mexico fare dominated by the ubiquitous chile pepper, Santa Fe has several nationally known restaurants specializing in the latest culinary trends, as well as a handful of good ethnic restaurants. Albuquerque's diversity is even more pronounced, with everything from Jamaican to Vietnamese fare. Befitting its ranching heritage, you can also find good steaks and other meats across the state. And if in dire need, a fast-food joint is almost always at hand.

HOW MUCH WILL IT COST?

Trips for almost any budget are possible in New Mexico. You can stay at posh resorts and rack up substantial bills or camp out and spend little more than gasoline and grocery money—if the weather's right, a night under the stars is the best bargain going. In between these two extremes are many moderate options—for instance, you might find a charming B&B you'll always remember for as little as $60 a night. If you can, sample a variety of accommodations. Santa Fe is the most expensive destination, with meals and lodging running substantially higher than any other sector of the state. Taos and

Albuquerque follow. Outside of these urban areas, prices are quite moderate—even cheap, by national standards.

Since many of the state's prime sightseeing highlights are found inside national parks and monuments, it's a good idea to purchase the Golden Eagle Pass, which costs $50 and provides free admission for a year to almost all national parks and monuments. U.S. residents over 62 can purchase a Golden Age Passport, offering the same benefits, for $10. Either can be obtained at most park and monument visitors centers or admission booths.

Gas will be a major expense if you cover all the destinations described in this book. As the nation's fifth-largest state, New Mexico covers a lot of ground!

TRANSPORTATION

Air service into and within the state is constantly increasing. New Mexico's major jetport is in Albuquerque (the Albuquerque International Sunport), but regular air service is also available in Farmington and Las Cruces, and, on a more limited basis, in Santa Fe, Taos, Carlsbad, Roswell, and Ruidoso. There are also modern airports in Alamogordo, Silver City, Socorro, Gallup, Raton, Las Vegas, and Clovis.

Bus lines crisscross the state, but with many attractions far from cities and towns, and generally limited public transportation within cities, bus travel isn't very practical. Nor is train travel. The region is served by the historic Southwest Chief (operated today by Amtrak), which runs between Chicago and Los Angeles, passing near Santa Fe at the Lamy depot, on through Albuquerque, and westward to Gallup. While this scenic rail line is a great way to arrive, it leaves you without local mobility.

The most practical way to get around New Mexico is with your own set of wheels. A four-wheel-drive vehicle is ideal because it allows you to cut through a winter storm or get off the blacktops onto dirt roads without getting stranded, but a standard road car will do. Rentals are available throughout the state, particularly in large urban centers. Rental RVs are also more and more commonly available, especially in Albuquerque. Rates vary widely, from $380 to $1,100 a week. Winter road travel in New Mexico can be difficult, and summer thunderstorms can also create hazardous conditions, flooding arroyos and bottomlands. To check on road conditions and closures, call 800/432-4269.

RECOMMENDED READING

New Mexico has produced a surprisingly rich body of wonderful literature, both fictional and expository, over the centuries. It's hard to know
where to begin with recommendations that might help visitors better
understand the region, but the following provides a good overview.

Fiction

Willa Cather wrote a beautiful and rich portrait of a thinly disguised
Archbishop Lamy of Santa Fe during the transition from Mexican rule
to U.S. rule in *Death Comes to the Archbishop*. It is one of the most
enduring and popular books set in New Mexico.

Ruth Laughlin produced a fictional account of the life of the
remarkable Dona Tules set in Santa Fe in the 1840s called *The Wind
Knows No Shadow*. Richard Bradford's *Red Sky at Morning* is a very
funny and accurate account of coming of age in Santa Fe during World
War II. Among the late, great Harvey Fergusson's many novels is *Rio
Grande*. Another renowned early author was Eugene Manlove Rhodes,
whose "Pasó por Aquí" is a classic. Another seminal figure in Santa
Fe's literary world was Mary Austin, whose many works include *The
Land of Journey's Ending* and *Land of Little Rain*. Oliver La Farge wrote
a Pulitzer Prize–winning, touching tale of a displaced Navajo youth in
Laughing Boy.

For a magical look at the Indio-Hispanic soul of New Mexico see
Rudolfo Anaya's *Bless Me, Ultima*. John Nichols produced a hilarious,
dead-ringer glimpse into New Mexico of the 1960s and early 1970s in
The Milagro Beanfield War. Frank Waters, one of the Southwest's pre-
mier authors, penned a story set in Taos Pueblo called "The Man Who
Killed the Deer." Edward Abbey got his start in New Mexico with
books including the powerful *Fire on the Mountain* and *The Brave
Cowboy*. Conrad Richter produced a moving portrait in 1936 of the tra-
vails of a ranching family in *Sea of Grass*, a subject explored further in
Riders to Cibola by contemporary author Norman Zollinger.

Tony Hillerman has become a one-man publishing empire with
his carefully researched series of contemporary thrillers set on the
Navajo reservation, including *The Blessing Way*, *Skinwalkers*, and *A
Thief of Time*.

Among the state's many Indian authors is Leslie Marmon Silko.
Her novel *Ceremony* is a moving account of an Indian army veteran

returning to Laguna Pueblo. In a similar vein is *House Made of Dawn*, which secured a Pulitzer Prize for Scott Momaday. Poet Simon Ortiz of Acoma has many fine works; I especially like "Going for the Rain."

Non-Fiction

Great River, which won Paul Horgan the Pulitzer Prize, will undoubtedly remain the primary historical reference for the Spanish Southwest as a whole; it's also an engrossing read.

David Grant Noble is the author of the best overview of the prehistoric Indian ruins scattered across the region: *Ancient Ruins of the Southwest*. For an inside look at the Taos Society of Artists in the 1920s and '30s, see Mabel Dodge Lujan's *Edge of Taos Desert*. A sensitive and evocative look at the lives and customs of a secretive penitent sect of Roman Catholics in New Mexico's small Hispanic communities is found in the great Fray Angelico Chavez' *My Penitente Land*. Read it along with Sabine Ulabari's *My Grandmother Smoked Cigars* and Stanley Crawford's still-resonate *Mayordomo*, about the lives along a small irrigation ditch in north-central New Mexico.

An accurate insight into the state's contemporary Hispanic communities of the Sangre de Cristos is William deBuys' *Enchantment and Exploitation: The Life and Hard Times of a New Mexico Mountain Range*. Speaking for contemporary urban Hispanics is the powerful, insightful, and evocative Jimmie Santiago Baca of Albuquerque; his "Martin & Meditations on the South Valley" is particularly fine.

John Sinclair put together a great collection of true stories about rawhiders and homesteaders in south-central New Mexico in the 1920s in *Cowboy Riding Country*. A look at the fascinating life of Edith Warner, friend to early Los Alamos scientists and Pueblo people, is found in Peggy Pond Church's *House at Otowi Bridge*. A closer look at the making of The Bomb and its creators is found in *The Day the Sun Rose Twice*.

One of the earliest attempts at regional description was written by Charles Lummis during his walk from Cincinnati to Los Angeles in the late 1800s, *The Land of Poco Tiempo*. It begins, "Sun, silence and adobe—that's New Mexico in three words." Even older—in fact it was the first literature penned in America—is *History of New Mexico*, written in 1610 by Gaspar Perez de Villagra.

Many works have been written on the Santa Fe Trail: for a unique perspective read Susan Shelby Magoffin's *Down the Santa Fe Trail and into Mexico*. The state's leading historian today is Marc Simmons; his *Following the Santa Fe Trail* is a great guide to this important route, but all of his work is worthy. For a colorful insight into the region's early trappers and mountain men, see the *Personal Narrative of James O. Pattie*, first released in 1831. Among the many works about the Kid are *Time for Outrage*, by Amelia Bean, and *Billy the Kid: A Short and Violent Life*, by Robert Utley.

New Mexico Place Names by T. M. Pearce is my most-used reference book. You might also want to have a good pair of binoculars and a bird identification book on this journey, as well as field guides to cactus and wildflowers. For getting off the main roads, I suggest the wonderfully detailed atlas *Roads of New Mexico*, by Shearer Publishing of Fredericksburg, Texas.

1
ALBUQUERQUE

The quintessential Southwestern city, Albuquerque is a bit raw and gangly, like an adolescent going through a major growth spurt. Yet, unlike Phoenix or Las Vegas, it is also akin to an old man with a long and colorful past. As the natural gateway into New Mexico, with its busy international airport and two bisecting interstate highways, and as my hometown, it's a logical place to begin our New Mexico tour.

Fueled in part by the computer giant Intel's production plants, Albuquerque is booming, characterized by a young population and a Phoenix-like sprawl beginning to occur at its edges. The center of the state's financial, medical, educational, manufacturing, and retail industries, with a metro area population pushing 650,000, it feels like a new city, but actually it's one of the nation's oldest, founded in the Old Town district in 1706. Like much of New Mexico, the city has a multicultural flavor, with its old Spanish/Hispanic core, the subtle influences of the area's original Indian cultures, and the Anglo elements developed largely since World War II; the people are friendly and unpretentious, and they mix together comfortably.

However, for a modern metropolis, Albuquerque is refreshingly close to nature. From almost anywhere in the city you can see the looming face of the Sandia Mountains, their colors shifting with the light throughout the day. A string of dormant volcanic cones dots Albuquerque's western skyline, and the city is bisected by the green swath of the fabled Rio Grande.

ALBUQUERQUE—OLD TOWN AREA

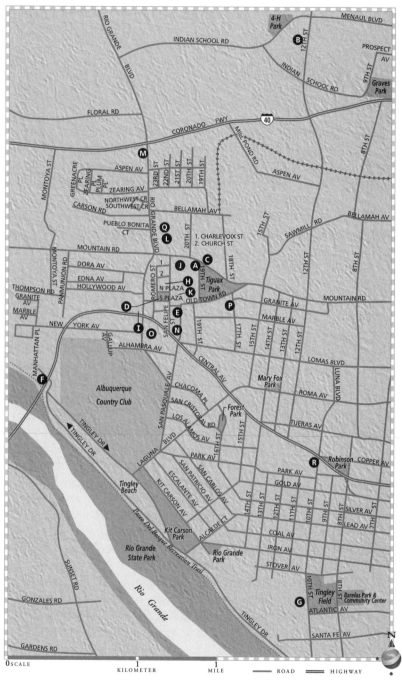

1. CHARLEVOIX ST
2. CHURCH ST

Sights

Ⓐ Albuquerque Museum of Arts, History and Science

Ⓑ Indian Pueblo Culture Center

Ⓒ New Mexico Museum of Natural History

Ⓓ Old Town Plaza

Ⓔ Rattlesnake Museum

Ⓕ Rio Grande Botanic Garden and Albuquerque Aquarium

Ⓖ Rio Grande Zoo

Ⓗ San Felipe de Neri Church

Ⓘ Turquoise Museum

Food

Ⓙ La Crepe Michele

Ⓚ La Placita

Ⓛ Maria Teresa's

Lodging

Ⓜ Best Western Rio Grande Inn

Ⓝ Bottger Mansion

Ⓞ Casas de Sueños

Ⓟ Old Town Bed-and-Breakfast

Ⓠ Old Town Sheraton

Ⓡ Route 66 Hostel

A PERFECT DAY IN ALBUQUERQUE

After an early breakfast at Garcia's Kitchen, visit Petroglyph National Monument on the West Mesa to get an overview of the city and some grounding in its prehistoric past. Then visit Old Town to soak up its Hispanic flavor, shop, visit museums, and have lunch at La Crepe Michele or La Placita. A short drive takes you to the Indian Pueblo Cultural Center for an introduction to the art, culture, and history of the state's 19 Pueblo tribes. End the day with a ride on the tramway to Sandia Crest for a spectacular sunset. Then take a drive through the North Valley to Corrales for dinner at Casa Vieja.

OLD TOWN AREA SIGHTSEEING HIGHLIGHTS

★★★ Indian Pueblo Cultural Center—This is a great place to introduce yourself to New Mexico's Pueblo Indians, arguably the most culturally intact of all the nation's Indian people. The center is owned and run by the Pueblo people themselves, which alone makes it unique. Here you can tour permanent exhibits on the arts and history of each of the 19 different pueblos, see changing contemporary art shows, watch live dances and arts-and-crafts demonstrations on weekends, and even take in a meal, all in the Indian way. The center also houses a children's museum, an excellent gift shop, and a bookstore. *Details: 2401 12th St. NW (a few blocks north of I-40—Exit 157B— at the corner of 12th St. and Indian School Rd.); 505/843-7270 or 800/766-4405. Open daily 9–5:30. $3 for adults, $1.50 for students, children under 6 free. (2 hours)*

★★★ **Old Town Plaza**—Here is where Albuquerque got its start, as a small village founded by Hispanic farmers in 1706. Around the charming, shady plaza—much calmer and prettier than the highly touted central plazas of Santa Fe and Taos—and down side streets perfect for strolling are hundreds of one-of-a-kind retail stores, art galleries, craft shops, tacky-but-fun souvenir dives, and a handful of restaurants. Bargain directly with the Indian arts-and-crafts vendors who display their excellent goods on blankets under the portal on the east side of the Plaza.

On Sundays, **Wild West Shootouts** are held on Romero Street, and on special occasions, mariachi and other music is played on the central bandstand. Christmas Eve is particularly memorable here, as tens of thousands of *luminarias* (votive candles placed in small brown paper sacks with sand in the bottom) are set along walks and walls. The **Old Town Visitors Center** offers tips on the area's attractions and distributes a free walking-tour guide. *Details: Visitors center at 305 Romero St. NW; 505/243-3215. Open Mon–Sat 9–5, Sun 10–5. Free guided walking tours conducted by the Albuquerque Museum (see below) Apr–Oct Tue–Sun 11 a.m. Tours last about an hour. (30 minutes–2 hours)*

★★ **Albuquerque Museum of Arts, History and Science**—This museum houses the nation's largest collection of Spanish Colonial artifacts, including a pair of life-size conquistadors in original chain mail and armor. Interesting photos and artifacts from the city's past accompany major touring exhibitions and excellent historical and contemporary exhibits drawn from the city's vibrant art community. Outside, visit the museum's terrific sculpture garden. *Details: 2000 Mountain Rd. NW (on the eastern edge of Old Town); 505/243-7255. Open Tue–Sun 9–5. Free. (2 hours)*

★★ **New Mexico Museum of Natural History**—This outstanding museum has fascinating and fun displays on the region's prehistoric

critters and landforms, from life-size dinos (including a model of one of the largest specimens ever found) to "erupting" volcanoes. Several beautiful dioramas include one depicting New Mexico in the last ice age, with a real woolly mammoth skeleton beside it. Kids love the Evolator, a shaking, baking box that simulates a descent into the Earth and back in time. The museum also has a decent lunch room, a **Dynamax Theater**, and a great educational gift shop.
Details: 1801 Mountain Rd. NW (on the eastern edge of Old Town); 505/841-2800. Open daily 9–5. 4 adults, $3 seniors, $1 children 3–11. (2 hours)

✫✫ **Rio Grande Botanic Garden and Albuquerque Aquarium**—Opened to great and deserved fanfare in December 1996, this $33-million facility includes 450,000 gallons of exhibition aquariums and 10 acres of landscaped gardens. The gardens and the aquariums portray the life forms of the Rio Grande from the Colorado mountains to the Gulf of Mexico (thus the sharks!), as well as plants native to the Mediterranean, South Africa, Australia, Chile, and world deserts.
Details: 2601 Central Ave. at New York Ave. NW; 505/764-6200. Open daily 9–5. $6 adults, $4 children. (2–3 hours)

✫✫ **Rio Grande Zoo**—A few minutes' drive from the botanic gardens is one of the nation's better mid-sized zoos. Set on 60 acres under ancient, arching river cottonwoods are spacious, naturalistic settings for some 1,300 different species of mammals, reptiles, and birds, including rare lobos (Mexican wolves), California condors (the world's largest flighted bird), orangutans, and buffalo. There's also a rainforest and a wonderful seal tank with underwater viewing ports. The museum has a decent cafeteria, a snack counter, and a gift shop.
Details: 903 10th St. NW; 505/764-6200. Open daily 9–5. $4.25 adults, $2.25 seniors and children. (2 hours)

✫✫ **San Felipe de Neri Church**—On the north side of Old Town Plaza is this attractive, historic 1706 church. The sparse interior has a quiet elegance, with a spiral staircase winding up to a small balcony and an altar with hand-carved *retablos* (carved and painted panels). The church also maintains an attached museum and gift shop.
Details: 2005 N. Plaza, 505/243-4628. Church open daily 7 a.m.–6 p.m., with Sunday mass at 7, 8:30, and 10:15 a.m.; museum open Mon–Fri 1–4, Sat 12–3. Free. (30 minutes)

✯ **Rattlesnake Museum**—Housing the world's largest collection of live rattling snakes from around the Southwest and the world, this private museum in Old Town is popular with kids. The owner stresses the ecological importance of rattlesnakes.
> *Details: 202 San Felipe St. NW; 505/242-6569. Open daily 10 a.m.–9 p.m. in summer, 10–6 otherwise. $2 adults, $1 under age 17. (30 minutes)*

✯ **Turquoise Museum**—This eye-popping small museum displays an amazing array of the state's official gemstone: the sky-matching turquoise. There are immense nuggets, examples of fake turquoise, and samples from different mines worldwide.
> *Details: 2107 Central Ave. NW; 505/247-8650 or 800/821-7443. Open Mon–Sat 9–5. $3. (1 hour)*

GREATER ALBUQUERQUE SIGHTSEEING HIGHLIGHTS

✯✯✯ **Rio Grande Nature Center**—This 270-acre preserve is set amidst the largest river cottonwood forest in the world, stretching along the Rio Grande from Cochiti Pueblo in the north to Socorro in the south. Here, city thoughts quickly disappear. A wonderful nature center is sunk into ground of the *bosque* (Spanish for "woodland"), providing an underwater glimpse into a wetland pond where migratory ducks bob for food and turtles dive. A foot trail winds through the forest and along the great irrigation channel locals call the Clear Ditch.
> *Details: 2901 Candelaria Rd. NW (off Rio Grande Blvd. NW); 505/344-7240. Open daily 9–5. $4.25 adults, $2.25 under age 16. (1–2 hours)*

✯✯✯ **Sandia Mountains**—Rearing up in the east like a wave whose colors and form constantly shift with the light, the Sandias are Albuquerque's ever-changing artistic canvas. Their name is Spanish for "watermelon," a color they often assume at dusk. They offer both a visual orientation for the city and a nearby getaway for walks, hiking, picnicking, skiing, bird watching, and other outdoor activities.

The **Sandia Peak Aerial Tramway** rises some 3,000 feet up the fractured western face of the Sandias in a ride that thrills both kids and adults. One of North America's longest cable tramways, it requires at least 90 minutes for a round-trip, more if you plan to walk one of the rim trails. You can also drive to **Sandia Crest** via NM 536, a national scenic byway, which cuts off of NM 14 (see the Turquoise Trail scenic route, described at the end of this chapter). From the summit, at an elevation of 10,678 feet, you seem to see half of New Mexico: 125-mile views in all directions are often possible. The rim is frequently 30 to 40 degrees cooler than town, a welcome break in summer or a teeth-chattering encounter in winter, so dress appropriately. The **Sandia Crest House**, 505/243-0605, carries snacks, sandwiches, and small gifts. The Crest also hosts the Steel Forest, one of the world's greatest concentrations of radio and television antennas in the world—not the place to be in a summer lightning storm! A number of cars have also had their car alarms go wacky here, in some cases shutting down their ignition systems. Know how to override your car's security system.

Details: *For driving directions, see the scenic route described at the end of this chapter. To get to the tram's base station, take I-25 north to Tramway Blvd., head east to Tramway Loop, and turn left; 505/856-7325. Hours of operation shift seasonally; call ahead. Round-trip ticket $13.50 adults, $11.50 kids. Additional information on the Sandias is available from the Cibola National Forest, 505/842-3292, or the Sandia Ranger Station, located in Tijeras village on NM 337, 505/281-3304. (1–3 hours)*

✹✹ **Petroglyph National Monument**—Long before there was an Albuquerque, Indian people recorded their habitation and travel on the dark basalt rock cliffs and boulders of the West Mesa in one of the world's greatest assemblages of petroglyphs. Among the 15,000 or so drawings pecked into the dark surface of boulders and cliff overhangs are a tropical parrot, reflective of prehistoric trade with Mexico; spirals believed to represent the cosmos or eternity; and the hunchbacked flute-player Kokopelli, a god of fertility and frivolity. The images span more than 3,000 years, including some rare Spanish and Territorial period petroglyphs.

Details: *4735 Unser Blvd. NW; 505/839-4429. Take I-40 west over the Rio Grande to NM 448, then a left off Coors onto Unser Blvd. Open daily 8–5. $1 per car weekdays, $2 weekends. (2 hours)*

✹ **National Atomic Museum**—This unique tribute to technology will either thrill or appall you, depending on your view of nuclear energy and weaponry. It includes replicas of Fat Man and Little Boy, the bombs dropped on Hiroshima and Nagasaki. *Ten Seconds That Shook the World*, about the making of the atomic bomb, is shown four times daily.

Details: Kirtland Air Force Base, through the Wyoming Blvd. gate; 505/284-3243. Open daily 9–5. Free. (1 hour)

✧ **University of New Mexico Art Museum**—Believe it or not, this relatively small institution houses one of the nation's better photo collections, including both American and world masters, in many photographic and print media. It also hangs ambitious, often-excellent, changing fine art exhibitions, as well as faculty and student shows. *Details: Fine Arts Building next to Popejoy Hall, just off Central Ave. at Cornell Dr.; 505/277-4001. Open Tue–Fri 9–4, Sun 1–4, closed Sat. Admission by donation.* (1 hour)

KIDS' STUFF

Kids particularly like the already-noted Museum of Natural History, Rattlesnake Museum, Rio Grande Zoo, Rio Grande Botanic Garden and Albuquerque Aquarium, and the dances at the Indian Pueblo Cultural Center. Also popular are Petroglyph National Monument, the Sandias, and Rio Grande Nature Center. The **Albuquerque Children's Museum**, 800 Rio Grande Blvd. NW, 505/842-5525, within a shopping arcade attached to the Old Town Sheraton, is also outstanding. In the summer heat there's **The Beach**, 3 Desert Surf Circle at Montaño and I-25, 505/345-6066. Outside of town, on the Turquoise Trail, is the **Tinkertown Museum** (see Turquoise Trail senic route, below).

FITNESS AND RECREATION

Albuquerque has a host of outdoor recreation possibilities, as well as many public and commercial fitness centers. Walking, biking, and jogging trails can be found along the forested Rio Grande valley floor and in the foothills of the Sandias. A five-mile public asphalt trail in the valley, **Paseo del Bosque** is a great place to stretch your legs or ride a bike. Bike rentals and guided tours can be secured at **Old Town Bicycles**, 2209-B Central Ave. NW, 505/247-4926.

On the city's eastern edge is **Elena Gallegos-Simms Park**, 505/291-6224, a 640-acre preserve of lovely grasslands overlooking the city, set beneath the towering Sandias, with hiking, biking, and picnic areas. The **Domingo Baca Trail** leads to an area frequented by mule deer. Its water tank with a blind is a good place to view bird life. The park entrance is on the east side of Tramway Boulevard, about ⅛-mile north of Montgomery Boulevard. It's open from seven in morning to nine at night in summer, seven to seven otherwise.

The **Sandias** offer wonderful short to multi-day hikes, both along the high rim (good in summer) and at lower elevations close to the city (good in winter). A terrific seven-mile hike can be had on **La Luz Trail**, which switchbacks up from high desert terrain in the foothills to subalpine forests at the summit, opening up views of the Rio Grande Valley below. Ideally, you'd have a car waiting for you at the Crest. Be sure to bring along your own water, and be extremely alert for ice on the trail, even in spring. To get to the trailhead, take I-25 north to the Tramway Exit and head east; at the first left turn, proceed on Forest Service Road 444, which runs to the trail parking lot. For additional trail information, contact the **Sandia Ranger Station**, 505/281-3304.

In winter, the wedge-shaped range also provides for cross-country and downhill skiing on its eastern slope at **Sandia Peak Ski Area**, 505/242-9133, a small but surprisingly good beginner/intermediate area that receives more than 100 inches of snow a year. I stepped into cable bindings for the first time here in 1961, and the mountain has introduced thousands to the sport before and since. Weekends can be quite crowded in nice weather. In summer, you can rent mountain bikes at the ski area; the chairlift operates from 10 a.m. to 4 p.m. on weekends.

If you like horseback riding, check out **Sandia Trails**, 10601 Fourth St. NW, 505/281-1772, in the valley, or **Turkey Track Stables**, 1306 U.S. 66 East, Tijeras, 505/281-1772, in the Manzano Mountain foothills.

The city also maintains four public golf courses, numerous indoor and outdoor pools, and tennis courts. For details on city walking and biking trails or these other activities, call the **Albuquerque Cultural and Recreation Services Department**, 505/768-3550.

SPECTATOR SPORTS

Albuquerque *loooves* its sports. Especially popular are the **University of New Mexico Lobos**, 505/277-2116 or 800/905-3315, in particular their basketball games in the infamous 18,000-seat Pit at the corner of University Boulevard and Avenida César Chavez. It's also hard to beat a summer night at the **Albuquerque Dukes'** baseball stadium, 1601 Avenida César Chavez, 505/243-1791, with a soft breeze accompanying the crack of bat on ball. This is the Los Angeles Dodgers' Triple-A farm team; Orel Hershiser is an alumnus.

The city is also home to the world's largest hot-air balloon gathering, the **Kodak Albuquerque International Balloon Fiesta**. Held annually from the first through the second weekends in October, it draws more than 850 balloonists from across the globe. Highlights are the weekend morning mass ascensions and the Special Shapes events, when balloons of almost every imaginable form—hot dogs, wine bottles, rolled-up newspapers, castles, pigs, and spaceships—take to the air. The $4 admission allows you to wander among the launching balloons. With more than 1.5 million spectators, finding a room or dining reservation in the city on short notice is almost impossible. Shuttle buses run between major hotels and the site. For information, call 888/422-7277 or visit the Web site at www.aibf.org.

FOOD

Albuquerque may not be a dining mecca, but its sheer size and growing sophistication provide it with an ample selection of restaurants. Right on the Plaza is **La Placita**, 206 San Felipe St. NW, 505/247-2204, serving traditional New Mexican dishes, plus a wide selection of American dishes including fine steaks, with a full bar. The wonderful building dates to 1706. Also exuding historic flavor is **Maria Teresa's**, 618 Rio Grande Blvd. NW (next to the Old Town Sheraton), 505/242-3900. This national landmark property serves pricey but delicious Continental specialties as well as New Mexican fare and features a pleasant courtyard. **La Crepe Michele**, 400 C-2 San Felipe St. NW (tucked into the intimate Patio del Norte), 505/242-1251, is an excellent French bistro offering something different for those burned out on chile. Its proximity to San Felipe de Neri church precludes liquor.

For some excellent New Mexican food outside the plaza area, check out the **M&J Sanitary Tortilla Factory**, 403 Second St. SW, 505/242-4890, which supplies Air Force One with takeout. They have incendiary salsa and the best sopaipillas in the state. Another locally beloved spot is **Garcia's Kitchen**, 1113 N. Fourth St. NW, (505) 247-9149. You won't believe the oddball collectible decor. A seat at the counter provides quick service, or dive into a booth and dig into a bowl of steamy *carne adovada* (pork marinated in red chile) with a fried egg for breakfast. It's guaranteed to clear the cobwebs!

In Nob Hill, a popular shopping and nightlife district, many a revealing comment has been dropped around the animated tables of **Scalo Northern Italian Grill**, 3500 Central Ave. SE, 505/255-8781. Meals range from salmon salads to veal scaloppine with toasted almonds and cranberries. Elsewhere in the city, locals head to the **Artichoke Café**, 424 Central Ave. SE, 505/243-0200, a saucy little bistro, for some of the city's best French, new American, and Italian fare, such as grilled duck or pumpkin ravioli with fresh spinach. It's open for lunch and dinner daily, except Sundays.

Oasis, 5400 San Mateo, 505/884-2324, presents modestly priced fine Greek and Mediterranean food, including dolmas, spanikopita, Greek salads, moussaka, and skewered lamb. A relatively new arrival is the **Jamaican Grill**, 5555 Zuni SE, 505/265-5816, with spicy fare down tradewinds way: jerk plates, brown chicken stew, and mango sorbet. For a meal in a genuine, 1930s-era diner, drop into the **Tic Toc**, 601 Osuna NE, 505/345-0202.

Outside Albuquerque, my favorite local restaurant is in the charming village of Corrales: **Casa Vieja**, 4541 Corrales Rd., 505/898-7489. Housed in a building almost three centuries old, its small dining rooms, several with fireplaces, envelop one in the relaxing atmosphere of old New Mexico. The French and northern Italian food is outstanding, as is the service. A jacket and tie are required. Not open for lunch. In nearby Bernalillo is the less expensive but outstanding **Range Café**, 264 Camino del Pueblo (the main drag), 505/867-1700, with meatloaf like Mom used to cook, all fresh ingredients, and excellent breads, pastry, breakfasts, and desserts.

LODGING

The city and surrounding area have a diverse selection of accommodations, ranging from all the major brand-name hotels and motels to many one-of-a-kind bed-and-breakfasts.

The nicest of the corporate hotels is the four-diamond **Hyatt Regency**, 330 Tijeras Ave. NW, 505/842-1234. Located downtown, it's popular with business travelers and has a slick art deco interior and restful ambiance. Within it is a good restaurant, McGraths's, an outdoor pool, health club, and shopping arcade. Rates are $135 to $175. While not as fancy as the Regency, the **Old Town Sheraton**, 800 Rio Grande Blvd. NW, 505/842-9863, is a nice place offering accommodations close to Old Town, museums, the North Valley, and downtown. Amenities

ALBUQUERQUE

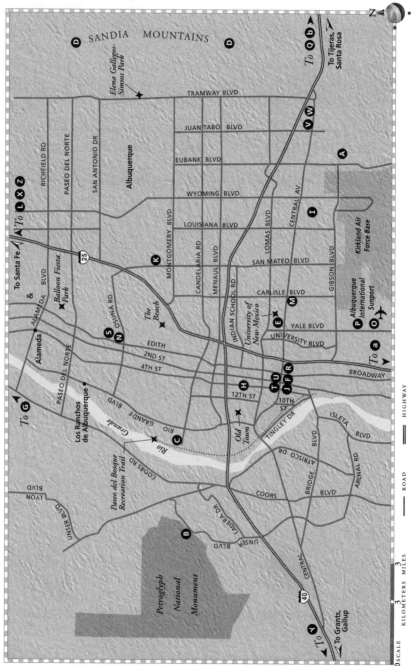

SANDIA MOUNTAINS

Elena Gallegos–Simms Park

TRAMWAY BLVD

JUAN TABO BLVD

EUBANK BLVD

WYOMING BLVD

Albuquerque

RICHFIELD RD

PASEO DEL NORTE

SAN ANTONIO DR

LOUISIANA BLVD

MONTGOMERY BLVD

CANDELARIA RD

MENAUL BLVD

CENTRAL AV

LOMAS BLVD

SAN MATEO BLVD

CARLISLE BLVD

Kirkland Air Force Base

To Santa Fe

To Santa Fe &

Balloon Fiesta Park

ALAMEDA BLVD

Alameda

OSUNA RD

The Beach

PASEO DEL NORTE

EDITH

2ND ST

4TH ST

INDIAN SCHOOL RD

University of New Mexico

YALE BLVD

UNIVERSITY BLVD

GIBSON BLVD

Albuquerque International Suport

To G

Los Ranchos de Albuquerque

GRANDE BLVD

RIO GRANDE BLVD

12TH ST

Old Town

TINGLEY DR

10TH ST

BROADWAY

To a

Paseo del Bosque Recreation Trail

Rio Grande

COORS RD

ISLETA BLVD

ATRISCO DR

BRIDGE BLVD

ARENAL RD

LYON BLVD

UNSER BLVD

LADERA DR

UNSER BLVD

COORS BLVD

Petroglyph National Monument

CENTRAL

To Grants, Gallup

To Tijeras, Santa Rosa

To Tijeras, Santa Rosa

0 SCALE   3 KILOMETERS   3 MILES

ROAD   HIGHWAY

Sights

Ⓐ National Atomic Museum

Ⓑ Petroglyph National Monument

Ⓒ Rio Grande Nature Center

Ⓓ Sandia Mountains

Ⓔ University of New Mexico Art Museum

Food

Ⓕ Artichoke Café

Ⓖ Casa Vieja

Ⓗ Garcia's Kitchen

Ⓘ Jamaican Grill

Ⓙ M&J Sanitary Tortilla Factory

Ⓚ Oasis

Ⓛ Range Café

Ⓜ Scalo Northern Italian Grill

Ⓝ Tic Toc

Lodging

Ⓞ Best Western Wyndham Albuquerque Hotel

Ⓟ Comfort Inn

Ⓠ Elaine's

Ⓡ Gas Light

Ⓢ Hacienda Antigua

Ⓣ Hyatt Regency

Ⓤ La Posada de Albuquerque

Ⓥ Motel 6

Camping

Ⓦ Albuquerque KOA Central

Ⓧ Albuquerque North KOA

Ⓨ American RV Park

Ⓩ Coronado State Monument

ⓐ Isleta Lakes

ⓑ Turquoise Trail Campground

include two on-site restaurants, an outdoor pool with a hot tub, and the attached Albuquerque Children's Museum. Rates are $100 to $120.

Also downtown is the charming **La Posada de Albuquerque**, 125 Second St. NW, 505/242-9090 or 800/777-5732. Opened in 1939 by New Mexico native Conrad Hilton (see Chapter 14, the Middle Rio Grande Valley) as his first endeavor outside of Texas, it is now an independent property undergoing a $4.5-million expansion to add a six-floor, 90-room tower. The hotel's older section boasts many attractive features, from murals to architectural elements, reflecting the early decades of Southwestern tourism. The on-premises Conrad's restaurant features good food from the Mexican Yucatán region. Rates are $69 to $115.

At the airport is **Best Western Wyndham Albuquerque Hotel**,

2910 Yale Blvd. SE, 505/843-7000 or 800/227-1117, which completed an $8-million renovation in 1997; rooms are $89. The **Comfort Inn**, 2300 Yale Blvd. SE, 505/243-2244 or 800/221-2222, has rooms for less than $65 a night. Another mid-priced option is the **Best Western Rio Grande Inn**, 1015 Rio Grande Blvd. NW, 505/843-9500 or 800/959-4726, offering easy access to the Old Town area, rooms with handmade furniture and local art, a laundry facility, and dining at the Albuquerque Grill. Rates are $88.

Among the cheapest accommodations is the **Route 66 Hostel**, 1012 Central Ave. SW, 505/247-1813, with dormitory bunk beds at $12 for members, $14 for nonmembers. Central Avenue has a slew of cheap motels, including the **Gas Light**, 601 Central Ave. NE, 505/242-6020, with doubles for around $30. On the far eastern edge of town is one of several **Motel 6**s, 13141 Central Ave. NW, 505/294-4600, with rooms for $36.

If you dare to leave the beaten path, you'll find many excellent and unusual bed-and-breakfasts in and around Albuquerque. Within Old Town is the **Bottger Mansion**, 110 San Felipe St. NW, 505/243-3639, a historic and handsome American foursquare home built in 1912. Victorian-era rooms have original pressed-tin ceilings and roomy brass beds. Try the breakfast burritos smothered in green chile. Rates are $79 to $139.

Adjacent to Old Town in the Country Club district, **Casas de Sueños**, 310 Rio Grande Blvd. SW, 505/247-4560 or 800/242-8987, has 17 comfortable casitas that ramble over two acres dotted with gardens, patios, and fountains. Some feature fireplaces, kitchens, and private hot tubs. Rates are $90 to $250. The **Old Town Bed-and-Breakfast**, 707 17th St. NW, 505/764-9144, is on the edge of Old Town in a quiet residential neighborhood. Built by adobe residential design pioneer Leon Watson, this comfortable residence has one outstanding new suite with a kiva fireplace, and an inexpensive, small but pleasant second-floor room with good views. Rates are $65 to $80.

Out in the pastoral, cottonwood-shaded North Valley, you'll find the 200-year-old **Hacienda Antigua**, 6708 Tierra Dr., 505/345-5399 or 800/201-2987. The building features a lovely courtyard with gardens and a pool. A hearty Southwestern breakfast is served. Rates are $105 to $160.

To the east of the city, on the "backside" of the Sandias and along the Turquoise Trail (see the scenic route described below), is **Elaine's**, 72 Snowline Rd., Cedar Crest, 505/281-2467 or 800/821-3092, a three-story log structure with massive stone fireplaces that perfectly suits its mountain setting. Rates are $80 to $90.

CAMPING

Several commercial campgrounds in and near town include the **Albuquerque KOA Central**, 12400 Skyline Rd. (Exit 166 off I-40 on the city's eastern edge), 505/296-2729, with 169 RV sites, 30 tent sites, and 16 cabins. Amenities are hot showers, LP gas, a grocery and pool, and miniature golf; however, you'll find little shade in summer. **Albuquerque North KOA**, 555 Hill Rd., 12 miles north of the city in Bernalillo, 505/867-5227 or 800/624-9767, has 57 RV sites and 36 tent sites, an outdoor café, horseshoes, and a heated pool. Another option is **American RV Park**, 13500 Coronado Freeway SW (at the top of Nine-Mile Hill, Exit 149 off I-40), 505/831-3456 or 800/282-8885, with 184 full hookup sites, pool, and food store.

Out of town, **Isleta Lakes**, 15 miles south of Albuquerque at Isleta Pueblo (take I-25 Exit 215 south onto NM 47), 505/877-0370, has 40 RV sites and 100 tent sites next to fishing and boating lakes, along with hot showers and grocery and laundry facilities. **Turquoise Trail Campground**, 22 Calvary Rd., in the Sandias at Cedar Crest (head east on I-40 15 miles to Exit 175, then follow NM 14 north for 5 miles), 505/281-2005, has 57 RV sites and two tent sites. **Coronado State Monument**, 14 miles north of Albuquerque in Bernalillo, 505/867-5351, has 24 sites and showers. The closest Forest Service campgrounds are in the Manzano Mountains, almost an hour from central Albuquerque. Primitive camping is allowed, however, in the Sandias; for details, call the Sandia Ranger Station, 505/281-3304.

NIGHTLIFE

Surprisingly, Albuquerque hosts many cultural groups and events. To find out more about these events, call the **New Mexico Symphony Orchestra**, 505/881-9595; **Albuquerque Civic Light Opera**, 505/345-6577; **Albuquerque Little Theater**, 505/242-4750; or the bilingual drama troupe **La Compania de Teatro de Albuquerque**, 505/242-7929. For events in the University of New Mexico's fine **Popejoy Hall**, call 505/851-5050 or 800/905-3315.

The city has two main entertainment areas: downtown along

Central Avenue, and the Nob Hill district. In the downtown area is the **KiMo Theater**, 423 Central Ave. NW, 505/848-1370, a former movie palace of fantastic Pueblo Deco design that now hosts live music, dance, performance, and other cultural events. It's usually open for free tours during the day. **La Posada de Albuquerque**, 125 Second St. NW, 505/242-9090, a historic hotel (see Lodging, above), has a lobby bar that features jazz and blues on weekend nights and piano on weekdays. Also downtown, **The Zone** and **Z-Pub**, 120 Central Ave. NE, 505/343-7933, present live shows occasionally. At the **Launchpad**, 618 Central Ave. SW, 505/764-8887, you can hear local and touring bands in a space-age environment. The venerable **El Rey** and **Golden West Saloon**, both on Seventh and Central, 505/764-2624, offer live music and atmosphere.

In Nob Hill, **Pulse**, 4100 Central Ave. SE, 505/255-3334, caters to the gay and gay-friendly crowd with occasional touring shows and the city's cutting-edge DJs. This is also ka-boy country; don't miss one of the West's longest-running pointy-toed shuffle spots, with more than 30 years of service, the **Caravan East**, 7605 Central Ave. NE, 505/265-7877, offering two live bands a night and a free buffet and half-price drinks during the 4:30-to-7 p.m. happy hour. The state's best comedy club, **Laff's**, 3100 Juan Tabo NE, 505/296-5653, is also a full-service restaurant and bar.

There are also a number of Indian casinos just outside Albuquerque, all offering poker, blackjack, craps, roulette, slots, and Bingo. To the south at 11000 Broadway SE (take I-40 south to Exit 215) is the **Isleta Gaming Palace**, 505/869-2614 or 800/460-5686; to the northwest of Bernalillo on NM 44 is the **Santa Ana Star**, 505/867-0000.

Scenic Route: The Turquoise Trail

You can zip up I-25 from Albuquerque to Santa Fe in about an hour. It's actually a beautiful drive; I've done it countless times, and it still holds my attention. But if you're looking to get off the beaten track and see a slice of life in rural New Mexico, check out the Turquoise Trail. It's dotted with ghost towns that are springing back to life, old mines, and landscapes that vary from bone-dry flats to piñon-juniper hill country.

From the "Big I" in Albuquerque (where I-40 and I-25 intersect), head east 15 miles on I-40 to the village of **Tijeras** and take Exit 175. Turn north (left) onto NM 14. Six miles up the road in Sandia Park, past the small rural communities of San Antonio, Cedar Crest, and **Cañoncito,** you'll pass the turnoff to NM 536, a **National Scenic Byway** that winds through lovely forests to **Sandia Crest.**

You may want to make a quick detour here to visit the charming **Tinkertown Museum,** featuring an immense, animated Western town and circus carved entirely out of wood. Tinkertown is open April to October daily from 9 to 6. Admission is $2.50 for adults and $1 for

THE TURQUOISE TRAIL

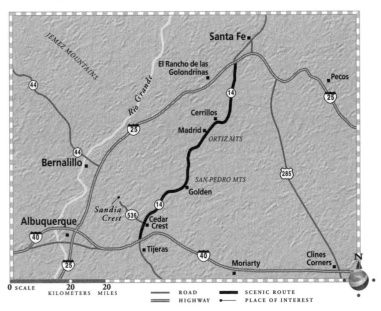

children. To get there, turn left off NM 14 at the Triangle Grocery Store, head up the road leading to Sandia Peak (NM 536), and follow the signs.

Back on NM 14 North, just a shout down the road, is **Pete's Mexican Restaurant** (a favorite with the locals). Next you'll roll on into tiny **Golden**. It sits in the foothills of the nearby **San Pedro Mountains**, site of the first gold strike (1825) west of the Mississippi. There's a rock shop, mercantile store, and pretty **St. Francis of Assisi** adobe church built in the 1830s. **La Casita**, the shop at the north side of town, serves as the unofficial information center.

Outside of Golden, you'll ascend a narrow pass through the mountains and then descend into a valley with breathtaking views toward Santa Fe. At the bottom of the valley lies the small, funky village of **Madrid**, a thriving coal-mining company town in the 1800s, with 2,500 residents. By the early 1960s it was almost totally abandoned, but by the end of the decade, it was reoccupied by hippies and today is home to many artists and craftspeople. On its main street you'll find the venerable **Mine Shaft Tavern**, which fronts the **Old Coal Mine Museum**, both 505/473-0743, where you can tour an underground mine. Also adjoining is the **Engine House Theate**r, 505/438-3780, which presents summer melodramas. If you have time, explore Madrid's many shops; but if you have only a few minutes, make sure you stop at **Primitiva**, specializing in Mexican furniture and crafts, located on the town's main street.

Last stop is **Cerrillos**, an 1880s boom town of silver, gold, and turquoise mines. Several film projects have been shot here (*Young Guns* and *Lonesome Dove* among them), and it harbors a few interesting shops, including **Casa Grande**, 505/438-3008, which contains mining exhibits, a gift shop, and a petting zoo. Between Cerrillos and Santa Fe on NM 14 is an area called **Garden of the Gods**, where beautiful sandstones have been stood on end by New Mexico's various uplifts. You can pull off the road at a turnout to marvel at these incredible rocks. NM 14 hits I-25 on Santa Fe's southern edge. The entire drive, without stops, takes about 90 minutes. For additional information write P.O. Box 303, Sandia Park, 87047. ◼

2
SANTA FE

S anta Fe has been described as America's most foreign capital, and with good reason. Founded circa 1608 as the political capital of what was once the northernmost province of New Spain, with territory encompassing almost all of the American Southwest, the city has a rich history resulting from the complex interplay of Indians, the Hispanic descendants of the Spanish and Mexican colonialists, and the Anglo or "gringo" influx that began in the mid-1800s.

This tricultural mix has created a vibrant city with a distinctive architecture and a flourishing arts scene that encompasses everything from opera to ethnic arts to haute cuisine. At the city's many outstanding museums, one can explore the region's Indian and Hispanic cultures and crafts, folk art from around the world, and some impressive modern art, including the work of Georgia O'Keeffe, whose desert landscapes are often seen as synonymous with northern New Mexico.

Above all, Santa Fe is beautiful: sitting at an elevation of 7,000 feet, with mountains at its back climbing to almost 13,000 feet, the city has an invigorating climate with four distinct seasons (including surprisingly cold, snowy winters). The high, generally dry climate gives the air a clarity and sparkle that is, well, enchanting. To the west and south, plateaus descend in steps to great dry basins, their distant edges 100 miles away punctuated by sawtooth mountain ridges. Visitors should make a point to get out of town and see some of the lovely countryside, pocketed with Indian ruins, pretty valleys with cool rivers running through them, Hispanic villages, and other hidden treasures.

DOWNTOWN SANTA FE

Sights

Ⓐ Canyon Road

Ⓑ De Vargas Street

Ⓒ Georgia O'Keeffe Museum

Ⓓ Institute of American Indian Arts Museum

Ⓔ Loretto Chapel

Ⓕ Museum of Fine Arts

Ⓖ Palace of the Governors

Ⓗ The Plaza

Ⓘ St. Francis Cathedral

Food

Ⓙ Anasazi Restaurant

Ⓚ Bistro 315

Ⓛ Bert's Burger Bowl

Ⓜ Carlos' Gospel Café

Ⓝ Cowgirl Hall of Fame

Ⓞ Coyote Café

Ⓞ Coyote Cantina

Ⓠ Dave's Not Here

Ⓡ Geronimo

Ⓢ Il Piatto

Ⓣ India Palace

Food *(continued)*

Ⓤ La Casa Sena

Ⓥ La Choza

Ⓦ The Palace

Ⓧ Pasqual's

Ⓨ Pink Adobe

Ⓩ Plaza Restaurant

ⓐ Pranzo

ⓑ Santacafé

ⓒ The Shed

ⓓ Zia Diner

Lodging

ⓔ Alexander's Inn

ⓕ Dunshee's

ⓖ Fort Marcy Compound

ⓓ Inn of the Anasazi

ⓗ Inn of the Turquoise Bear

ⓘ La Fonda

ⓙ La Posada

ⓚ Preston House

ⓛ Santa Fe Motel

ⓜ Water Street Inn

Note: Items with the same letter are located in the same place.

A PERFECT DAY IN SANTA FE

Begin on the Plaza with a stop at the Palace of the Governors. Shop on its portal for Indian arts and crafts, walk next door to the Museum of Fine Arts, then to the Georgia O'Keeffe Museum several blocks away. Drop into La Fonda hotel for a glimpse of its storied lobby, then saunter over to St. Francis Cathedral and its fascinating older *capilla* (chapel) located inside in the back left corner. After lunch at The Shed, head up Canyon Road for a walk. In the late afternoon take a drive up to the ski basin for a shot of the outdoors and, if you're lucky, a dramatic sunset. Have a drink at the Dragon Room of the Pink Adobe before eating at one of Santa Fe's many fine restaurants. On summer nights, the Santa Fe Opera beckons.

DOWNTOWN SANTA FE SIGHTSEEING HIGHLIGHTS

✯✯✯ **Canyon Road**—Nicknamed the "Art and Soul of Santa Fe," this narrow street running up the Santa Fe River canyon away from the Plaza was first an Indian trail; then a route for Hispanic woodcutters and berry-pickers traveling out of the Sangre de Cristo Mountains, rising to the east; and finally, in the 1920s, home to the residences of a handful of painters (including Fremont Ellis and other members of the Cinco Pintores), writers (including Mary Austin), and craftspeople who sparked the creation of the Santa Fe arts colony, which continues unabated today. The street houses many of Santa Fe's 120-plus art galleries, as well as unique shops and restaurants. It's a great street to walk, especially with parking hard to find.

Be sure to check out the **Bandelier Gardens** at **El Zaquan**, 545 Canyon Rd., one of the oldest residences in town and now home to the Santa Fe Historical Society. At the corner of Upper Canyon and Alameda, you'll find **Cristo Rey Church**, 1120 Canyon Rd., said to be the largest adobe structure in the nation, with an impressive Mexican-made stone altar.

Details: The bottom of Canyon Rd. begins on Paseo de Peralta just south of Alameda. There is a parking lot at the corner of Canyon and Camino de Monte Sol. (1–4 hours)

✯✯✯ **Georgia O'Keeffe Museum**—In July 1997 the world's first museum dedicated to a twentieth-century woman artist opened in Santa Fe. Georgia O'Keeffe was one of the many eastern-seaboard artists who emigrated to New Mexico from the 1920s through the 1940s. She proved to be the best of them all, and her legacy has created a one-gal mini-industry in north-central New Mexico. She lived an hour north, in Abiquiu (see Scenic Route, below). The museum manages at least 80 of O'Keeffe's pieces, making it the largest repository of her creations. Shows are supplemented by work lent from other collections. Many of her large signature oil paintings are here, but you'll also find some rarely seen sculpture, delightful watercolor sketches, and striking charcoal studies. The museum maintains a gift shop (no T-shirts!) on the premises. *Details: 217 Johnson St.; 505/995-0785. Open Tue–Sun 10–5, Fri to 8 p.m. $5 adults, free to under age 17; $1 for New Mexico residents on Sun (bring a driver's license); free to New Mexico seniors on Wed; free to all Fri 5–8. Four-day state museum pass good here. (1 hour)*

✭✭✭ **Museum of Fine Arts**—Arguably the Southwest's best museum, this graceful Isaac Rapp–designed adobe facing the northwest corner of the Plaza defined the Santa Fe form of Pueblo Revival architecture. Be sure to see selections from its second-floor permanent collection for a fine overview of the amazing array of artists who have worked in New Mexico. Downstairs are changing exhibitions, usually of high quality and interest. A very pretty patio contains precious murals by Will Shuster and fountains by Jesus Morales. If you have a chance to attend a performance of any kind at its St. Francis Auditorium, go—it's a beautiful building of classic Spanish Mission form and decor with fine acoustics. *Details: 107 W. Palace Ave. (kitty-corner to the Plaza); 505/827-4468. Open Tue–Sun 10–5, Fri to 8 p.m. $5 adults, free to under age 17; $1 for New Mexico residents on Sun (bring a driver's license); free to New Mexico seniors on Wed; free to all Fri 5–8. Four-day state museum pass good here. (1–2 hours)*

✭✭✭ **Palace of the Governors**—This humble-looking one-story building on the north side of the Plaza has seen an incredible number of bizarre and important events unfold within its thick adobe walls. The oldest government building in the United States (circa 1608), it has flown the flags of the Spanish empire, the Republic of Mexico, the Confederacy (for a few weeks), and the U.S. Territory that preceded its statehood in 1912. It was also ruled from 1680 to 1692 by an uneasy alliance of Pueblo people, who carried off one of the two successful

Indian revolts in all the Americas. Many men and women died within its walls, and plots were hatched for *coups d'état*. Zebulon Pike, the first U.S. explorer to enter New Mexico, was imprisoned here briefly, and the first U.S. territorial governor, Lew Wallace, author of *Ben Hur*, complained about the dirt settling out of its adobe ceilings as he tried to write.

Now the state history museum, it provides a great introduction to the region's past. Kids love the stage wagons in the interior patio. There's a working hand-press shop that produces beautiful books, a great gift shop, and a bookstore of local relevance. On the building's portal facing the Plaza, Pueblo artisans gather daily to display and sell their handmade jewelry, pottery, and other goods. Strict oversight by a panel ensures authenticity, so it's a reliable place to shop, and the money goes directly to the artists and craftspeople.

Details: *Palace Ave. between Washington and Lincoln Sts.; 505/ 827-6483. Open Tue–Sun 10–5, Fri to 8. $5 adults, free to under age 17; $1 for New Mexico residents on Sun (bring a driver's license); free to New Mexico seniors on Wed; free to all Fri 5–8. Four-day state museum pass good here. (1–2 hours)*

★★★ **The Plaza**—This was once the locus of the vast but poor province of New Mexico, the center of its politics, power, and pride, its commerce, culture, and social life. Indians were first attracted to the then-more-bountiful Santa Fe River, and they settled along it in small villages some 700 years ago. They had abandoned the area before the Spanish arrived to build their capitol around 1607, when the Crown decreed that an open square would front its government seat. English was not spoken here until the 1820s, when the air cracked with the snap of bullwhips as wagon trains rolled in at the terminus of the arduous Santa Fe Trail, which ran eastward to the American frontier in Missouri.

Today the roughest thing you're likely to encounter on the Plaza is an errant Hacky Sack. It's a nice place to sit on a bench under the shade of a tree and contemplate Santa Fe's past. Check out the interesting historical statues. While most of the Plaza's local stores have morphed into brand-name boutiques, it's still the focus of city celebrations of all kinds, including **Spanish Market** and **Indian Market** in summer, **Fiesta** in early fall, and Christmas farolitos and tree lights in winter. Even today, the Plaza is the heart of Santa Fe.

Details: *Bounded by San Francisco St., Old Santa Fe Trail, Palace Ave., and Lincoln St. The Santa Fe Visitor Center, 201 W. Marcy St. (between*

Lincoln and Grant Sts.), 505/984-6760, is one block away, in the Sweeney Convention Center, with public restrooms. (30 minutes)

★★ **Institute of American Indian Arts Museum**—This museum, known locally as "IAIA," showcases work from the nation's premier Indian arts educational facility of the same name. It houses a superb collection of more than 8,000 contemporary Indian art works created by the likes of Allan Houser, T.C. Cannon, Charles Loloma, Doug Hyde, Fritz Scholder, Earl Biss, Linda Lomahaftewa, Denise Wallace, and other alumni and faculty members. Don't overlook the sculpture garden. The museum also has traveling and revolving exhibitions, as well as a great fine arts and jewelry gift shop.
Details: *108 Cathedral Pl. (across from St. Francis Cathedral); 505/988-6211. Open Mon–Sat 10–5, Sun 12–5. $4 adults, $2 students and seniors, free to under age 16. (1–2 hours)*

★★ **St. Francis Cathedral**—This solid, handsome Romanesque building designed by the famous Archbishop Lamy and built by imported Italian stonemasons is a downtown landmark and testament to old Santa

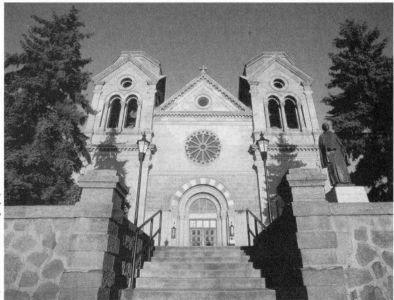

© John MacLean Photography

St. Francis Cathedral

Fe's Catholic soul. Lamy is buried here in a crypt. But perhaps most appealing is the tiny *capilla* (chapel) that the larger church was built around, located back in the left-hand corner of the interior. Its colorfully painted wooden altar and other details reflect its humble past and the style still found throughout the northern Hispanic villages. Here the famous La Conquistadora (Nuestra Señora de la Paz) is kept in a nicho. The oldest Madonna statue in the United States, she accompanied Don Diego de Vargas in his 1692 reconquest of Santa Fe, a victory his followers attributed to the Señora's divine intervention. The quiet park outside is cool even on a hot summer afternoon and is great for picnics. *Details: 231 Cathedral Pl.; 505/982-5619. Open daily, with Mass Mon–Fri 7 and 8:15 a.m., 5:15 p.m.; Sun 6, 8, and 10 a.m., noon, and 7 p.m. Donations suggested. (1 hour)*

✷ **De Vargas Street**—Some of the town's oldest houses, noted with plaques, are located along a few blocks of this narrow, charming street running along the south bank of the Santa Fe River between Old Santa Fe Trail and Galisteo. At the corner of Old Santa Fe Trail and De Vargas is the **San Miguel Mission**, said to be the oldest church in continual use in the nation; its foundations date to 1625 or so. Its bell is believed to have been cast in Spain in 1356. Inside are priceless statues and paintings. *Details: Church at 401 Old Santa Fe Trail; 505/983-3974. Open daily May–Sept 9–4:30, Oct–Apr 10–4. Admission by donation. (1 hour)*

✷ **Loretto Chapel**—This delicate, pretty Gothic-style church is renowned for its "Miraculous Staircase," which corkscrews up gracefully without a single nail or central support post. The story goes that the Sisters of Loretto prayed for a carpenter, and a nameless man showed up, built the staircase without the use of nails or obvious support systems, and left without pay. Was he St. Joseph, patron saint of carpenters? Visit and decide for yourself. *Details: 211 Old Santa Fe Trail. Open daily 9–5 (on Sun after services at 10:30). $1. (30 minutes)*

GREATER SANTA FE SIGHTSEEING HIGHLIGHTS

✷✷ **El Rancho de las Golondrinas**—Once upon a time, the Ranch of the Swallows was the final *paraje* (overnight stop) on the longest and oldest road in North America, El Camino Real, which wound tortuously north from Mexico City through Chihuahua and into New Mexico. Soldiers, priests, traders, stock drivers, and other Royal Road travelers would spend their final night at this spring-fed oasis before pushing onto Santa Fe. Today the paraje is a living museum, the Williamsburg of the Southwest, with operating water mills, fields, and homes, livestock, even a Penitente *morada* (the church of New Mexico's anachronistic order of Catholic penitents). During fall and spring festivals, anvils ring out, loom shuttles fly, aromas waft out of open posole kettles, and fiddles hum. Guided tours and living-history weekends are also available.

Details: About 11 miles south of Santa Fe off I-25. At the La Cienega Exit, head west on the two-lane road into a verdant valley and follow the signs; 505/471-2261. Spring festival held the first weekend in April, summer festival the first weekend in June, and harvest festival the first weekend in October. Open June–Sept Wed–Sun 10–4 for self-guided tours; guided tours available Apr–Oct. $4 adults, $3 seniors and teens, $1.50 children; festivals $6 adults, $4 seniors and teens, $2.50 children; under age 5 free. (2 hours–full day on site)

★★ **Museum of Indian Arts and Culture**—This is an attractive, modern institution dedicated to the region's oldest arts—beautiful pottery vessels, stunning silver and turquoise jewelry, fine textiles, and other works created by the state's Pueblo, Apache, and Navajo artists—both historical and living. Its galleries display excellent short-term shows on contemporary Indian arts. There is also a good gift shop.

Details: 708 Camino Lejo (off Old Santa Fe Trail); 505/827-6344. Open Tue–Sun 10–5. $5 adults, free to under age 17; $1 for New Mexico residents on Sun (bring a driver's license); free to New Mexico seniors on Wed. Four-day state museum pass good here. (1–2 hours)

★★ **Museum of International Folk Art**—This gem of a museum shelters one of the world's largest collections of folk art and folk toys—everything from Mexican masks and milagros to Zairian hand drums and East Indian dolls. Its Hispanic Heritage wing contains an excellent collection of traditional Hispanic arts of New Mexico, including *retablos* (carved wood panels), *bultos* (carved and painted sculptures), tin, and colcha embroidery. In 1998 a new wing opened for the Neutrogena Collection, a world-class textile assemblage. The museum has a great gift shop.

Details: 706 Camino Lejo (off Old Santa Fe Trail); 505/827-6350. Open Tue–Sun 10–5. $5 adults, free to under age 17; $1 for New Mexico *residents on Sun (bring a driver's license); free to New Mexico seniors on Wed. Four-day state museum pass good here. (2 hours)*

★★ **Pecos National Historic Park**—This park preserves the remains of Pecos Pueblo, once a major New Mexican pueblo. Located at the mouth of Glorieta Pass, the gateway between the Great Plains and the Rio Grande Valley, it was a huge trading center centuries prior to Spanish arrival. Decimated by introduced diseases, occasional battles with the Spanish, and attacks by Apache, Comanche, and other nomadic tribes, it was finally abandoned in 1838. A self-guided walking tour includes a rare opportunity to enter a functional *kiva* (the sunken ceremonial chambers of the Pueblo culture), and the ruins of a huge mission church built by the Franciscans with Indian labor. An outlying unit, at Pigeon Ranch in Glorieta Canyon, encompasses a decisive Civil War battleground and faint remnants of the historic Santa Fe Trail. There is a visitors center with videos, books, and a ranger on duty to answer questions.

Details: 25 miles from Santa Fe via I-25 N. Get off at Exit 307 and head east into the village of Pecos, then south 2 miles on NM 63 to the short entrance road; 505/757-6032. Open Memorial Day–Labor Day 8–6, rest of the year 8–5. $2 per person or $4 per vehicle. (2 hours)

★★ **Wheelwright Museum of the American Indian**—Mary Cabot Wheelwright, the Eastern-raised contemporary of Taos' more famous Mabel Dodge Lujan, opened this wonderful, relatively small museum in 1937 to house the work of her close friend Hosteen Klah, a Navajo medicine man, weaver, and sandpainter. Its collections have continued to expand, and today it mounts impressive shows of contemporary and historical art by Native Americans. Its Case Trading Post is a great source for excellent Indian arts and crafts, books, and music.

Details: 704 Camino Lejo (off Old Santa Fe Trail); 505/982-4636. Open daily 10–5, Sun 1–5. Free. (1 hour)

GALLERIES

Santa Fe is the major art center between the nation's East and West Coasts, with artwork running from traditional Indian and Hispanic works through contemporary and abstract visual arts and sculpture. There are around 200 galleries in town, most of them concentrated on or near Canyon Road (see Sightseeing Highlights, above) and near the Plaza. For details on show openings, most of which occur on Friday evenings, consult "Pasatiempo," the weekly arts and entertainment supplement found in the Friday edition of the *New Mexican*.

Gerald Peters Gallery, 1011 Paseo de Peralta, 505/988-8961, in an enormous new building that has been somewhat snidely dubbed the "Ninth Northern Pueblo," carries American masters, running from Charles Russell to Georgia O'Keeffe, as well as leading figures of the Taos Society of Artists and New Mexico modernists.

For close to 30 years, **Nedra Matteucci's Fenn Galleries**, 1075 Paseo de Peralta, 505/982-4631, has specialized in nineteenth- and twentieth-century American art, including California and New Mexico regionalists. It also has a pretty sculptural garden, Spanish colonial furniture, and other unique works.

In contemporary art, **Charlotte Jackson**, 200 W. Marcy St., 505/989-8688, focuses on monochromatic works; **Horwitch LewAllen**, 129 Palace Ave., 505/988-8997, on art ranging from Southwestern pop to serious modernist works; while **Linda Durham**, in Galisteo, 505/466-6600, shows sculpture and abstract works on paper by appointment.

Dewey Galleries, 76 E. San Francisco St., 505/982-8632, carries a variety of regional works, including work of the late great Apache sculptor and visual artist Alan Houser, Spanish Colonial creations, and Navajo weavings. **Niman Fine Arts**, 125 Lincoln St., 505/988-5091, is a rare Indian-owned gallery, focusing on the outstanding work of Dan Namingha. For wonderful Indian antiquities, visit **Morning Star**, 513 Canyon Rd., 505/982-8187; and for superb historic Navajo and rare Pueblo textiles, **Joshua Bear & Co.**, 116 Palace Ave., 505/988-8944. Of the handful of excellent photo galleries, I like **Andrew Smith**, 203 E. San Francisco St., 505/984-1234, for its variety of living and deceased masters and regional photographers.

Though it's not a retail gallery, **SITE Santa Fe**, 1606 Paseo de Peralta (near the Railyards), 505/989-1199, was launched in 1995 to raise the profile of contemporary art in Santa Fe. It hosts a year-round schedule of major visual art exhibits as well as frequent lectures, readings, and musical events. It's open Wednesday through Sunday from 10 to 5; admission is $2.50 (free on Sunday).

KIDS' STUFF

Kids, and many an adult, enjoy the scenic train ride in the restored passenger cars and cabooses of the **Santa Fe Southern Railway**, 505/989-

8600. Trains run Tuesday, Thursday, and Sunday between Santa Fe and Lamy for $21 to $30. Kids also love the **Santa Fe Children's Museum**, 1050 Old Pecos Trail, 505/989-8359. Admission is $2.50. Also, check out the International Museum of Folk Art and Las Golondrinas (see Sightseeing Highlights, above); horseback riding and river rafting (see Fitness and Recreation, below); and the **Southwest Children's Theater**, 142 E. De Vargas, 505/984-3055.

FITNESS AND RECREATION

Name almost any outdoor recreation, save ocean activities, and you can probably find it near Santa Fe. Take skiing. You have many choices for cross-country outings in the Sangre de Cristos, which rise to more than 12,600 feet just above town, or in the gentler Jemez Mountains, an hour away. Or you can be on your alpine skis or a snowboard in half an hour at the **Santa Fe Ski Area**, 505/982-4429 or 800/776-7669; snowline 505/983-9155. This relatively compact area skis big, with something for everyone, on top of 250 inches of often light powder. There are buffed ballroom slopes for beginner and intermediate skiers, short chutes, trees, and mogul runs, as well as supreme powder skiing on Big Tesuque Peak. The area has rentals and an instructional program, a children's center, cafeteria, restaurant, bar, and apparel shop. Reach it by heading east on Artist Road from Bishop Lodge Road, which turns into NM 475—also known as Hyde Park Road (road can be tricky in bad weather).

The ski-area road also leads to access to the cool high country in summer, where you can hunt for wildflowers and mushrooms, go birding, or simply lie down in a grassy meadow and watch the thunderheads glide by. The ski-area parking lot and the **Winsor Trail** are jumping-off points for day and multi-day hikes into the 224,000-acre **Pecos Wilderness**, with its superb trout fishing on more than 15 lakes and numerous small rivers and creeks, hunting, horsepack opportunities, and mountain climbing. With elevations reaching 13,103 feet in the **Truchas Peaks**, one shouldn't just traipse off unprepared here. People can freeze to death in winter or get struck by summer lightning. About 20 minutes up the ski-basin road from town, at a wide pullout, is **Aspen Vista Trail**, an easygoing old Forest Service road now closed to vehicles that is popular with hikers and cross-country skiers. In town, you can stroll or hike the pretty grounds of the **Randall Davey Audubon Center**, Upper Canyon Road, 505/983-4609, open daily nine to five.

Free guided birding walks are conducted on summer weekend mornings. For further information on outdoor recreation, contact the **Santa Fe National Forest**, 1220 St. Francis, Box 1689, Santa Fe, NM 87501; 505/438-7840. Late spring and early summer are peak seasons for river-running. Many professional tour companies lead guided raft trips down the furious **Rio Grande Box** near Taos, through the more sedate **White Rock Canyon**, and along the tranquil and beautiful **Rio Chama**. There are many local river-running companies (see the phone book for listings). Horse lovers will enjoy rides at **Rancho Encantado**, 505/982-3537, in the Sangre foothills; the **Broken Saddle**, 505/470-0074, in the grasslands of Cerrillos, half an hour south of town; or **Galarosa Stable**, 505/983-6565 or 800/338-6877, in the see-forever Galisteo Basin. The **City Parks and Recreation Division**, 505/473-7236, maintains one outdoor and several indoor pools, tennis courts, and the new 18-hole city golf course. Private racquet clubs, golf courses, and fitness centers also exist (see the phone book).

FOOD

Santa Fe has the broadest and best dining possibilities in the state. However, most of the better restaurants are in the mid-high to high price range. If you're used to New York or San Francisco prices, you won't be shocked, but folks from, say, Truth or Consequences, New Mexico, may be stunned at what a decent meal costs here. Expect tabs of $25 to $45 or more per person (with drinks) at the best spots. But Santa Fe also has a handful of more moderately priced, good restaurants, along with the ubiquitous fast-food franchises along Cerrillos Road, so even those on a budget won't starve.

A handful of places vie for the coveted "best" (and most expensive) designation. I love the fireplaces, thick adobe walls, portal dining, and intimate bar of **Geronimo**, 724 Canyon Rd., 505/982-1500, which serves exquisite, pricey food matched by careful service. The appetizers, such as a crispy red corn chile relleno stuffed with roasted duck and black-bean mole and jalapeño-peach salsa, are meals in themselves. Geronimo serves wonderful Sunday brunches as well.

Another popular high-end spot is the **Coyote Café**, 132 Water St., 505/983-1615, which was the first of chef/owner Mark Miller's impressive establishments. A fixed-price dinner ($39.50) includes appetizer or salad, entrée, and dessert. The word here is "inventive." In warm

SANTA FE AREA

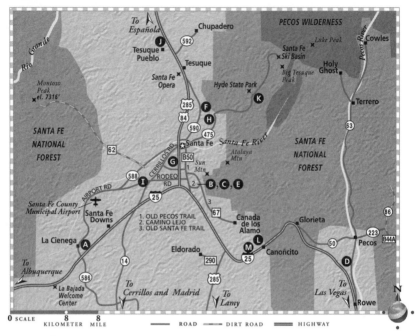

Sights

Ⓐ El Rancho de las Golindrinas

Ⓑ Museum of Indian Art and Culture

Ⓒ Museum of International Folk Art

Ⓓ Pecos National Historic Park

Ⓔ Wheelwright Museum of the American Indian

Lodging

Ⓕ Bishop's Lodge

Ⓖ El Rey Inn

Ⓗ Houses of the Moon

Camping

Ⓘ Babbitt's Los Campos RV Resort

Ⓙ Camel Rock RV Campground,

Ⓚ Hyde Memorial State Park

Ⓛ Rancheros de Santa Fe Campground

Ⓜ Santa Fe KOA

weather, the less-expensive rooftop **Coyote Cantina** serves equally exotic fare, such as sea bass tacos. The critically acclaimed **Santacafé**, 231 Washington Ave., 505/984-1788, serves fine food inspired by an eclectic array of local and international styles. The courtyard is a lovely spot for summer dining.

Yet another of the dining elite is the **Anasazi Restaurant**, 113 Washington Ave., 505/988-3236, with its fanciful blends of local and novel dishes, such as a cinnamon-chile tenderloin of beef, served on a fixed-price dinner basis. Located in the Inn of the Anasazi, this multiple award–winner is one of the nation's better hotel restaurants.

For a quiet dinner in a lovely adobe with one of the city's best classic New Mexico art collections, check out **La Casa Sena**, 125 E. Palace Ave. (in Sena Plaza), 505/982-1500, with its mix of fine local dishes and Continental fare. In summer, dining on the outdoor patio is delightful. There is something faintly decadent, in a pleasurable way, about **The Palace**, 142 W. Palace Ave., 505/982-9891. Its Continental Italian food is superb, and the service is impeccable, but the crushed red-velvet walls and the lingering air of the 1800s gambling hall and bordello suggest its former indolence. The painting of the Indian girl in the lounge says it all.

Underneath this stratospheric dining level are a host of less expensive but still excellent restaurants. A classic Santa Fe establishment that was *the* place to dine here for many, many years is the **Pink Adobe**, 406 Old Santa Fe Trail, 505/983-7712. Its animated atmosphere and tasty New Mexican and Continental fare keep 'em coming back. Across the street, **Bistro 315**, 315 Old Santa Fe Trail, 505/986-9190, is a classic, romantic French bistro that focuses on fresh organic vegetables, meats, and seafood. The well-prepared, diverse, and modestly priced Italian food of **Pranzo**, 540 Montezuma St., 505/984-2545, has been a hit since the day it opened. Another excellent midrange Italian choice is **Il Piatto**, 95 W. Marcy St., 505/984-1091, boasting terrific staff and food.

India Palace, 227 Don Gaspar (at the back of the El Centro shopping compound through the Water Street parking lot), 505/986-5859, serves wonderful East Indian meals in a serene setting, with some of Santa Fe's best waiters. Its lunch buffet is a real bargain, and dining on its covered patio in summer is a treat. Just down the street is **Pasqual's**, 121 Don Gaspar, 505/983-9340, which is particularly popular at breakfast, and for good reason. Homemade pancakes with fresh fruit, log-size burritos, and succulent corned-beef hash are just a few of the dishes that attract throngs of people to this downtown spot every weekend. Get there early or be prepared to wait.

Santa Fe also has a handful of decent restaurants with entrées for less than $10. The **Plaza Restaurant**, 54 Lincoln Ave. (right on the Plaza), 505/982-1664, is one of the best. It's been a fixture since 1918, and it still boasts red leather booths, black Formica tables, and a 1940s dining counter complete with soda fountain. The menu offers tuna sandwiches, burgers, New Mexico plates, and Greek dishes. Beer and wine are available. Another downtown spot, **Carlos' Gospel Cafe**, 125 Lincoln Ave. (inside the First Interstate Plaza), 505/983-1841, is still just open for lunch, despite its cadre of diehard local regulars. Fat sandwiches (half-orders available), fresh salads, the best corn chowder you'll ever find, and the always-beaming Carlos himself shine here. Closed Sunday.

For classic New Mexican food and superior deserts, head to **The Shed**, 113½ E. Palace Ave., 505/982-9030, which has been around since 1962. It's always full at lunch, and relatively recently it began to serve dinner on a limited basis. Its sister restaurant, **La Choza**, 905 Alarid St. (near the intersection of St. Francis and Cerrillos), 505/982-0909, has about the same menu in a less crowded part of town. West of St. Francis, **Dave's Not Here**, 1115 Hickox St., 505/983-7060, is a real neighborhood joint with two community tables and several private ones. Hearty burgers, perhaps the best chile rellenos in town, yummy tacos, and scrumptious chocolate pie are a few top choices.

In the Guadalupe area, the **Zia Diner**, 326 S. Guadalupe St., 505/988-7008, was a classic the day it opened, serving hearty home-style comfort food with a flair—meatloaf with green chile, fresh fish, thick mashed potatoes, and great fruit pies. Across the street, the **Cowgirl Hall of Fame**, 319 Guadalupe St., 505/982-2565, serves good grub amid lots of local color. Besides Southwestern standards, specials include wild-game dishes such as buffalo burgers and wild-boar burritos. During warmer months the large, pleasant patio is very popular; at night, live music often fills a hopping bar. For a burger above, try **Bert's Burger Bowl**, 235 N. Guadalupe St., 505/982-0215. The green chile cheeseburger is regularly voted the town's best, and you can't go wrong with the excellent posole, pressure-cooked chicken, and old-fashioned shakes.

LODGING

As with its dining, Santa Fe has lots of accommodation choices, but the best don't come cheaply. Expect to pay more than $150 a night for a double at the high end. Summer is peak season, as are winter holidays, and you'll pay more at these times. At the top of the luxury list is the **Inn**

of the Anasazi, 113 Washington Ave., 505/988-3030 or 800/688-8100, just a half-block off the Plaza. Attention was lavished on every detail of this relatively small hotel, and each one-of-a-kind room has handmade furniture, a kiva-style fireplace, hand-woven blankets, and a beamed ceiling. The hotel also houses one of Santa Fe's best restaurants (see Food section, above).

Bishop's Lodge, on Bishop's Lodge Road, 505/983-6377, is only five minutes from the Plaza, but it sits in a stream-fed valley and town seems far removed. First opened in 1918, it has lovely dining rooms, a grand bar, a large outdoor pool, and beautifully landscaped grounds. On the property is a tiny and exquisite chapel, once the private retreat of Archbishop Lamy. Daylong activity programs for kids allow parents to explore their own interests. Horseback riding and skeet shooting are also available.

On the road to the ski basin, four miles from the Plaza, is the Japanese-style **Houses of the Moon**, 505/989-5077, on the grounds of the Ten Thousand Waves spa. Six small houses each have brick floors, marble fireplaces, and futon beds. Guests receive discounts on spa services, which include community and private outdoor hot tubs, massages, facials, and herbal wraps.

Dropping down a notch in price, with doubles averaging $100 to $150 a night, is a raft of choice spots. Perhaps the classic hotel of the Southwest is **La Fonda**, 100 E. San Francisco St., 505/982-5511 or 800/523-5002. The only hotel facing the Plaza, it is believed to occupy a spot where a *fonda*, or inn, has stood since 1610. Both Kit Carson and John F. Kennedy stayed here. Each room is unique, there's a lively bar downstairs, and its lobby has seen many historic events and people pass by. Though only a few blocks from the Plaza, **La Posada**, 330 Palace Ave., 505/986-0000, has a country feeling, with its rambling casitas and gardens spread over six acres. An outdoor pool; cozy, historic bar; romantic patio; good restaurant; and even a ghost add to its appeal. Rates range from $89 (single) to $400 (deluxe suite).

One of the finest motels you'll encounter is the **El Rey Inn**. Founded in 1936, its whitewashed buildings with tile trim are flanked by large trees, lawns, and flower gardens. Some rooms have kitchenettes and fireplaces. Rooms can run from less than $65 to $150. About the least expensive decent accommodations in the downtown core is the **Santa Fe Motel**, 510 Cerrillos Rd., 505/982-1039. Expect rates of $65 to $100.

Bed-and-breakfasts are a great way to go in Santa Fe, with many eclectic, attractive, and comfortable choices. One of the best, and most expensive ($125 to $195), is the **Water Street Inn**, 427 W. Water St., 505/984-1193. It has imaginative, fun decor; fireplaces; private baths; cable TV in all rooms; and in-room breakfasts. The **Inn of the Turquoise Bear**, 342 E. Buena Vista, 505/983-0798 or 800/396-4104, markets itself toward the gay populace. Here previous owner Witter Byner hosted the likes of D.H. Lawrence, Willa Cather, Ansel Adams, Igor Stravinsky, Robert Frost, W.H. Auden, Rita Hayworth, and Errol Flynn. Rooms are $90 to $175, and the suite is $250.

You can also find many more moderate bed-and-breakfast options. A top choice is **Alexander's Inn**, 529 Palace Ave., 505/986-1431. This 1903 two-story Craftsman-style house has a country-cottage ambiance, with fresh flowers everywhere, a veranda shaded by apricot trees and wisteria, and wholesome, all-natural breakfasts. In the heart of the quiet Eastside area, a mile from the Plaza, **Dunshee's**, 986 Acequia Madre, 505/982-0988, is the pretty home of artist Susan Dunshee, including a suite in the main house and an adobe casita with two bed-rooms perfect for a small family. Rates are $120 to $130. **Preston House**, 106 Faithway St., 505/982-3465, is Santa Fe's only Queen Anne–style home. The main house has charming rooms, but for more privacy stay in a casita out back. Rates are $80 to $150.

A good choice for families is **Fort Marcy Compound**, 320 Artist Rd., 505/982-6636. It has 100 one- to three-bedroom suites with full kitchens, fireplaces, and VCRs. Other amenities include laundry facility, hot tub, and great hillside sunsets on a 10-acre site within walking distance of the Plaza. Rates range from $100 to $230.

CAMPING

Several options exist nearby for public camping, along with a handful of RV and commercial sites. The closest public land camping is at **Hyde Memorial State Park**, 505/983-7175, about eight miles up the ski-basin road (NM 475). There's a small fee. Free camping is available in nearby **Santa Fe National Forest**, 505/438-7840. Other options include **Camel Rock RV Campground**, 10 miles north of Santa Fe on U.S. 84/285, 505/455-2661. Owned by Tesuque Pueblo, it has 68 full hookups, 26 tent sites, a laundry, showers, and a gift shop. It has been closed but is expected to reopen in 1999. In town is **Babbitt's Los Campos RV Resort**, 3574 Cerrillos Rd., 505/473-1949, with a swimming pool, showers, LP gas, and picnic tables. Ten miles east of town is **Rancheros de Santa Fe Campground**, 736 Old Las Vegas Highway (NM 3), 505/466-3482. Set among piñon trees, it offers 95 RV sites, 37 tent sites, a few cabins, hot showers, LP gas, a grocery, laundry, and pool. Also in the area is the **Santa Fe KOA**, 11 miles east of town at I-25 Exit 290, 505/466-1419.

NIGHTLIFE

For a small city, Santa Fe has a lively nightlife, particularly in the summer, when there are more possibilities for fun than any one person can take in. For a current listing of what's happening, check out Friday's "Pasatiempo," the weekly arts and entertainment supplement of the *New Mexican*.

Probably the grandest event of all, drawing people from around the world, is the **Santa Fe Opera**, 505/986-5900. Located just north of town, the striking, recently remodeled opera house has open sides that allow fresh night air to enter and the sounds of thunder to roll in, adding to the pageant on stage. In addition to several classic operas, a world premiere is held every summer. If you find the ticket prices daunting, standing-room tickets can be purchased for eight dollars on Friday and Saturday, six dollars on weekdays, at 10 a.m. or an hour and a half before the performance. People often leave at intermissions, allowing you to grab a cheap seat for the second act.

Another summer event that has been drawing patrons from across the nation since 1973 is the **Santa Fe Chamber Music Festival**, 505/983-2075, which holds exquisite performances in the lovely St. Francis Auditorium at the Museum of Fine Arts. Launched in 1983, the **Santa Fe Symphony and Chorus**, 505/983-1414, presents nine or so performances a year, including a free holiday concert in early December.

Santa Fe has a budding theater scene. **Santa Fe Stages**, 505/982-6683, produces excellent contemporary and classic shows and dance performances. Throughout July and August on Friday, Saturday, and Sunday nights, the Bard comes alive through the **Shakespeare in Santa Fe** series, 505/982-2910, presented at St. John's College, 1160 Camino Cruz Blanca. Since 1922 the surprisingly good **Santa Fe Community Theater**, 142 E. De Vargas, 505/988-4262, has been offering a variety of works, including the annual Fiesta Melodrama.

Contemporary music can be heard at a number of venues. **Corazon de Santa Fe** is a series of free concerts on the Plaza, with music ranging from R&B and bluegrass to salsa, presented on Tuesday and Thursday evenings throughout the summer. Also during summer, outstanding shows are held at the wonderful **Paolo Soleri Amphitheater**, 1501 Cerrillos Rd. (on the grounds of the Santa Fe Indian School), which has fantastic sightlines and acoustics. See the local newspapers for details.

In 1998, Santa Fe's ailing club scene was given a serious boost with the opening of **The Paramount**, 331 Sandoval, 982-8999, which features both national touring acts and topnotch local bands; expect a moderate to pricey cover charge. The adjoining **Bar B**, by far and away Santa Fe's slickest joint (it cost more than $1 million to create), offers cool jazz in an intimate setting.

A number of other nightclubs and bars also offer live music. Recently reopened after a major fire, **El Farol**, 808 Canyon Rd., 505/983-9912, is a popular and historic hangout, where the likes of U2's Bono and Joan Baez have stepped out of the crowd and up to the mike. The regular line music ranges from flamenco to blues. El Farol is also a Spanish restaurant with a good selection of tapas and tasty paella; for a table, arrive early. The **Dragon Room** of the Pink Adobe, 406 Old Santa Fe Trail, 505/983-7712, is a longstanding place to see and be seen in Santa Fe. In winter, a fireplace creates a romantic mood, enhanced by flamenco guitar and other live music. Another romantic nightspot is the **Staab House Bar** at La Posada, 330 Palace Ave., 505/982-6950. If Chris Calloway, Cab's daughter, is singing, go! If you're in the mood for schmaltz, head for the piano bar at **Vanessie**, 434 W. San Francisco St., 982-9966, which serves up the old favorites nightly in a big gorgeous room full of swooning tourists. Several blocks down but miles away aesthetically, **Evangelo's**, downtown at 200 W. San Francisco St., 505/982-9014, has 200 varieties of imported beer, pool tables in its smoky basement, and live music upstairs on weekends.

Salsa fans might want to check out **Club Alegria**, on Agua Fria two blocks east of Siler Road, 505/471-2324, on Friday nights to hear a live salsa band led by a Catholic priest (Father Pretto). For great, danceable Latin jazz, check out Yoboso, who play every Monday and Tuesday at **La Fonda**, 100 E. San Francisco St., 505/982-5511. If you're in the mood for two-stepping, head for **Rodeo Nites**, 2911 Cerrillos Rd., 505/473-4138.

Both Indian gaming facilities near Santa Fe on U.S. 84/285 offer card games, roulette, craps, slots, and Bingo, along with restaurants and gift shops: **Camel Rock Casino**, 505/984-8414 or 800/GO-CAMEL; and **Cities of Gold**, 505/455-3313 or 800/444-3313.

Scenic Route: Abiquiu and O'Keeffe Country

Mounds of deep purple and rust-colored dirt. Pale yellow cliffs, banded above by pink and tan sandstone. A flat-topped peak, bones and crosses floating in the turquoise sky. Such are the images left to us by the late great American painter Georgia O'Keeffe, who settled in the once-remote village of Abiquiu in 1949 to pursue her art. Today the area is attracting movie stars building permaculture gardens, but a visit out this way is still well worth the time.

If you are coming from Santa Fe, stop at the site of the second oldest European colony in the United States, **San Gabriel**, founded in 1598 by Don Juan de Oñate, just outside present-day Española.

To get there, take U.S. 84/285 24 miles northwest from Santa Fe to Española. Staying on the east side of the Rio Grande, head north on NM 68 to the edge of town and turn west (left) onto NM 74, the access road to **San Juan Pueblo**. Wind north through the pueblo, past the **Oke Owenge** arts-and-crafts shop on the left, and a Gothic stone church and the **pueblo plaza** on the right. Bear left just past the **Eight Northern Indian Pueblos Center** and cross a bridge to the west bank

ABIQUIU AND O'KEEFFE COUNTRY

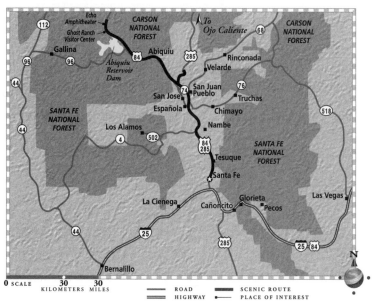

of the Rio Grande. San Gabriel once stood in the fields just to the south. Although almost nothing remains today, I think it's an interesting stop, certainly of immense historical significance.

Continue west on NM 74 for three miles to its intersection with U.S. 285 coming down from Ojo Caliente. Turn south (left), cross the Rio Chama, and at the intersection with U.S. 84, turn west (right). This road zips up the **Chama Valley** past beautiful bottom land of alfalfa, orchards, and cottonwood trees sheltering ancient adobe homes flanked by the earthen hills and cliffs often painted by O'Keeffe. In about 16 miles you roll into **Abiquiu**. Take a few minutes to visit **Bode's**, a still-functional general mercantile. Then turn off U.S. 84 to Abiquiu's plaza. **Georgia O'Keeffe's** house, 505/685-4539, is right across the street from Bode's. You can walk around the plaza, but there's not much to see, and some locals will greet you with less than open arms. O'Keeffe's home, however, can be visited on guided tours by advance reservation on Tuesday, Thursday, and Friday.

Another few miles west along U.S. 84 toward Chama is **Ghost Ranch**, a private retreat center where O'Keeffe also lived, and the **Ghost Ranch Living Museum**, 505/685-4312, with outstanding exhibits of native Southwestern animals and plant life. A few more miles up the road, on the left, tucked under the area's striking yellow, cream, tan, and even light purple cliffs, is **Echo Amphitheater**, a huge natural alcove that bounces your voice around with remarkable clarity. Kids love it.

The round-trip can take as little as four hours or as much as a full day, depending on how much you want to linger. On the way back, dine or recline at the **Abiquiu Inn** and its **Abiquiu Café** (Middle Eastern and Mediterranean dishes), on U.S. 84 just east of Abiquiu, 505/685-4378. Perhaps the nicest bed-and-breakfast in the entire region, **Rancho de San Juan**, is nearby—on U.S. 285 a few miles north of the Chama River, 505/753-6818. It has a gourmet restaurant, beautiful public spaces, and lovely, one-of-a-kind rooms, sporting great views of the countryside O'Keeffe immortalized. ◣

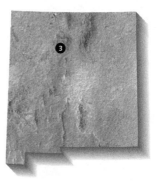

3

JEMEZ AREA

I f the Sangre de Cristo Mountains of north-central New Mexico are
young, bold, and dramatic, the Jemez Mountains are aged, friendly,
and inviting. It's natural, then, that their gently meandering summits
and valleys, plentiful water, and lush forests should have harbored the
seeds of the Pueblo Indian culture, as seen in the tens of thousands of
archaeological sites found throughout the range.

The immense Valle Grande once blew its top with a force that
scattered debris clear into Kansas. Today mesas drop off unexpectedly
in rugged pitches, and geothermal hot waters still bubble to its surface
here and there, attesting to the smoldering fires within. Ironically, its
eastern-facing Pajarito Plateau is also the site of one of the world's
most advanced technological centers, Los Alamos National
Laboratory, birthplace and ongoing nursery of nuclear weapons, and
the single greatest concentration per capita of supercomputers and
Ph.D.s on earth.

The adjoining town of Los Alamos is the commercial center of the
area, with a number of shops, restaurants, and lodging options, as well
as several interesting museums that document the lab's role in the
development of the atomic bomb. The town's preoccupation with the
atomic age is evidenced by the call letters of a popular oldies station—
KBOM. All in all, it's an unlikely place: a slice of high-tech suburban
America plunked down in the middle of a beautiful mountain range,
ancient Indian ruins, and Hispanic people who have inhabited the area
for centuries.

JEMEZ AREA

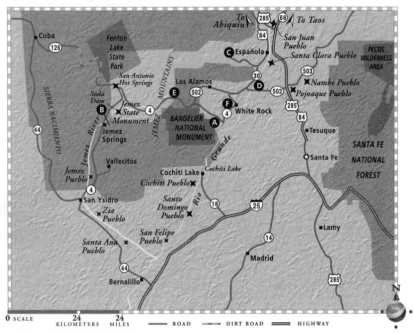

Sights

A Bandelier National Monument

B Jemez Springs

C Puye Cliff Dwellings

D San Ildefonso Pueblo

E Valle Grande

Food

F Katherine's

G Los Ojos

Lodging

F Back Porch

F Bandelier Inn

G Jemez River

Camping

A Juniper Campground

Note: Items with the same letter are located in the same town or area.

A PERFECT DAY IN THE JEMEZ AREA

Pack a picnic and start your day at San Ildefonso Pueblo. Cross the Rio Grande and wind over the mesas to Bandelier National Monument. After touring the ruins and eating your lunch, take a drive along high and cool NM 4 at least as far as the stunning Valle Grande, then return to Los Alamos and visit the technically oriented Bradbury Science Museum or the Fuller Lodge History Museum for more of a social version of local history. If you're staying in the area, try dinner at Katherine's, in White Rock.

SIGHTSEEING HIGHLIGHTS

★★★ **Bandelier National Monument**—This National Park Service site protects the cultural remnants of the Anasazi, ancestors of today's Pueblo Indians. Protected from fierce winter storms, narrow **Frijoles Canyon** has south-facing cliffs perfect for absorbing warming sunlight. Its perennial stream and abundant game once enabled its residents to build elaborate cliff dwellings, canyon-floor residences, ceremonial kivas, and other stone structures along more than a mile of the canyon. A one-mile asphalt trail winds through the fourteenth-century ruins, making this an accessible, and—in summer—almost oppressively popular place.

However, 23,000 backcountry wilderness acres lie outside of this main valley, with some 75 miles of hiking and backpacking trails leading to more isolated ruins and wonderful views. One of the most frequented trails is **Falls Trail**, which leads to lovely waterfalls 1.5 and 2 miles from the trailhead. The visitors center contains some beautiful murals, good interpretive displays, and a gift shop.

Details: 40 miles west of Santa Fe. Take U.S. 84/285 north to Pojoaque, then exit onto NM 502 and proceed past San Ildefonso Pueblo. Four miles west of the Rio Grande, exit onto NM 4, and then watch for the entrance sign on your left. Prior to reaching the main monument, you'll pass an outlier, Tsankawi, which offers a beautiful half-hour hike to some unexcavated ruins; 505/672-3861. Bandelier is open daily Memorial Day–Labor Day 8–6, rest of the year 8–5. $10 per vehicle. (2 hours– full day)

★★★ **Bradbury Science Museum**—Los Alamos National Laboratory and the town of Los Alamos are the offspring of America's drive to build the world's first nuclear bomb. This World War II effort ultimately did end the war when the United States bombed Hiroshima and Nagasaki in 1945. Whether you are a hawk or a dove, this fascinating museum reveals something of the effort that went into the project even though it tends to glorify the incredible technology and downplay the moral questions surrounding the development and use of weapons of mass destruction. Other displays show Los Alamos' involvement in other sciences, from building space probes to energy research, though weaponeering remains its tour de force today.

Details: 15th St. and Central Ave.; 505/667-4444. Open Tue–Fri 9–5, Sat–Mon 1–5. Free. (1 hour)

★★★ **San Ildefonso Pueblo**—Scientists like Robert Oppenheimer, director of the atomic bomb project, occasionally used to come down off "The Hill" (as Los Alamos National Laboratory was euphemistically called as late as the 1970s) to watch the age-old ceremonial dances at San Ildefonso Pueblo. What an odd juxtaposition. Around 1919 San Ildefonso potter Maria Martinez helped spark the revival of traditional Pueblo arts when she perfected the process of creating the beautiful black-on-black polished pottery now seen throughout the region and in the impoverished tribal museum. At a handful of pottery studios/galleries you can purchase work from the pueblo's many active ceramic artists. The pueblo also has a fishing pond. The dawn **Winter Hunting Dance** (January 22) is truly memorable. Deer dancers slowly filter down out of the surrounding hills and through the village streets to gather on the main plaza.

Details: Off NM 502 just east of the Rio Grande (see directions to Bandelier, above); 505/455-3549. Open daily except occasional ceremonial days and major holidays. $3 per vehicle. A still camera permit costs $5; a video camera permit, $15. (1 hour)

★★ **Fuller Lodge/Los Alamos County Historical Museum**—Fuller Lodge was once the main facility of a boys' school attended by Robert Oppenheimer, a fact that circuitously led to his selection of Los Alamos as the perfect "hideaway" for the atomic bomb project. Today the building, with its unique vertical log structure, houses an arts center; in an adjoining building is the Los Alamos County Historical Museum. For people interested in this chapter of U.S. history, it's a fascinating stop.

Details: 2132 Central Ave.; (505) 662-9331. Open Mon–Sat 10–4, Sun 1–4. Free. (1–3 hours)

★★ **Valle Grande**—This is one of the world's largest volcanic calderas, the collapsed rim of an ancient volcano that blew its top a million years ago in an immense cataclysm. You cannot fathom its size until you realize that the specks you see off in the distance are actually elk. You can't enter the privately owned caldera's lush meadows or fish its meandering streams, but pullouts along the road make for grand viewing. The drive to Valle Grande from Bandelier or Los Alamos is lovely, winding through dense stands of quaking aspen, ponderosa pine, Douglas fir, and blue spruce. The aspen make for a great fall-color outing. The National Forest and Park Services hope to acquire this area and open it to the public.

Details: Head west along NM 4 from Bandelier National Monument; from Los Alamos, take Trinity Dr. to Diamond Dr., turn south (left) and then west (right) onto West Jemez Dr. (NM 501). The roads are open year-round, though winter storms can be treacherous. For further information on the surrounding national forests, contact the Los Alamos Ranger Station, 505/667-5120. (2–3 hours)

★ **Jemez Springs**—This small, rural town is 73 miles southwest of

© Daniel B. Gibson

The "Red Place" along NM4, south of Jemez Springs

Santa Fe on the southwestern edge of the Jemez; it's equally accessible from Albuquerque via NM 44 and NM 4. Nearby are excellent ruins, along with hiking, fishing, cross-country skiing, and mountain biking opportunities. En route on NM 4 from Valle Grande, just before Jemez Springs and alongside the Jemez River, you'll pass the travertine deposit known as the **Soda Dam**, popular with swimmers. Don't try jumping the cliff—several people have died here. One mile further you'll pass **Jemez State Monument**, 505/829-3530, which contains impressive Indian and Spanish mission ruins. In town is the **Jemez Springs Bath House**, 505/829-3303, which has indoor and outdoor mineral pools. Indoor pools cost $8 an hour, a private tub $30 an hour. Massages, herbal wraps, facials, and other services are also available.

Details: Continue west and south on NM 4 past Valle Grande. (2–4 hours)

✯ **Puye Cliff Dwellings**—This historical site is run by Indians, in this case Santa Clara Pueblo, whose ancestors once lived in the stone and cave structures lining a south-facing canyon wall. A trail takes visitors from the canyon floor up pole ladders to the mesa top. You can also visit the pueblo itself, which includes a historic Catholic church and several shops selling Santa Clara's acclaimed pottery.

Details: Drive north on NM 30 (the road that runs between Española and the Los Alamos bridge on the west bank of the Rio Grande) for 7 miles, turn west (left) onto a gravel Forest Service road, and proceed 4 miles to the site entrance; 505/753-7326. Hours vary. $5 adults, $4 seniors and children. (2 hours)

FITNESS AND RECREATION

Jemez has a myriad of recreation possibilities. As already noted, within **Bandelier National Monument** are more than 60 miles of backcountry trails that access remote sections of the park. Several of these trails descend and ascend major canyons, which can be extremely hot in midsummer or buried under snow and ice in winter. Prime time for the monument's backcountry is in the late spring or fall. Permits available through the visitors center (see Sightseeing Highlights) are required for backcountry outings.

Just outside of Los Alamos is the **Pajarito Ski Area**, 505/662-5725. For decades the private ski stash of physicists and other Hilltoppers, the area is now open to the general public on weekends,

Wednesdays, and federal holidays throughout the season. It has a 1,400-foot vertical drop, and is noted for its monstrous moguls and occasional major snow dumps of four feet or more. Call ahead for conditions and driving directions. These mountains have a relatively gentle profile, making them ideal for cross-country skiing. A network of Forest Service dirt roads, closed to winter traffic, provides excellent routes. One leads to the **San Antonio Hot Springs**, others into Bandelier. Great hiking, mountain biking, and fishing are other attractions throughout the range and in the **Jemez National Recreation Area**. For details, contact the **Santa Fe National Forest**, in Los Alamos at 505/667-5120; the Jemez Springs Ranger Office at 505/829-3535; the **Coyote Ranger District** at 505/638-5526; or the **Española Ranger District** at 505/753-7331.

The **Los Alamos Ice Rink**, at 4475 West Rd., 505/662-4500, is one of the state's few outdoor ice-skating rinks, complete with rentals and snack bar. Hours of operation vary with the weather. The nation's highest-altitude indoor Olympic-size pool is at the **Larry Walkup Aquatic Center**, 505/662-8170.

A few Santa Fe–based rafting companies lead daylong float trips through **White Rock Canyon** of the Rio Grande. This little-visited but significant canyon at the foot of the Jemez has petroglyphs, ruins, and some exciting but relatively tame white water.

FOOD

Bandelier National Monument has a snack bar, but for a sit-down meal, stop in White Rock or Los Alamos. A real surprise is **Katherine's**, 121 Longview Dr., White Rock, 505/672-9661, which offers such fine meals as filet mignon with béarnaise sauce and fresh seafood, table-made Caesar salads, and excellent desserts, including a mouth-watering lemon mousse.

Los Alamos has several decent possibilities, besides a slew of fast-food joints. The **Blue Window**, 800 Trinity Dr., 505/662-6305, serves soups, crêpes, and New Mexico plates at lunch, and homemade pasta and fresh fish at night. The **Central Avenue Grill**, 1789 Central Ave., 505/662-2005, dishes up gourmet pizza, salads, and vegetarian lasagna, as well as microbrews. **De Colores**, 820 Trinity Dr., 505/662-6285, specializes in New Mexico fare but also cooks chicken and steak. It's closed on Sunday. The **Hill Diner**, 1315 Trinity Dr., 505/662-9745,

LOS ALAMOS

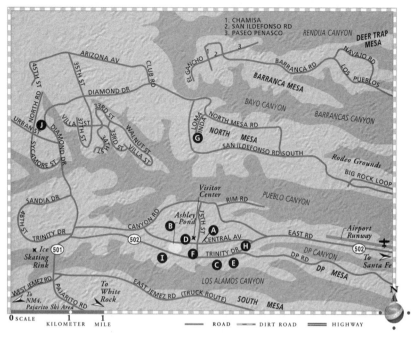

Sights

Ⓐ Bradbury Science Museum

Ⓑ Fuller Lodge/Los Alamos
History Museum

Food

Ⓒ Blue Window

Ⓓ Central Avenue Grill

Ⓔ De Colores

Ⓕ Hill Diner

Lodging

Ⓖ Adobe Pines

Ⓗ Hilltop House

Ⓘ Los Alamos Inn

Ⓙ North Road Inn

serves classic diner dishes in a cozy mountain cabin setting. Banana cream pies like you remember!

In Jemez Springs, don't miss **Los Ojos**, downtown, 505/829-3547, the bar/restaurant nerve center of this community, with pool tables, a huge stone fireplace topped by an elk rack, a jukebox, and wonderful log bar stools that call out for a lazy afternoon sipping brews. Tasty burgers!

LODGING

The lodging closest to Bandelier National Monument is found in White Rock, at the **Bandelier Inn**, 132 NM 4, 505/672-3838 or 800/321-3923. It offers reasonably priced rooms, and suites with kitchenettes, cable TV, a hot tub, free breakfasts, and a coin-op laundry for $61 a night. The **Back Porch**, 13 Karen Circle, 505/672-9816, is a White Rock B&B where the rooms, which overlook lush gardens and a forested arroyo, have private baths. Rates are $50 to $75.

In Los Alamos, you have the **Hilltop House**, 400 Trinity Dr., 505/662-2442 or 800/462-0936, which provides rooms, suites, and kitchenettes, as well as a 24-hour food mart and gas service, outdoor pool, hot tub, and sauna, for $78 a night. Also on the premises is the Trinity Sights Restaurant and Lounge. Another option is the **Los Alamos Inn**, 2201 Trinity Dr., 505/662-7211 or 800/279-9279, with an outdoor pool, hot tub, and room service for $79. The inn has two restaurants: Ashley's, with seafood and steaks, and Ashley's Pub.

Los Alamos hosts a handful of bed-and-breakfasts, all with double rooms in the $50-to-$75 range. Options include the **Adobe Pines**, 2101 Loma Linda Dr., 505/662-6761, a modern, elegant adobe with an indoor pool overlooking the Los Alamos Golf Course; the **North Road Inn**, 2127 North Rd., 505/662-3678 or 800/279-2898, which features seven suites with private bath, phone, and cable TV.

In Jemez Springs, a lovely bed-and-breakfast, **Jemez River**, 16445 NM 4, 505/829-3262 or 800/809-3262, is a certified hummingbird sanctuary set on five riverfront acres. The rooms feature coved ceilings and tile floors opening onto a patio. Rates are $80 to $110.

CAMPING

Juniper Campground, 505/672-3861, at Bandelier National Monument, is a pretty spot on the rim of Frijoles Canyon, with 100 sites (no RV hookups) available on a first-come, first-served basis. The grounds have running water, and rangers lead nightly campfire talks in summer. There are also a few developed campgrounds and dispersed campsites in the surrounding **Santa Fe National Forest** (see Fitness and Recreation, above).

Scenic Route: The High Road to Taos

Most folks heading north from Santa Fe or the Jemez area take the "river route" along the Rio Grande through Española, the Velarde Valley, and lower Taos Canyon. While this is a beautiful drive, there's an even prettier route known as "the High Road." It weaves in and out of the high alpine valleys of the Sangre de Cristos and many small Hispanic villages, as well as past the most isolated of the pueblos, Picuris. In fall the aspens and scrub oak create vast swaths of color; in winter soft snow blankets the adobe walls and orchard trees; in spring wildflowers erupt; and in summer green alfalfa and high grass fields shimmer.

The route is best begun in Pojoaque, north of Santa Fe where NM 503 intersects U.S. 84/285. Turn east (right) onto NM 503 and amble up the **Nambe River Valley**. Some two miles along you'll pass a short side road leading into the **Nambe Pueblo** plaza. NM 503 continues north across some eroded and striking "badlands." Next make a 90-degree turn to the north (left) off NM 503 onto NM 520, which takes you over a rise and into the next valley and the town of **Chimayó**. Just after entering the valley, keep your eyes

THE HIGH ROAD TO TAOS

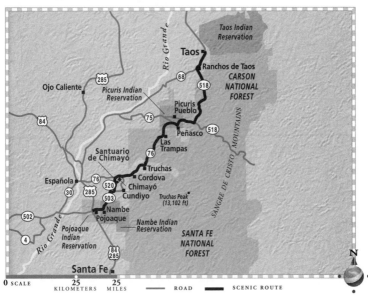

peeled to your right and you'll see a little plaza and a sign announcing the **Santuario de Chimayó**. This is one of America's most famous and popular points of pilgrimage. Every Easter tens of thousands of faithful walk, crawl, and crank wheelchairs to it—many from as far away as Albuquerque! The tiny, humble chapel with its brightly painted wooden altar is representative of the rural chapels found throughout the region. However, most come to dip their hands in the tiny *pozito*, or well, found in a side room, whose dirt is supposed to hold miraculous powers. A small gift shop sells intriguing religious articles. Continuing north, stop at the neighboring **Rancho de Chimayó**, on the main road, 505/351-0444, for some good New Mexican food served up in a charming old farmhouse.

A few miles farther along the main road, you might also wish to stop at **Ortega's Weaving Shop**, 505/351-4215, for a look at the work of this renowned, centuries-old, Hispanic weaving center. At the intersection of NM 76, turn east (right). You might want to drop off this road in about four miles into the village of **Cordova**, which is famed for its *santeros* who carve and paint incredible folk images of Catholic saints. Next stop is the village of **Truchas**, which has several more art galleries and weaving studios. Seven miles past Truchas is **Las Trampas**, home to the striking adobe church of **San Tomas**, which dates to 1751.

At the T-intersection with NM 75, turn west (left) if you wish to detour into **Picuris Pueblo**, perhaps the state's most isolated pueblo and the only one found in a mountain setting. The pueblo has a small museum and visitors center with a restaurant featuring Native foods, 505/587-2957. Its big to-do is the San Lorenzo Feast Day on August 10, which includes dances, foot races, pole climbing, and a procession. Return to NM 75 and continue east through the villages of Peñasco, Vadito, and Placitas. Turn north (left) onto NM 518, which joins NM 68 just south of Taos at Ranchos de Taos. The drive, without stops, takes about two hours. ◼

4
TAOS

Taos is the younger sibling of Santa Fe. Like Santa Fe, it has a strong Hispanic and Indian feel, along with frontier and hippie-holdout elements, but without the rarefied atmosphere and (some would say) pretension of Santa Fe. Also like Santa Fe, it is set in an area of tremendous scenic beauty. On one side of the city rises the often snowcapped and mystical Taos Mountain, said to be a power point of the planet. On the other side slices the impressive Taos Gorge, carved by the Rio Grande. To the west great vistas open.

For centuries Taos has been a trading and visiting center. Tribes of the Great Plains, when they weren't at war with the Pueblo Indians, came into Taos to barter with both the Indians of Taos Pueblo and the Spanish, who founded the town of Taos in the early 1600s. In 1898 two American artists, Bert Phillips and Ernest Blumenschein, were on their way to Mexico for a painting trip, when their vehicle broke down outside of Taos. They ended up falling in love with the area and became the nucleus of an art colony that grew to include matron Mabel Dodge Lujan, photographers such as Ansel Adams, painters such as Nicolai Fechin and Georgia O'Keeffe, author D.H. Lawrence, and a slew of lesser-known but highly talented artists in the 1920s through the 1940s. Art remains a major force in the town today.

In the late 1960s the area became a haven for the "back to the country" movement, and world-class skiing was born at nearby Taos Ski Valley. Today elements of all these cultures coexist in the somewhat funky but charming community of greater Taos.

TAOS PLAZA AREA

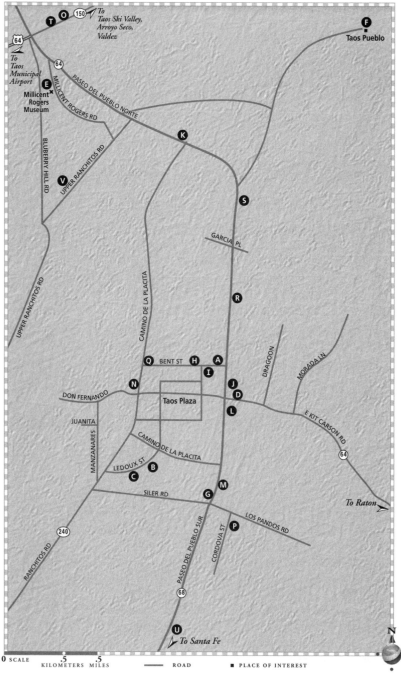

To
Taos Ski Valley,
Arroyo Seco,
Valdez

Taos Pueblo

To
Taos
Municipal
Airport

Millicent
Rogers
Museum

PASEO DEL PUEBLO NORTE

MILLICENT ROGERS RD

BLUBERRY HILL RD

UPPER RANCHITOS RD

UPPER RANCHITOS RD

GARCIA PL

CAMINO DE LA PLACITA

DRAGOON

MORADA LN

BENT ST

Taos Plaza

DON FERNANDO

E KIT CARSON RD

JUANITA

MANZANARES

CAMINO DE LA PLACITA

LEDOUX ST

SILER RD

LOS PANDOS RD

CORDOVA ST

PASEO DEL PUEBLO SUR

RANCHITOS RD

To Raton

To Santa Fe

0 SCALE   .5   .5
KILOMETERS MILES   ——— ROAD   ■ PLACE OF INTEREST

N

Sights

Ⓐ Bent Street

Ⓑ Blumenschein Home

Ⓒ Harwood Foundation

Ⓓ Kit Carson Home

Ⓔ Millicent Rogers Museum

Ⓕ Taos Pueblo

Food

Ⓖ Amigos Natural Grocery & Deli

Ⓗ Apple Tree

Ⓘ Bent Street Deli

Ⓙ Doc Martin's

Ⓚ El Pueblo Café

Ⓛ Eske's

Food (continued)

Ⓜ Lambert's

Ⓝ Main St. Bakery

Ⓞ Tim's Chile Connection

Lodging

Ⓟ Casa de las Chimeneas

Ⓠ Casa Feliz

Ⓡ Fechin Inn

Ⓢ Kachina Lodge

Ⓣ Quail Ridge Inn

Ⓤ Sun God Lodge

Ⓥ Taos Country Inn

Ⓙ Taos Inn

Note: Items with the same letter are located in the same town or area.

A PERFECT DAY IN TAOS

During the summer, visit Taos Pueblo early or late in the day to avoid crowds and heat. In town, check out museums, galleries, shops, and historic sites, with lunch at the Main Street Bakery or Bent Street Deli. If you're into outdoor recreation, mix a half-day in town with a half-day of skiing, white-water rafting, hiking, or mountain biking. Finish the day with a drive to the Gorge Bridge and the D.H. Lawrence Ranch, and have dinner at one of the town's many fine restaurants.

SIGHTSEEING HIGHLIGHTS

★★★ **Bent Street**—Just off the town's main plaza, Bent Street has become a center for small galleries, unique retail shops, and restaurants. It also shelters a small but interesting museum. The **Governor Bent Museum** preserves the home of the state's first territorial governor appointed by U.S. authorities, Charles Bent, whose family played a critical role in the success of the Santa Fe Trail. Bent's head was cut off by a mob in this house during the failed Taos Revolt of 1847, while his wife and children escaped by digging a hole through an adobe wall into an adjoining home. *Details: Museum at 117A Bent St.; 505/758-2376. Open daily 10–5. $2 adults. For further general information on Taos, contact the Taos Visitors Center on the corner of Paseo del Pueblo Sur and Paseo del Canon, 505/758-3873 or 800/732-8267. (1 hour)*

★★★ **Martinez Hacienda**—Within the massive, straw-flecked adobe walls of this compound, a prominent Taos family rose and fell from fortune. The property provides a rare look into the sparse, often harsh, yet fulfilling life on the Spanish frontier, with period rooms re-creating life in the early 1800s. Parts of the home date to the seventeenth century, when it was used as a neighborhood shelter during Comanche raids. During the last weekend in September it hosts the annual Old Taos Trade Fair, when its looms, blacksmith shop, kitchens, and other facilities really come to life. *Details: Head away from the Plaza on Ranchitos Rd. (NM 240) and follow a small creek a few miles through the picturesque countryside; 505/758-1000. Open daily 9–5. $5 adults. (1 hour)*

★★★ **Taos Pueblo**—The five-story Taos Pueblo is an icon of New Mexico's Pueblo Indian culture. A national historic landmark and UNESCO World Heritage Site, the Pueblo is perhaps the best-preserved of its peers in New Mexico. Built circa A.D. 1000–1400, it still lacks electricity or plumbing. Only a handful of families live here year-round today, but many families maintain homes within its condo-like structure for use during their many religious and secular ceremonies.

A dozen or so artists' galleries and shops are scattered about the pueblo. Do not enter any structure unless it is clearly marked as a public facility. Also of note is **San Geronimo Church**. Built in 1850, it's a lovely example of Spanish Colonial Mission–style architecture.

Prime days for visiting include the Fiesta de San Antonio on June 13, the Taos Pueblo Powwow on July 25 and 26, the Fiesta de San Geronimo on the evening of September 29 and daylong on September 30, Christmas Eve, Christmas Day, and January 1. *Details: Head north through Taos on Paseo del Pueblo (NM 68). Just past the Kachina Lodge and post office, take the marked fork to the right and* *continue a few miles into the pueblo parking lot; 505/758-9593. Open Apr–Nov daily 8–5:30; Dec–Mar 8:30–4:30; closed one month in late winter. $5 per vehicle; $5 for camera permit, $10 for video permit. (2 hours)*

★★ **Blumenschein Home**—This funky old adobe, built around 1797, was the home and studio of one of the pioneers of the Taos art colony, Ernest Blumenschein. His terrific work, contents of the house (including an interesting kitchen), and changing displays provide insight into the early days of Taos' still-thriving arts community.

    Details: 222 Ledoux St.; 505/758-0505. Open daily 9–5. $5 adults, $2.50 children ages 6–15. (1 hour)

★★ **Kit Carson Home**—As interesting and contrary a figure to be found anywhere in the annals of the West was trailblazer, mountain man, family man, trader, trapper, and U.S. Cavalry officer Kit Carson. This low-slung, 12-room adobe preserves the home in which he resided from 1843 to 1868. Personal and family effects are displayed along with a gun collection and mountain-man artifacts.

    Details: Kit Carson Rd., near the Plaza; 505/758-4741. Open Nov–Mar daily 9–5, Apr–Sept 8–6. $5 adults, $2.50 children ages 6–15. (1 hour)

© John MacLean Photography

Rancho de Taos Church

✯✯ **Millicent Rogers Museum**—This excellent, smallish museum, with strong holdings of Pueblo pottery (including those of famed San Ildefonso potter Maria Martinez), Indian silver jewelry and weavings, as well as Hispanic religious and secular arts and crafts, contains some of the more than 5,000 objects in the personal collection of deceased Standard Oil heiress Millicent Rogers, another of Taos' colorful historical characters. There's also a good gift shop and bookstore.

Details: Take U.S. 64 north. Just before the stoplight north of town, turn west (left) onto Millicent Rogers Rd. and continue several miles south; 505/758-2462. Open year-round daily 10–6. $6 adults, $5 students, $1 children. (1 hour)

✯✯ **Rio Grande Gorge Bridge**—Once the highest bridge on the U.S. highway system, this structure spanning the Rio Grande's Taos Gorge will put your heart in your mouth if heights scare you. The thin line of the river flowing beneath your feet is some 650 feet down. Park at either side and walk on the sidewalks to reach observation points.

Details: Drive north out of town on U.S. 64, turn left at the stoplight, and continue on U.S. 64 toward Tres Piedras. You can't miss it. It's free and always open. (30 minutes)

✯✯ **San Francisco de Asis Church**—Better known as the Ranchos de Taos Church, after the humble farming community just south of Taos, this eighteenth-century Spanish Colonial church is one of the most-photographed and -painted religious structures in the world. Almost every major artist who has ever lived in or passed through New Mexico has tried to capture its oddly appealing, earthy, abstract form. Mass is still presented here regularly, so don't barge in.

Details: U.S. 68, Ranchos de Taos (south of Taos). Its buttressed west wall (best seen in late afternoon) is visible from the highway; 505/758-2754. Open Mon-Sat 9–4. Donation requested. (30 minutes)

✯✯ **Harwood Foundation**—In almost any other region this would be a top attraction, but in northern New Mexico it is just one of a plethora of good art museums. Opened in 1923, it houses a knockout collection of early Taos artists, as well as work by their contemporaries and a room recently built expressly for Agnes Martin. A $1.5-million addition in 1997 expanded its galleries from two to seven.

Details: 238 Ledoux St.; 505/758-9826. Open Tue–Sun 10–5. $3.50 adults. (1 hour)

✦ **D.H. Lawrence Ranch**—A must-see for the literary pilgrim, this 160-acre property was the famed English author's home for some 22 months between 1922 and 1925. The buildings are not open to the public, but one can visit the small shrine where his ashes are buried, and the nearby grave of his wife, Frieda Lawrence. He wrote of this place, "I think New Mexico was the greatest experience from the outside world that I have ever had."

Details: *Take U.S. 64 and NM 522 north of Taos about 10 miles. Just before the village of Cristobal, look for a sign on the right, and continue along this gravel road for 4.5 miles. The shrine is about 100 yards uphill from the parking area; 505/776-2245. Open daily. Free. (1 hour)*

FITNESS AND RECREATION

Taos is a terrific locale for outdoor recreation. Sitting on a plateau flanked by mountains topping 13,000 feet and one of America's deepest canyons, the Rio Grande Gorge, its microclimates and geography make a wide range of activities possible. In fact, because of the vast differences in altitude, you can both ski and run white water on the same day.

Alpine skiers from around the world head to **Taos Ski Valley**, 505/776-2291, about 45 minutes from Taos Plaza. This area pioneered the concept of extreme inbounds skiing off the hike-to ridge of Highline and West Basin, and it's renowned for its phenomenally light powder (312 inches a year, average!). But it is a large area with lots of terrain for all ability levels. In summer, its chairlift provides hikers and sightseers with a ride into the Sangre de Cristo's highest peaks. To get there, take U.S. 64 to the light at the edge of town, then turn east (right) onto NM 150 through Arroyo Seco; it's about a 30-minute drive from town. Many options exist for cross-country skiing, too. Contact the **Carson National Forest**, 505/758-6200, in Taos, for details; or check out **Enchanted Forest Cross Country Ski Area**, 505/754-2374, located near Red River.

The other major recreational draw is hour-long, half-day, and full-day white-water outings on the Rio Grande. Various sections run from mild to white-knuckle. For options and information on guided services, or permits to run it yourself (not recommended for amateurs), contact the Taos Visitor Center (see Bent Street, above) or the **Bureau of Land Management** area office, 505/758-8851.

Superb options for backpacking and hiking also exist. Some 30 minutes from town is the edge of the 20,000-acre **Wheeler Peak Wilderness Area**. The **Williams Lake Trail**, popular on weekends,

TAOS REGION

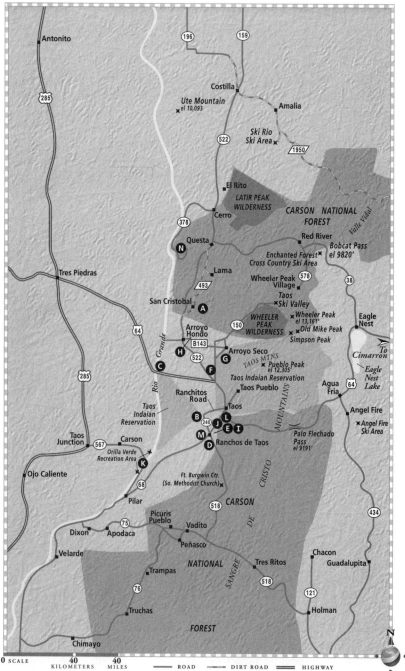

Antonito

196   159

285   Costilla
       Ute Mountain   Amalia
       el 10,093
                  Ski Rio
                  Ski Area
       522   1950

              El Rito
              LATIR PEAK
              WILDERNESS   CARSON NATIONAL
       378 Cerro   FOREST   Valle Vidal
Tres Piedras N Questa   Red River   Bobcat Pass
                                         el 9820'
                    Lama   Enchanted Forest
                            Cross Country Ski Area
       493   Wheeler Peak   578
                  Village   38
       San Cristobal A   Taos
                          Ski Valley
64   Wheeler Peak   Eagle
       150   WHEELER   el 13,161'   Nest
       Arroyo   PEAK   Old Mike Peak
285   Hondo   WILDERNESS Simpson Peak   To
       B143   Cimarron
       H   522 G Arroyo Seco TAOS MTNS   Eagle
       C   F   Pueblo Peak   Nest
                              el 12,305'   Lake
                  Taos Indaian Reservation
       Ranchitos   Taos Pueblo   Agua   64
       Road   Fria
       Taos   B Taos
       Indaian   240 Angel Fire
       Reservation J L   Palo Flechado Angel Fire
Taos   M E I   Pass   Ski Area
Junction Carson   D Ranchos de Taos el 9191'
567   434
       Orilla Verde
       Recreation Area K
Ojo Caliente   Ft. Burgwin Ctr.
                    (So. Methodist Church) CARSON
       68   518
       Pilar
       Picuris   DE
       Pueblo   Vadito
       75   Chacon
Dixon Apodaca   Peñasco   Guadalupita
Velarde   NATIONAL
         Trampas SANGRE Tres Ritos
                          518
       76
                         121
       Truchas   Holman

       FOREST   N

Chimayo

0 SCALE   40   40
       KILOMETERS MILES   ━━ ROAD ┅┅ DIRT ROAD ═══ HIGHWAY

Sights

Ⓐ D.H. Lawrence Ranch

Ⓑ Martinez Hacienda

Ⓒ Rio Grande Gorge Bridge

Ⓓ San Francisco de Asis Church

Food

Ⓔ Trading Post Café

Ⓕ Villa Fontana

Lodging

Ⓖ Abominable Snowmansion

Ⓗ Mountain Light

Lodging (continued)

Ⓘ Old Taos Guesthouse

Ⓙ Sagebrush Inn

Camping

Ⓚ Orilla Verde National Recreation Area

Ⓛ Taos RV Park

Ⓜ Taos Valley RV Park and Campground

Ⓝ Wild and Scenic Rivers National Recreation Area

---

climbs four miles from the Taos Ski Valley parking lot to a beautiful lake fronting the state's highest summit—13,160-foot **Wheeler Peak**. Mountain biking is also becoming a major draw, with several trails recently opened, including the **West Rim Trail** along the edge of the **Taos Gorge** (9.5 miles one way, with its northern terminus at the Rio Grande Gorge Bridge). For details, including routes and rentals, contact **Gearing Up**, 505/751-0365, or **Hot Tracks**, 505/751-0949.

FOOD

For a small community, Taos has amazingly diverse and high-quality dining options. Topping the price range but well worth a visit is **Doc Martin's**, in the Taos Inn, 125 Paseo del Pueblo Norte, 505/758-1977, the 1998 Zagat survey award–winner for northern New Mexico restaurants. Nightly specials vie with staples including roasted pheasant or penne pasta with mushrooms, bell pepper, and eggplant. Its wine list is quite impressive. **Lambert's**, 309 Paseo del Pueblo Sur, 505/758-1009, is known for its contemporary American dishes prepared with fresh ingredients. **Villa Fontana**, on NM 522 five miles north of the plaza, 505/758-5800, serves some terrific classic northern Italian fare in a

country-inn setting. A relatively new, highly regarded entry is the
Trading Post Café, 4179 NM 68 near its intersection with NM 518,
in Rancho de Taos, 505/758-5089, where I recently had a delicious half
duck with apple chutney.

In the moderate range is the **Bent Street Deli**, 120 Bent St.,
505/758-5787, with great soups, salads, and sandwiches; dinners feature
pasta or fish. Nearby is the **Apple Tree**, 123 Bent St., 505/758-1900,
with an international menu. Heading north to the ski valley, on NM
150, is **Tim's Chile Connection**, 505/776-8787, a sure bet for tasty
New Mexican fare, home-brewed beer, and infamous margaritas.

In the inexpensive category, some of the best handcrafted beer found
anywhere is tipped into mugs at **Eske's**, 106 DesGeorges Lane (one
block southeast of Kit Carson and Paseo del Pueblo), 505/758-1517. Six
to eight brews are on tap at any moment, hauled out of the basement
where 22 or so are nursed to life by brewmeister Steve Eskeback and his
wife, Wanda. Sandwiches, soups, and other fine pub fare is served, with
fresh sushi on Tuesday. Live music often plays at night. No smoking.

The aroma of fresh-baked breads and pastries wafts over you at
Main St. Bakery, just west of the Plaza off Camino de la Placita,
505/758-9610. Specialties include homemade granola, datenut/orange
French toast, and huevos rancheros. For New Mexican food as well as
chicken, hamburgers, and such, check out **El Pueblo Café**, 625 Paseo
del Pueblo Norte, 505/758-2053. **Amigos Natural Grocery & Deli**,
326 Paseo del Pueblo Sur, 505/758-8493, is a good place to stock up
on food treats or to sit at the counter for a great sandwich.

LODGING

The **Taos Inn**, 125 Paseo del Pueblo Norte, 505/758-2233 or
800/826-7466, has a lot going for it. It's set in the heart of town within
walking distance of most of Taos' interesting sites. A historic property
composed of centuries-old homes now linked together, it was completely renovated in 1981–82. All rooms have fireplaces, phones, and
private baths; rates are $75 to $225. The inn has a great restaurant,
Doc Martin's (see Food, above), and a fun bar, often with live music.

The **Sagebrush Inn**, 1508 Paseo del Pueblo Sur, 505/758-2254 or
800/428-3626, has been Taos' other classic dig since its opening in 1929.
Famed painter Georgia O'Keeffe lived for extended periods in one room
here, and its lobby with comfortable leather chairs, Hispanic and Pueblo
art and artifacts, a large stone fireplace, and exposed vigas epitomizes the

Taos ambiance. Rates start at $85. The Sagebrush has a rustic bar (often sporting country-western bands at night) and a decent restaurant.

The newest addition to the town's leading hotels is the attractive **Fechin Inn**, 227 Paseo del Pueblo Norte, 505/751-1000 or 800/811-2939. Named after renowned artist Nicolai Fechin, its 85 rooms and suites incorporate the artist's original home and reflect his eclectic style and tastes. Amenities include a fitness center, bar, and free Continental breakfast. Pets are allowed. Rates range from $109 to $179.

Popular with skiers and families is **Quail Ridge Inn**, just outside of town off the Ski Valley road, 505/776-2211 or 800/624-4448. This 110-unit Pueblo-style complex has a 20-meter heated pool, indoor tennis courts, saunas, hot tubs, a coin-op laundry, fireplaces, phones, and maid service. A basic double is $89; condos are $120. A restaurant and bar are also on the premises.

The **Kachina Lodge**, 413 Paseo del Pueblo Norte, 505/758-2275 or 800/522-4462, is another unique property, an upscale motel opened in 1961 with a kind of Pueblo Deco decor. Though its bedrooms are nothing special, its lobby, cool Kiva Coffee Shop, and other public spaces feature a superb collection of Indian arts and crafts. Rates are $100 to $130. On the north edge of town, it provides quick access to the ski valley road.

For those on a budget, the **Sun God Lodge**, 919 Paseo del Pueblo Sur, 505/758-3162 or 800/821-2437, has small rooms with Mexican furniture, sculpted walls dividing the bedrooms and bathrooms, and other thoughtful touches. Rates are $59 to $82. Taos' least expensive lodging is the **Abominable Snowmansion**, on the Ski Valley road in Arroyo Seco, 505/776-8298. It's a pleasant no-frills hostel with private rooms and dormitory rates from $16 to $22.

Taos has a great collection of bed-and-breakfasts, each with its own distinct character. The **Taos Country Inn**, off Upper Ranchitos Road set in fields a few miles west of downtown, 505/758-4900, has stunning views of sacred Taos Mountain. Saltillo tile floors, local wooden furniture and art, Southwestern textiles, and the adobe structure provide a perfect New Mexico experience. Try the Deveaux Room, with windows on three sides and a fireplace. Rates are $110 to $140. **Casa de las Chimeneas**, 405 Cordoba Rd., 505/758-4777, is one of Taos' luxury B&Bs. Inside its seven-foot-thick adobe walls are outstanding regional art, tiled hearths, French doors, and lovely furniture. All rooms have private entrances, fireplaces, telephones, mini-refrigerators, and cable TV. In spring, a beautiful garden comes alive. Rates are $130 to $160.

Downtown, on historic Bent Street, is **Casa Feliz**, 505/758-9790.

The former home of artist Becky James (who was once married to famed photographer Paul Strand), it radiates charm and tranquillity. Each room has its own bathroom and New Mexico handcrafted furniture. Rates are $85 to $110. Overlooking town on its southeast edge is the **Old Taos Guesthouse**, off Kit Carson Rd., 505/758-5448. Each of the eight rooms has a private entrance and private bath. The friendly owners also cook up a great breakfast. Rates are $70 to $110. A simple, inexpensive B&B with see-forever views is **Mountain Light**, out of town in Arroyo Hondo, 505/776-8474. Rates are $52 to $62.

CAMPING

Nine campgrounds sit within 20 miles of Taos in the **Carson National Forest**, 505/758-6200. Developed sites also exist in the **Orilla Verde National Recreation Area**, 505/758-8851, along the Rio Grande near Pilar (30 minutes south of town off NM 68), administered by the BLM. About 45 minutes north of town is the spectacular **Wild and Scenic Rivers National Recreation Area**, 505/758-8851, where you can camp high above the confluence of the Rio Grande and Red River or hike into the canyon for primitive camping. In Ranchos de Taos, the **Taos RV Park**, 505/758-1667 or 800/323-6009, offers 29 sites with full hookups. In Taos, try the **Taos Valley RV Park and Campground**, 505/758-4469, with 92 sites. It's closed November through February.

NIGHTLIFE

In winter, several bars in Taos Ski Valley can be a lot of fun; particularly, **The Bistro**, in the venerable Hotel St. Bernard, 505/776-2251; the **Martini Tree**, on the third floor of the Resort Center, 505/776-2005; and **The Thunderbird**, 3 Thunderbird Rd., 505/776-2280. In town, you can usually do the country shuffle out at the **Sagebrush Inn**, 1508 Paseo del Pueblo Sur, 505/758-2254 or 800/428-3626. Downtown, **Eske's**, 106 DesGeorges Lane (one block southeast of Kit Carson and Paseo del Pueblo), 505/758-1517, often has live music, too. See the *Taos News* for shows held occasionally at the rocking **Old Martinez Hall** in Rancho de Taos, 4140 NM 68, 505/758-2091. **Taos Mountain Casino**, on the Taos Pueblo reservation, 505/758-4460 or 888-WIN-TAOS, has smoke-free card games, slots, and roulette, as well as a nice deli restaurant.

5

NORTHEAST CORNER

This corner of New Mexico hides many secrets. Behind its quiet facade is a tempestuous history of boom-and-bust farming cycles, a bloody tussle known as the Union County War, mining fortunes, gunslingers, and the Santa Fe Trail, which ran from Missouri into what was then Mexico. The one-time home of thousands of dryland farmers driven out by the Great Drought of the 1930s, it seems a bit forlorn and forgotten today. It slumbers on toward the millennium, its towns eking out an existence.

But the area has its appeal. A mingling of the westernmost fringe of the Great Plains and the eastern foothills of the Sangre de Cristos, it has clean bracing air, mountain-fed streams and ponds, abundant wildlife, magnificent views off high mesas, and endlessly rolling grasslands under a blue dome of sky. Capulin Volcano National Monument, the massive Canadian River Canyon, and a state park with dinosaur tracks trapped in stone await the visitor here. The area also holds historical gems; if you are drawn to odd, sometimes finely done historic buildings and homes, you'll find much to admire here, from the Dorsey Mansion and Villa Philmonte to Raton's historic district and the stockade compound of Kit Carson.

A PERFECT DAY IN THE NORTHEAST CORNER

A great day in this region begins at Raton's Red Violet Inn B&B. Be on the road by 9 a.m., and head northeast out of town and east across Johnson Mesa to the small town of Folsom. Visit its museum before

NORTHEAST NEW MEXICO

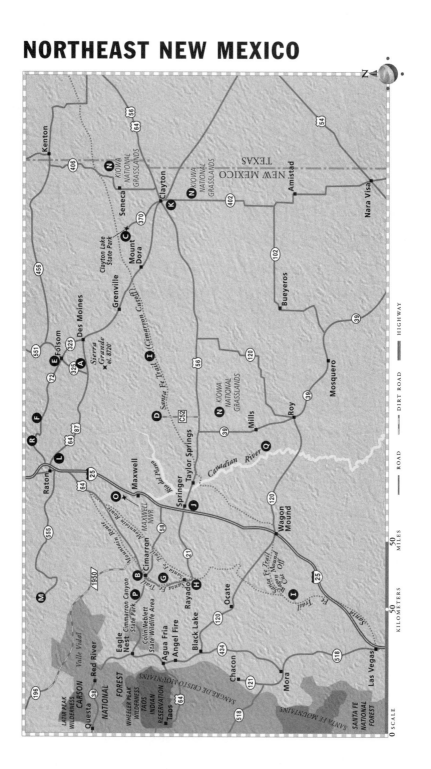

Sights

Ⓐ Capulin National Monument

Ⓑ Cimarron

Ⓒ Clayton Lake State Park

Ⓓ Dorsey Mansion

Ⓔ Folsom

Ⓕ Johnson Mesa

Ⓖ Philmont Ranch

Ⓗ Rayado

Ⓘ Santa Fe Trail

Ⓙ Santa Fe Trail Museum

Food

Ⓚ Eklund Dining Room & Saloon

Ⓙ El Taco

Ⓛ Mel's Texas Bar-B-Q

Ⓑ Porch Deli

Ⓑ Simple Simon's Pizza

Ⓑ St. James Hotel

Lodging

Ⓑ Casa de Gavilan B&B

Ⓑ St. James Hotel

Ⓚ Sunset

Ⓜ Vermejo Park Ranch

Camping

Ⓑ Cimarron Inn & RV Park

Ⓚ Clayton KOA

Ⓒ Clayton Lake State Park

Ⓝ Kiowa National Grasslands

Ⓞ Maxwell National Wildlife Refuge

Ⓟ McCrystal Creek/Cimarron

Ⓠ Mills Campground

Ⓡ Sugarite Canyon State Park

Note: Items with the same letter are located in the same town or area.

dropping south for a picnic on the summit of Capulin Volcano National Monument. Continue on to Clayton and camp in the Kiowa National Grasslands along the old Santa Fe Trail north of town. Another good day would begin in Cimarron, followed by a visit to the Philmont Ranch, Kit Carson's place at Rayado, and then on to Springer.

SIGHTSEEING HIGHLIGHTS

✸✸✸ **Capulin National Monument**—Sometime between 8,000 and 2,500 years ago, powerful earthquakes, belching smoke, and fire emerged from the earth here as geologic forces began to build a mountain of ash and magma. By the time the disturbance was over, a thousand-foot-high, beautifully symmetrical peak, Capulin (Spanish for "chokecherry"), rose from the plains below.

A two-mile road spirals to its summit. Here you'll find a short trail—a fifth of a mile long—that drops to a vent at the bottom of the crater; another one-mile trail makes a short climb to the rim and encircles it. The hikes offer close-up glimpses of volcanic geology, the hardy and pretty plant life of this windswept point, and tremendous views of five states. A visitors center, at mile 0.6 from the park entrance, has audiovisual displays, literature, and restrooms.

Details: *Entrance is from NM 325, 3 miles north of the town of Capulin, 30 miles east of Raton on U.S. 64/87; 505/278-2201. The park is open year-round, although snow closes the summit road a few times each winter. Visitors center open Memorial Day–Labor Day daily 7–7. $4 per vehicle. For details, write P.O. Box 40, Capulin, NM 88414. (2 hours)*

★★★ **Philmont Ranch**—The Philmont Ranch actually encompasses three separate but related sights of interest for visitors: the Philmont Scout Ranch, Villa Philmonte, and the Seton Memorial Library and museum.

The **Philmont Scout Ranch** is the national training center for the Boy Scouts of America. Each summer 25,000 scouts converge on this lovely 137,493-acre site in the rugged east-facing flank of the Sangre de Cristos.

The **Villa Philmonte** has been called the "frontier Xanadu." The astonishing 17,000-square-foot Spanish-Mediterranean mansion was built in the 1920s by Phillips Petroleum co-founder Waite Phillips. Its 15 major rooms—filled with a wonderful collection of art by members of the Taos Society of Artists, Pueblo pottery, and European antiques— both dazzle and charm. My favorite room is the hunting lair found tucked away in one corner, where it appears the guys have just stepped out to get a breath of fresh air and are about to return to their poker game. Outside are lovely gardens and lawns. In donations made in 1938 and 1941, Phillips gave 127,000 acres of his land here to the Boy Scouts for the ranch described above. Today the Scouts administer his home as a museum.

Within the Philmont Museum, the **Seton Memorial Library** contains many of the paintings, drawings, and books written by acclaimed Canadian-born naturalist and artist Ernest Thompson Seton (1860–1946), who spent the end of his life in New Mexico.

Also on the Philmont Ranch is a herd of 100 to 150 buffalo. They can be viewed occasionally west of NM 21 between Cimarron and the ranch headquarters. Don't enter the pasture. The **Philmont Trading Post** carries camping and souvenir items. It's open summers daily from 7:30 a.m. to 6:45 p.m.

Details: Scout encampment 4 miles south of Cimarron on NM 21; 505/376-2281. Adjoining Villa Philmonte, 505/376-2281, can be visited only on guided tours—arranged at the nearby Philmont Museum. Tours held May–Aug daily every half hour 8–4:30, Sept–mid-October at 10:30 a.m. and 2:30 p.m., mid-Oct–Apr by appointment; $4 adults. Philmont Museum, 505/376-2281, open June–Aug daily 8–5, Sept–May Sat and Sun; free. (2–3 hours)

★★ **Cimarron**—The James brothers, Wyatt Earp, Annie Oakley, and other famous figures of the pioneer-era West spent time in this small town located at the foot of the Sangre de Cristos. It shelters a number of interesting and historic buildings, including the **Aztec Mill**, which serves today as a local history center. Other notable properties include the **Old Town Jail**, the **St. James Hotel** (see Lodging, below), the **Wells Fargo Station**, **Swink's Gambling Hall**, and an operational 1930s-era soda fountain in the drug store. A visitors center is located on U.S. 64 in town.

Details: Aztec Mill 1 block off NM 21; 505/376-2913. Open summer daily—except Thu—9–5, spring and fall Sat and Sun 1–5. $2 adults, $1 seniors and children. (2 hours)

★★ **Dorsey Mansion**—Here is a fascinating example of the way time has bypassed this corner of New Mexico. This structure was once the bustling headquarters of an isolated ranch spanning 64 square miles, owned by Arkansas-born U.S. Senator Stephen Dorsey and his wife, Helen. They abandoned it in 1892 after personal and legal tragedies, and he died in poverty, but the house is still quite extraordinary. Outside, Gothic stone gargoyles peer down from the roof while a bobcat and rattlesnakes twine about a fountain. Inside are found the first gas lights in the region, a dining room seating 60, Italian marble fireplaces, crystal chandeliers, a billiard room, and an art gallery. The property is currently a llama and horse ranch. It is open for public tours, but call ahead.

Details: Take U.S. 56 20 miles east from Springer to the village of Abbott, proceed another 4 miles east on U.S. 56, then head north on a dirt *road 12 miles to the residence, 505/375-2222. Exactly 7 miles north of U.S. 56 you cross the tracks of the Cimarron Cutoff of the Santa Fe Trail. If you look closely, you may be able to discern the original wagon routes. $5 adults. (1 hour for tour)*

★★ **Johnson Mesa**—For a beautiful drive with little or no traffic across dramatic terrain east of Raton, cross Johnson Mesa to the small town of Folsom. The 32-mile excursion passes abandoned wooden homesteads, thousands of acres of wildflowers, and the **Folsom Man Site** (on private property at mile 25 or so), where archaeological discoveries in 1928–29 pushed back human occupation of the New World to the then-unheard-of antiquity of 12,000 B.C.

Details: The road is paved but is closed in winter. There are no services between Raton and Folsom. (1 hour)

★★ **Raton Historic District**—This somnolent town of 7,500 people was once a boom town plump from its role as a county seat, a regional rail and mining center, and a "gateway" to New Mexico. Then the railroad pushed farther south to Las Vegas and Raton began a slow slide. Its lack of industry, however, has left it with a fantastic assemblage of century-old buildings and homes. A five-block National Historic District between First and Third Streets and Clark and Rio Grande Avenues protects some 70 structures, including the rail depot, the **Roth Building**, the **Marchiondo Building**, the **Labadie House**, and the **Schuler Theater**. Guides to the district are available at the Raton Museum or Chamber of Commerce. Also in the district is the **Raton Museum** with dioramas and relics of the railyard era, the former coal camps, and local ranch life.

Details: Museum at 216 S. First St., 505/455-8979. Open Oct–Apr Wed–Sat, May–Sept Tue–Sat. (2 hours)

★★ **Rayado**—This village was the frontier home of famous trapper, scout, and military commander Kit Carson in the 1850s before he married Josefa Jaramillo and moved to Taos. Built as a walled compound to withstand armed attacks, it is run today as a living history museum by the Boy Scouts. You'll see a working blacksmith shop, kitchen, armory, living quarters, and outdoor activities. You'll discover tidbits of frontier life, such as treatment of floors with oxblood preservatives. Also in Rayado is one of the former homes of Lucien

B. Maxwell, one of New Mexico's most prominent citizens, who controlled a land grant of more than 1.7 million acres in the nineteenth century. *Details: 8 miles south of Villa Philmonte on NM 21; 505/376-2281. Carson's compound open in summer daily 8–5. Free. (1 hour)*

★★ **Santa Fe Trail**—Two branches of the Santa Fe Trail—the Mountain Route, which crossed over Raton Pass from Colorado into New Mexico, and the Cimarron Cutoff, which angled across Union County from Oklahoma—once bisected this corner of the state. Original wagon ruts are still evident on the plains. *Details: Potential viewpoints include U.S. 87/64 between Grenville and Mt. Dora, the town of Rayado, at mile 26 on NM 120 east of Wagon Mound, and along NM 406 north of Clayton. Call 505/988-6888 for details. (30 minutes on site)*

★ **Clayton Lake State Park**—Set among rolling grasslands, this 420-acre park features a half-mile trail with interpretive signs overlooking a set of 100-million-year-old dinosaur tracks containing nearly 500 footprints from eight different species—including those of a pterodactyl taking off in flight. *Details: 13 miles north of Clayton via NM 370; 505/374-8808. Open daily. $3 per vehicle for a day. (1 hour for dino trail)*

★ **Folsom**—A small town that serves outlying ranches, Folsom was the scene decades ago of a flood that largely destroyed it. A switchboard operator stayed at her post warning residents of the impending flood until she was swept away. This and other stories are presented and preserved at the **Folsom Museum,** along with a fascinating array of everyday household and work materials, photos, and a collection of Folsom Man spear points and stone tools. *Details: Museum is on main street, 505/278-2477. Open Memorial Day–Labor Day 10–5. Free. (30 minutes)*

★ **Santa Fe Trail Museum**—This facility, housed in the old Colfax County Courthouse in Springer, contains a collection of odds and ends, including a Trail-era covered wagon, high-school graduation pictures, and an electric chair. *Details: Located on Maxwell St.; 505/483-2341. Open June–Aug daily with varying hours. $1.50 adults, $1 seniors. (30 minutes)*

FITNESS AND RECREATION

The northeast corner of New Mexico, with its scarcity of people and variety of terrain—12,000-foot-high mountains, huge mesas, and the rolling High Plains—is a great place for outdoor activities. A spectacular feature many people overlook—even lifelong residents—is **Mills Canyon**, a major red sandstone-tiered gash cut by the Canadian River as it drops out of the mountains onto the plains. A rough road bumps to the canyon bottom and provides a remarkable outing for those equipped with a four-wheel-drive vehicle. Bear, cougar, bobcat, mule deer, exotic Barbary sheep, smaller wildlife, and birds are abundant. There is fishing in the river, and opportunities for remote mountain biking, hiking, and white-water sports.

It is located west of Roy within the **Kiowa National Grasslands**, and administered by **Cibola National Forest**, 505/374-9652. To get there, head north 10 miles from Roy on NM 39 to the village of Mills; turn left onto Forest Road 600, a dirt road that heads almost due west. The canyon will appear unexpectedly in front of you.

Another outstanding area for hiking, viewing wildflowers, birding, fishing, cross-country skiing, and ice fishing is **Sugarite Canyon State Park**, 505/445-5607, located northeast of Raton almost on the Colorado border. The park also contains remains of an important old coal mining camp where more than 1,000 people once lived and worked. The day use fee is three dollars per vehicle. To get there, head out of town six miles on NM 72 (the Johnson Mesa road) and then turn left onto NM 526 and head five miles up the canyon.

A premier spot for bird watching is the **Maxwell National Wildlife Refuge**, 505/375-2331, where more than 50,000 ducks typically gather in late fall, along with geese and bald eagles. It is open year-round and entry is free. To get here exit I-25 at mile marker 426 and drive into the village of Maxwell. Go 0.75 mile north on NM 445, then west on NM 505 for 2.5 miles to the refuge entrance. The refuge headquarters is 2.5 miles north.

Elk hunters and aspen viewers flock to the **Valle Vidal** in fall while anglers vie for elusive and rare Rio Grande cutthroat trout in summer on this high and lonesome land tucked under the Colorado border to the north of the town of Cimarron. Some 100,000 acres of mountain valleys and thick pine and aspen forest administered by the **Carson National Forest**, 505/586-0520, protect a plethora of wildlife, including a small buffalo herd in the McCrystal Creek area. Dirt ranch roads also make for excellent hiking and biking. To get here, from Cimarron take U.S. 64 east. At 4.7 miles turn north (left) and proceed northeast on the gravel road some 20 miles to the Vidal Unit boundary, and another 10 miles or so to McCrystal Creek.

A popular fishing destination is **Cimarron Canyon State Park**, 505/377-6271, west of the town of Cimarron on U.S. 64. A few ponds and the waters of the Cimarron River running beneath an impressive palisade of cliffs make for a nice day outing or picnic.

The 33,000-acre **Whittington Center**, 505/445-3615, is a popular shooting range and guided hunting reserve run by the National Rifle Association. It is located 10 miles southwest of Raton off U.S. 64. Kitchenettes, snacks, and bedding are provided.

FOOD

This area is no dining mecca, but there are a few pleasant surprises out yonder in them thar hills. For an old-time ambiance, head over to the **Eklund Dining Room & Saloon**, 15 Main St., 505/374-2551, in Clayton. Housed in the former Eklund Hotel, which was built in the late nineteenth century, the restaurant has been restored to its former elegance and serves up Mexican and American fare for $10 to $20.

Along I-25 in Springer is **El Taco**, at the north end of Maxwell Street, serving up excellent New Mexico fare, from tacos to rellenos. Another find is **Mel's Texas Bar-B-Q**, nine miles east of Raton on U.S. 64/87, where Mel Johnson smokes up some delightful ribs, chicken, dinner combos, and beef sandwiches. All the meats are slow-smoked on hickory, oak, and pecan woods with secret family sauces.

Pappa's Sweet Shop, 1201 S. Second St, Raton, 505/445-9811, serves up tasty French toast made from their own bread, and at night steaks, seafood, and Mexican dishes. It was founded in 1923. Also in Raton are the **Shanghai**, 160 S. Second, 505/754-2952, with surprisingly good Chinese food; and a low-budget option, **Domingo's**, 1903 Cedar, 505/445-2288, which has a Tuesday night all-you-can-eat buffet and a beer and wine license.

Cimarron also has a few places to eat. Dependable vittles are found at the venerable **St. James Hotel** (see Lodging, below), which has a dining room, coffee shop, and bar. The **Porch Deli**, Ninth Street, 505/376-2228, serves soups, sandwiches, lunch specials, salads, and baked goods. **Simple Simon's Pizza**, also on Ninth Street, 505/376-2130, has carry-out pizza.

RATON

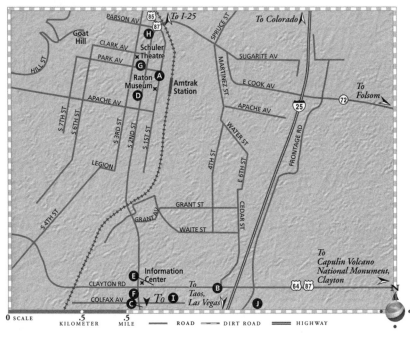

Sights

Ⓐ Raton Historic District

Food

Ⓑ Domingo's

Ⓒ Pappa's Sweet Shop

Ⓓ Shanghai

Lodging

Ⓔ Best Western Sands Motel

Ⓕ Colt Motel

Ⓖ Portal Hotel

Ⓗ Red Violet Inn

Camping

Ⓘ I-J & N Campground

Ⓙ Summerlan RV Park

LODGING

The **St. James Hotel**, on NM 21 at 17th and Collison in Cimarron, 505/376-2664 or 800/748-2694, is worth a visit even if you don't spend the night. Built in 1873, the hotel housed Annie Oakley, Wyatt Earp, Buffalo Bill, and Jesse James, and Zane Grey worked on a book while residing here. It was once a wild place: 26 men are reported to have been killed in the downstairs bar and restaurant. I've noted the bullet holes in the stamped tin ceiling and the bar itself, and there is one room that the management refuses to rent due to its distressing female ghost. Rooms run $60 to $95. You can also reserve rooms in a motel annex for $45 to $70. Summer brings lots of Boy Scouts.

Near Cimarron is the **Casa de Gavilan B&B**, P.O. Box 518, Cimarron, NM 87714, 505/376-2246, housed in a turn-of-the-century adobe. It was once owned by Waite Phillips, of Philmont Ranch fame. Rooms run $75 to $105 for two.

One of the priciest accommodations in New Mexico is found here as well—on the immense **Vermejo Park Ranch**, 505/445-3097, located 45 miles or so west of Raton near the high peaks of the Sangre de Cristos. The historic guest lodge is now part of Ted Turner's vast New Mexico holdings. The ranch is trout nirvana and also shelters large herds of elk, deer, and other wildlife. Rates are around $300 a day, which includes meals and non-hunting activities.

The **Portal Hotel**, 101 N. Third St., 505/445-3631, is perhaps Raton's most historic lodging. It began as a livery, then was expanded into the Seaburg European Hotel in 1904—once New Mexico's largest. Doubles, with baths but no TV, cost $40. For a Raton B&B, try the **Red Violet Inn**, 344 N. Second St., 505/445-9778 or 800/624-9778, set in a 1902 brick home. Rates range from $40 to $60. The inn is closed in February.

Also in Raton is the **Best Western Sands Motel**, with a pool, playground, and restaurant. Large rooms with queen- or king-sized beds run $70 in summer. At the low end of the price scale is Raton's **Colt Motel**, 1160 S. Second St., 505/445-2305, with doubles for $25. Clayton also has some inexpensive motels, including the **Sunset**, 702 S. First, 505/374-2589.

Note: Raton sports a horseracing track, La Mesa, with races every weekend from May to September; rooms can be hard to find on Friday and Saturday nights during these months.

CAMPING

Mills Campground, 505/374-9652, in Mills Canyon (see Fitness and Recreation, above), is an isolated and beautiful spot with free camping in a national forest from late spring through early fall. Another beautiful camping area off the beaten path is the Valle Vidal (see Fitness and Recreation), which contains national forest campgrounds **McCrystal Creek** and **Cimarron**. They are closed late fall to late spring. The Vidal also allows backcountry hiking and camping. You can also camp for free on the **Kiowa National Grasslands** (see Fitness and Recreation), though I've found almost no one does.

Sugarite Canyon State Park (see Fitness and Recreation) is open May through October for camping with $7 tent sites and RV sites with hookups for $11. Water, but not showers, is available. Camping is usually allowed on the **Maxwell National Wildlife Refuge** (see Fitness and Recreation). **Clayton Lake State Park** (see Sightseeing Highlights, above) also allows camping. Sites go for $7 for tents and $11 for RVs with hookups.

There are also a few RV parks in Raton, among them **Summerlan RV Park**, just to the southeast of I-25 and Clayton Road, 505/445-9536, with sites for $14; and the **I-J & N Campground**, 1330 S. Second St., 505/445-3488, with sites for $14 as well. The **Clayton KOA**, 903 S. Fifth St., 505/374-9508, has tent spaces for $13, RV sites with hookups for $15, and Kamping Cabins for $21. There is a laundry and playground. Another option is the **Cimarron Inn & RV Park**, at the corner of U.S. 64 and NM 58, 505/376-2268 or 800/546-2244, with 12 RV hookups for $14.50.

NIGHTLIFE

The historic **Schuler Theater**, 131 N. Second, Raton, 505/445-5520, is still in operation, with occasional music and variety shows. The elaborate European Rococo interior has surprisingly good acoustics; also check out the lobby murals painted in the 1930s by Manville Chapman. Raton's **Pioneer Bar**, at Clayton Road and S. Second, has bands on weekends and dollar beers on weeknights.

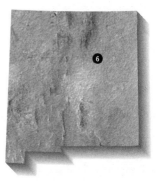

6
LAS VEGAS AREA

While eclipsed by Nevada's city of the same name, Las Vegas, New Mexico, is actually the much older of the two communities. Here, where the Great Plains meet the Rocky Mountains among meadows of luxurious grasses (*vegas* in Spanish), Plains Indians, Spanish explorers and settlers, French mountain men, Anglo cattlemen, and Jewish merchants have mingled. In the 1880s, it was the state's premier town and the San Miguel County seat, boasting opera houses, lavish saloons, hotels, and bustling businesses. Then the railhead pressed onto Albuquerque, Fort Union closed, and Las Vegas fell into a deep slumber.

Voilà! It's the 1990s and the town is awakening. Buildings that were never torn down by "urban renewal"—the 1970s blight that wiped out many New Mexico downtowns—two-story stone houses with wraparound porches, and other remnants of its affluent past are being restored and reoccupied. The town is attracting people who appreciate its history, its beautiful setting at the foot of the Sangre de Cristo Mountains, and the tenacity of its original Hispanic settlers. The population has swelled past 17,000.

Though not far from Santa Fe, Las Vegas has a much slower, untrampled feel, with much to be discovered. With the Sangre de Cristos at the town's backside, recreation opportunities abound, as do rich historical and cultural resources. Surrounding the town are a host of interesting day trip destinations, including Fort Union, various Hispanic villages, and scads of wildlife.

LAS VEGAS AREA

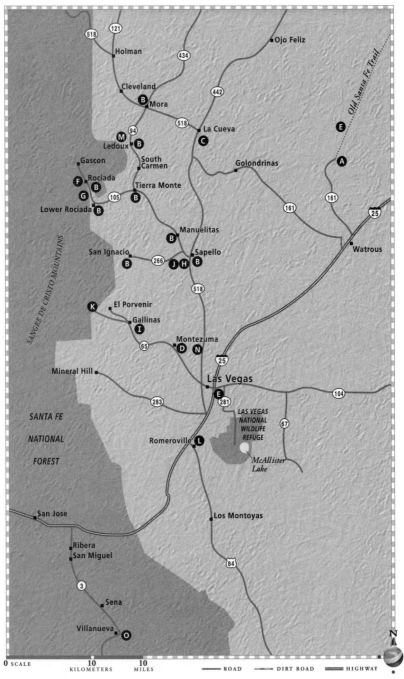

Sights

Ⓐ Fort Union

Ⓑ Hispanic Villages

Ⓒ La Cueva National Historic Site

Ⓓ Montezuma Castle

Ⓔ Santa Fe Trail

Food

Ⓕ One Stop

Ⓖ Pendaries Country Club

Ⓖ Pendaries Lodge

Ⓒ Salman Ranch

Lodging

Ⓗ Cerro Pelon Guest Ranch

Ⓘ Mountain Music Guest Ranch

Lodging *(continued)*

Ⓖ Pendaries Lodge

Ⓙ Star Hill Inn

Ⓕ Totem Ranch B&B

Camping

Ⓚ Big Pine/EV Long/Oak Flats/El Porvenir

Ⓛ Las Vegas KOA

Ⓜ Morphy Lake State Park

Ⓖ Pendaries RV Park

Ⓝ Storrie Lake State Park

Ⓞ Villanueva State Park

Note: Items with the same letter are located in the same town or area.

A PERFECT DAY IN THE LAS VEGAS AREA

After spending the night at the Plaza Hotel, have breakfast downstairs before heading out to explore the wonderful old buildings around the plaza area. Then drive down to the railroad district and tour the town's lovely residential neighborhoods. Spend the afternoon visiting Fort Union or touring the mountain villages. Take in the sunset at the national wildlife refuge or at the Montezuma Hot Springs.

SIGHTSEEING HIGHLIGHTS

★★★ **Fort Union**—I first approached this national monument on a summer afternoon as a huge rainstorm gathered. Great beams of sunlight filtered through the clouds over a vast, treeless plain at the base of a high range of mountains. We drove up to the fort and seemed to

be its only visitors. Taking pictures, I stumbled into a camp of reenactment folks dressed in period clothes. They were holed up in tents and
offered me something to drink. Rain was beginning to splat down in
great drops, so I gladly accepted. It seemed like I'd stepped back in
time. The time would have been somewhere between 1851 and 1891,
when the fort protected trade and travelers along the nearby Santa Fe
Trail. As one of the largest military outposts in the American
Southwest, it played a major role in the life of the region.

Today slumped adobe walls, some brick fireplaces, wagons, and
wagon wheel ruts radiating out across the High Plains remain. There is
a self-guiding trail through the fort's ruins, which include warehouses,
a hospital, offices, quarters, parade ground, workshops, and sutler
store. On summer weekends living history and interpretive programs
are presented. A visitors center has excellent displays on the fort and
area history.

Details: 28 miles northwest of Las Vegas; 505/425-8025. Take I-25
north from town to Exit 366 at Watrous, then head northwest on NM 161 to
the entrance. Open summer daily 8–6, winter daily 8–5. $2 per person or $4
per carload. (1 hour on site)

★★★ **Las Vegas Historic Districts**—In 1835 a handful of Hispanic
families from the Pecos River town of San Miguel del Bado were provided a land grant in an area of lush meadows along the banks of the
Gallinas River. With the coming of the Santa Fe Trail, the village
grew into a prosperous small town of Las Vegas. Then on July 4,
1879, the Atchison, Topeka and Santa Fe Railroad steamed into town
for the first time, amid great hoopla. As the railroad's first port-of-
entry into New Mexico, the town quickly grew into the state's largest
and most prosperous.

During this period, many fine and often elaborate or whimsical
stone, brick, and wood frame buildings not commonly found in New
Mexico were erected here. When the train pushed on further south
and Albuquerque became the new Cinderella, Las Vegas slipped back
into obscurity. But its idleness allowed it to be spared major urban
renewal projects, and today it retains many of its fine old homes and
commercial buildings.

In fact, Las Vegas boasts more than 900 properties on the National
Register of Historic Places and not one but *seven* National Historic
Districts—including one near the railroad tracks and another around the
town's original plaza. The plaza is a pretty spot with trees and a music

gazebo in the center. Around it face a charming array of historic multi-story buildings, including the eye-catching **Plaza Hotel**; the Italianate **Veeder Buildings**; the **Charles Ilfeld Building**, named for the pioneering American Jewish merchant; and the **First National Bank**. Elsewhere in town are the Neoclassical Revival **Carnegie Library**, one of the few still in use in the nation; the **Castaneda Rail Depot**, which is closed but still intriguing; and residential areas full of lovely Queen Anne, Tudor, Picturesque Italianate, Mansard, and other fanciful buildings.

Details: The chamber of commerce (see Resources, pages 245–247) has a series of illustrated, free walking guides to Las Vegas' historic homes, churches, and commercial buildings. For additional information, contact the Citizens Committee for Historic Preservation, 505/425-8803. (1–4 hours)

★★ **Hispanic Villages**—There are a number of villages dotting the stream-fed valleys of the Sangre de Cristos just to the west and north of Las Vegas, some settled by Hispanic farmers as early as the 1830s. Most feature a pretty Catholic church and cozy houses that have weathered many a snowy winter and enjoyed many a glorious flower-popping spring and summer.

A drive along NM 518 and offshoots makes for a pleasant day of sightseeing. The route begins on the town's north side, where NM 518 intersects Mills Avenue. Head north on NM 518 past Storrie Lake State Park some 13 miles to the village of **Sapello**. Turn northwest onto NM 94 for nine miles, passing through the smaller villages of **Manuelitas** and **Tierra Monte**. Here turn west onto NM 105 for a seven-mile detour into villages tucked right under the spine of the mountains: **Rociada, Gascon**, and **Upper Rociada** (reached via a backtrack to NM 276). The laid-back resort of **Pendaries Village** is also found here at another branch off NM 105. Return to Tierra Monte and NM 94, and proceed another four miles north through **South Carmen** to **Ledoux**, and another four miles to **Mora**—by far the largest of these mountain communities.

Details: Total drive distance is about 50 miles one-way. Return via NM 518 through La Cueva (home of historic Cleveland Roller Mill and Museum, 505/387-2645) and NM 161 to I-25 South. (3–6 hours)

★★ **La Cueva National Historic Site**—This site preserves several properties erected by an early Hipanic land grant settler, Vincente Romero, including his so-called **Big House**—with its gun slots in the walls for fending off Comanche, Ute, and Apache raiders; and **The**

Mill, a water-driven flour mill that operated up to 1949. Here too is **San Rafael Mission**, which contains exquisite French Gothic windows, a visible reminder of the important role once played in the area by the French priests brought to New Mexico by Bishop Lamy.

The Spanish settlers of the area discovered many *mora* (blackberries) here, and today berries, particularly raspberries, retain their prominence. The **Salman Ranch Store**, originally established by Romero, today carries on the mercantile tradition, selling jars of delicious raspberry jams, syrup, and vinegar made from local fruit, as well as vegetables and hand-crafted goods. The Big House, Mill, San Rafael Mission, and Salman Ranch Store are all on the National Register of Historic Places. Today they are all owned and operated by the Salman family.

Details: The sites are all located in the village of La Cueva (see Hispanic Villages entry, above), 505/387-2900. Interior access of the historic properties is restricted to tours only, but mercantile open May–Oct daily, Nov–Apr shorter hours. Free. (1–2 hours on site)

★★ **Santa Fe Trail**—Twenty years older than the famed Oregon Trail, this trail was the artery to America for the Mexican province of New Mexico from 1821 to the 1860s. Along it passed New Mexican traders, the Yankees from Missouri, New Mexico militia, and U.S. cavalry in later years. At its height in 1866, more than 5,000 freight wagons rolled along it. Las Vegas was the first town found along the 900-mile stretch running northeast across Kansas.

A century and a half ago, as weary, dusty travelers approached the town they could stop for a refreshing drink and splash of water at the spring-fed **Hays Well**. In the 1930s Dust Bowl, the spring became the town's sole source of water, and still flows steadily. The well was recently restored and is open to the public. Wagon rut trails can be seen at several locations on the town outskirts. Las Vegas celebrates **Rails 'n' Trail Days**, one of its major festivals, annually in June as a salute to the Santa Fe Trail and the railroad that made the town.

Details: Well at 2213 Hot Springs Rd. (NM 65). To view wagon ruts, drive east on NM 104 from downtown Vegas, and at the top of the bridge over I-25 look onto the plains to the northeast. The same tracks can be seen by traveling 2 miles north on I-25 from the NM 104 on-ramp. Look to your right. Call 505/988-6888 for details. (1–2 hours)

★ **Montezuma Castle**—Originally built in the 1880s as a luxury resort overlooking a series of natural hot springs, this imposing and magnificent pink sandstone towered structure has seen a lot of hard times, including fires that destroyed it more than once. At one time it served as a monastery for Mexican priests; it is now the **Armand Hammer United World College of the American West**. The springs are still in use, open to the general public. The historic structure, however, needs millions of dollars of restoration and is closed. It can be seen from a distance.

Details: Head north out of Las Vegas 6 miles on Hot Springs Rd. (NM 65). You'll see the castle rising above the Gallinas River valley. (30 minutes on site)

✻ **Rough Riders Museum**—When Teddy Roosevelt needed to form a cavalry regiment for the Spanish American War, he went looking for some of the nation's toughest cowboys. He found hundreds of them in northeastern New Mexico. Many of these soldiers' and Roosevelt's personal mementos and professional artifacts associated with their famous 1898 charge up Kettle Hill in Cuba were gathered into this museum, which opened in 1965.

Details: 727 Grand Ave.; 505/425-8726. Open year-long Mon–Fri 9–5. Free. (1 hour)

FITNESS AND RECREATION

Storrie Lake State Park, 505-425-7278, is one of the state's most popular spots for windsurfing. Its 1,100 surface acres enjoy consistent summer winds and persistently cold water! The park is located four miles north of Las Vegas. To get there head out of town on Hot Springs Road (NM 518). It is open year-round for fishing and bird watching. There is a three-dollar day use fee.

Also in the area is a small family-run ski resort, **Sipapu**, 505/587-2240, with an 865-foot vertical drop, a triple chair- and two surface lifts. Rentals and instruction are also available, as well as a day lodge with restaurant and lounge. Adult lift tickets are only $27. Their season usually runs from December through mid-March. It is located 55 miles northwest of Las Vegas on NM 518 in Vadito.

Don't miss the free outdoor natural **Montezuma Hot Springs**, located next to the Gallinas River just north of Las Vegas. On the property of the World College, they are maintained by volunteers. From the roadway they look a bit funky, but the water is divine. I gratefully found myself sitting in one of the cement pools recently on a

New Year's Day morning. They are open daily until midnight. Nudity is not permitted. To get there head six miles north out of town on Hot Springs Road, NM 65.

About a half a mile further along NM 65 is a pond that is cleared of snow in winter for ice skaters. It's free, but if you're used to smooth indoor rink ice, you're in for a rough ride. A friend who claims to be a good skater cut himself pretty good on our last outing here.

One of the state's prettiest golf courses—an 18-hole, par 73 layout—is found at **Pendaries Village Country Club** (see Hispanic Villages, above), 505/425-3561, high in the Sangre de Cristos about 25 miles northwest of Las Vegas. Pendaries also has summer horseback riding and fishing in private stocked ponds (no state license required). Call 505/425-6076 for details. There is also a public course at **Highlands University**, 505/425-7711.

I have also enjoyed visits to **Las Vegas National Wildlife Refuge**, 505/425-3581. I saw an eagle dive on a flock of ducks here and capture one that broke from the flock. I also watched a coyote try in vain to catch a goose. Clouds of waterfowl overwinter here, and the refuge's ponds, timbered canyons, and stream attract lots of migrating songbirds. Its bird list carries more than 271 species. Fishing is allowed year-round on the refuge's **McAllister Lake**. It is located east of town. To get here, drive east out of Las Vegas 1.2 miles on NM 104; turn right (south) onto NM 281 and proceed four miles to the refuge office, then another 0.5 to Crane Lake overlook. Access is free.

There are also great opportunities for fishing, hiking, and backpacking in the mountains just west of town. Anglers will enjoy the headwaters of the **Gallinas River** and its tributaries. To get there leave town to the north on Hot Springs Road (NM 65). Trailheads from paved roads lead high into the **Pecos Wilderness**. Trail maps and details are available from the Santa Fe National Forest's **Las Vegas Ranger Station**, 1926 Seventh St., 505/454-0560. A popular hike is up **Hermit's Peak**, the prominent stone outcropping that towers over town to the west. It is only eight miles round-trip, but involves a 3,000-foot elevation gain. Its trailhead is located 15 miles northwest of Las Vegas at El Porvenir Campground off NM 65.

Finally, **Villanueva State Park**, 505/421-2957, is worth a visit. Set in a rocky canyon carved by the Pecos River, it has hiking trails, fishing, and picnic areas beneath large river cottonwoods that turn a golden yellow in fall. It is located some 34 miles southwest of Las

Vegas just off NM 3 near the isolated picturesque Hispanic farming village of Villanueva.

FOOD

Las Vegas has many restaurants. Probably the best is the **Landmark Grill** in the Plaza Hotel (see Lodging, below), which serves reasonably priced breakfast, lunch, and fine dinners daily. I had a green salad with lightly grilled Portobello mushrooms and an almond-crusted salmon filet to die for here. In summer or on holidays, dinner reservations are recommended.

Other dependable Vegas restaurants include **El Rialto**, 141 Bridge St., 505/454-0037, open for lunch and dinner daily; it also has a full bar. Especially popular are their steaks ($15 to $20) and New Mexican food (a combo plate under $10). **Dick's Liquor & Deli**, 705 Douglas Ave., 505/425-8261, is a friendly, inexpensive joint for catching sports broadcasts and chowing down on tasty sandwiches. It has a full bar, including 20 kinds of tequila and a whopping 50-plus varieties of beer. It's closed on Sundays. **Estella's Cafe**, 154 Bridge (no phone), serves up good, modestly priced New Mexican dishes in a room filled with religious icons.

For lunch, drop into **Murphey's**, 600 Douglas Ave., 505/425-6811, which has a great old soda fountain as well as daily specials and homemade desserts. For breakfast, try the **Spic and Span Bakery & Cafe**, 713 Douglas Ave., 505/425-6481, where each booth has its own hat rack.

Outside Las Vegas, the **Salman Ranch** (see La Cueva National Historic Site, above) serves ice cream, sandwiches, tamales and chile, fresh fruit drinks, fresh bread, and other items in summer. In tiny Rociada, visit **One Stop**, NM 105, 505/454-1435, for tasty hamburgers, deli sandwiches, and groceries. Also in the mountains near the village of Rociada (see Hispanic Villages, above) are the **Pendaries Country Club**, 505/425-3561, which serves lunch and dinner from May to mid-October, and the **Pendaries Lodge**, 505/425-6076.

LODGING

Las Vegas has one of the state's nicest and most unique lodgings, the **Plaza Hotel**, 230 Old Town Plaza, 505/425-3591 or 800/328-1882. Opened in 1882, it offers both old-time elegance and modern amenities. Facilities include 36 tastefully furnished rooms with private baths

LAS VEGAS

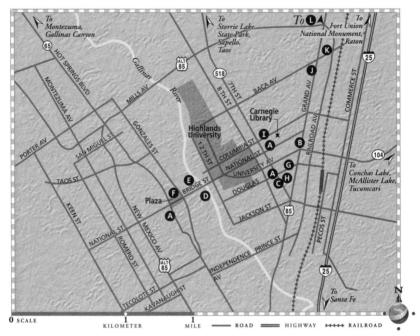

Sights

Ⓐ Las Vegas Historic Districts

Ⓑ Rough Riders Museum

Food

Ⓒ Dick's Liquor & Deli

Ⓓ El Rialto

Ⓔ Estella's Cafe

Ⓕ Landmark Grill

Ⓖ Murphey's

Ⓗ Spic and Span Bakery & Cafe

Lodging

Ⓘ Carriage House

Ⓙ Inn on the Santa Fe Trail

Ⓚ Palomino

Ⓕ Plaza Hotel

Ⓛ Super 8

Note: Items with the same letter are located in the same place.

or showers, room service, cable TV and in-room phones, a 24-hour front desk, the Victorian-style bar Byron T's, and perhaps the town's best restaurant, the Landmark Grill. The staff is also very hospitable; I spent New Year's Eve of 1997 here and they put on quite a party! Doubles range from $60 to $115 for a two-room suite (the second-story southwest corner room is a beaut).

Las Vegas also has a few nice B&Bs. The **Carriage House**, 925 Sixth St., 505/454-1784, is a century-old Victorian with elegant furnishings in a pretty residential section of town. Rooms range from $55 to $75. The **Inn on the Santa Fe Trail**, 1133 Grand Ave., 800/425-6791, is a Pueblo-Territorial style hacienda with a pool, spa, gardens, nicely furnished rooms and suites, and a good restaurant open May to September: Blackjack's Grill. Rooms run $49 to $89.

From late spring through fall, the **Mountain Music Guest Ranch**, in the Gallinas River Canyon northwest of town, 505/425-7008, is a nice place for riding and fishing, with cabin accommodations ranging from $85 to $125. Also in the mountains is **Pendaries Lodge**, some 26 miles from Las Vegas (see Hispanic Villages, above, for directions), 505/425-3561 or 800/733-5267. It is open early May through late October. The log cabin facility has a full-service dining room and 18 guest rooms, with doubles $59 to $69; townhouses/condominiums are also available for $175.

Another unusual mountain retreat is the **Star Hill Inn** near Sapello, 505/425-5605, which caters to amateur stargazers. Each of the six cottages has a fireplace, complete kitchen, and private porch; rates are $70 to $140. You can bring your own scope, rent one, or use a group instrument. Also at the foot of the Sangres is the **Totem Ranch B&B**, in Rociada, 505/425-8929, with doubles running $45 to $65; and the **Cerro Pelon Guest Ranch** in Sapello, 505/425-7169, with on-site fishing and a nicely furnished cabin for five people at $65 or a duplex for $55.

There is also a handful of motels in Vegas, including the **Super 8**, 2029 N. U.S. 85, 505/425-5288, with rates from $41 to $52; and the **Palomino**, 1330 Grand Ave., 505/425-3548, with rates from $26 to $60.

CAMPING

Storrie Lake State Park (see Fitness and Recreation, above), just north of Las Vegas, has 11 RV hookup sites at $11, 21 tent sites with shelters and grills for $7, restroom with hot showers, and drinking water. Park gates are locked at sunset. **Morphy Lake State Park**, five miles southwest of Mora near Ledoux, has primitive camping, and fishing. There's no potable water and it is accessible only with four-wheel-drive vehicles. **Villanueva State Park** (see Fitness and Recreation, above) has tent sites for $7 and RV hookups for $11.

There is also dispersed, primitive camping in the nearby **Santa Fe National Forest**, 505/425-3534, as well as in a handful of public campgrounds along the Gallinas River near the village of El Porvenir: **Big Pine**, **EV Long**, **Oak Flats**, and **El Porvenir** with a total of 46 campsites, none with RV hookups. There is a six-dollar fee at Porvenir and Long; the others are free. They all have tables, fire pits, and pit toilets (Oak Flats has no water) and are open May through October. To get to them, head north from town on Hot Springs Road (NM 65) about 16 miles.

The **Las Vegas KOA**, in Romeroville, five miles south of Las Vegas on the Anton Chico road off I-25 at Exit 339, 505/454-0180, has a pool, showers, laundry, and playground, and sites from $14 for tents and slightly more for RVs. Another camper option is the **Pendaries RV Park** (see Hispanic Villages, above, for directions), 505/425-6578, which also has some motel and condo units for $65 to $150.

NIGHTLIFE

As northeastern New Mexico's major town and home to one of the state's leading colleges, Highlands University, Las Vegas doesn't roll up its sidewalks at night. Among the places to catch live music on weekends are **Dick's** (see Food, above) and **Byron T's** in the Plaza Hotel (see Lodging, above). The **Bottle Shop Lounge**, 1130 Grand Ave., 505/454-0373, plays live country tunes Wednesday to Saturday. There's even a "disco"—yes, they still exist— at the **El Fidel Hotel**, corner of Grand and Douglas, 505/425-6761. It attracts the college and younger set of the area.

7

EAST CENTRAL PLAINS—
LLANO ESTACADO

In this fringe of the Great Plains, characterized by featureless rolling hills and flatlands broken occasionally on its northern edge by dramatic mesas and plateaus, early Spanish explorers drove stakes into the ground to mark their way back to civilization. Thus, the area became known as the Llano Estacado, or Staked Plains. Today people are still few and far between; the land has not yielded riches easily. Cattle ranchers, farmers, and people serving these industries are the primary inhabitants, battling bitter winter cold, dusty spring winds, and hot summer days.

But the area does have pockets of great beauty—such as the refreshing spring-fed lakes of Santa Rosa, the irrigated farmlands of the Pecos River Valley, and the caprock plateaus. There are also some historically important places here, including the graveyard where Billy the Kid is buried; the haunting ruins of the Salinas missions; the tragic Bosque Redondo, where thousands of Navajos died in the 1860s; and the recording studio where Buddy Holly worked. Along the far western edge, in the lovely and underappreciated Manzano Mountains, are some outstanding recreational opportunities, while large reservoirs on the Canadian and Pecos Rivers beckon to boaters. On the flats are game birds, and mountain lions still prowl the rocky canyons.

EAST CENTRAL PLAINS

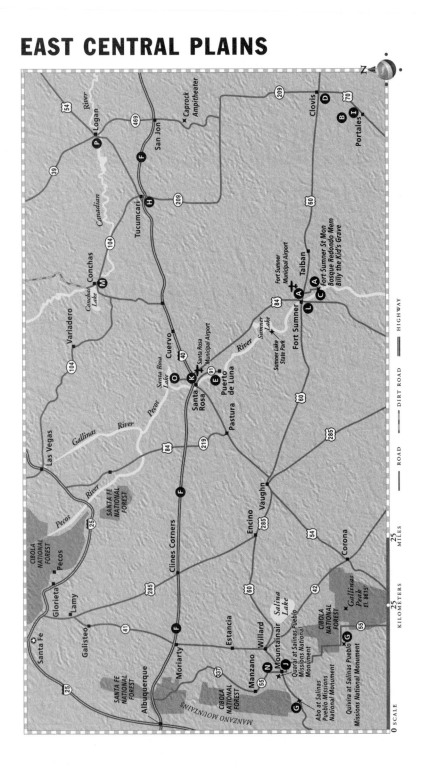

Sights

- **Ⓐ** Billy the Kid Trail
- **Ⓑ** Blackwater Draw
- **Ⓒ** Fort Sumner State Monument
- **Ⓓ** Norman Petty Studio
- **Ⓔ** Puerto de Luna
- **Ⓕ** Route 66
- **Ⓖ** Salinas Pueblo Missions National Monument
- **Ⓗ** Tucumcari Historical Museum
- **Ⓘ** Windmill Collection

Food

- **Ⓙ** Ancient Cities Café
- **Ⓙ** Carol and Company
- **Ⓚ** Country Pride
- **Ⓓ** Foxy Drive-in
- **Ⓘ** Juanito's
- **Ⓘ** Pizza Mill
- **Ⓙ** Pueblo Café
- **Ⓘ** Wagon Wheel Café

Lodging

- **Ⓗ** Best Western Aruba
- **Ⓗ** Blue Swallow Motel
- **Ⓛ** Coronado Motel
- **Ⓘ** Morning Star Inn
- **Ⓓ** Motel 6
- **Ⓛ** Oasis Motel
- **Ⓙ** Shaffer Hotel
- **Ⓘ** Super 8

Camping

- **Ⓓ** Clovis KOA
- **Ⓜ** Conchas Lake State Park
- **Ⓝ** Manzano Mountains State Park
- **Ⓞ** Santa Rosa State Park
- **Ⓗ** Tucumcari KOA
- **Ⓟ** Ute Lake State Park

Note: Items with the same letter are located in the same town or area.

A PERFECT DAY IN THE LLANO ESTACADO

One great day would begin with a tour of the Salinas Mission ruins, followed by a picnic lunch in Mountainair, then a drive east to the Fort Sumner State Monument and Billy the Kid sites. Another day would include stops in Santa Rosa for a swim in the lovely springs, the Norman Petty Studio in Clovis, and the Blackwater Draw archaeological site.

SIGHTSEEING HIGHLIGHTS

✯✯✯ **Billy the Kid Trail**—The Kid's wandering trail of desperation and death across New Mexico ended at Fort Sumner on the night of July 14, 1881, at the ranch house of his friend, Pete Maxwell. According to one version, his nemesis, Sheriff Pat Garrett, shot him in bed; others say Billy heard Garrett come in and was on his feet in the dark when his former friend gunned him down, ending the saga of this reviled and celebrated Western icon.

He was buried in the **Fort Sumner Graveyard** between his buddies Charlie Bowdre and Tom O'Folliard, his passing marked by a small headstone. This gravestone was subsequently stolen and recovered twice. Today it is held in place by steel straps inside a cage. Even in death, Billy remains behind bars. The graveyard is located right behind the **Old Fort Sumner Museum**, 505/355-2942, a privately owned tourist facility with diverse collections including paintings of the Kid and Sheriff Garrett, a series of interesting paintings depicting highlights of Billy's checkered life, historic photos, old firearms, and bits and pieces of local history. The museum has a souvenir shop. The **Billy the Kid Museum** outside the town of Fort Sumner has 17,000 square feet of exhibitions, including a rifle that supposedly belonged to the Kid, other Kid memorabilia, and a collection of antique buggies and wagons. This museum also has a gift shop. (For more on the Kid, see Chapter 9, Ruidoso Area.)

Details: To get to the Fort Sumner Museum and Fort Sumner Graveyard, follow the directions noted below for Fort Sumner State Monument. Fort Sumner Musem open Memorial Day–Labor Day daily 7:30–7, shorter hours off-season. $2.50 adults, $2 children. Billy the Kid Museum at 1601 Sumner Ave., 2 miles east of the town of Fort Sumner on U.S. 60/84; 505/355-2380. Open mid-May–Sept daily 8:30–5; Oct–mid-May Mon–Sat 8:30–5, Sun 11–5; closed Jan 1–15. $4 adults, $3.50 seniors, $2 children ages 6–11. (2–3 hours)

✯✯✯ **Fort Sumner State Monument**—In the mid-1800s, conflicts between settlers and the Navajo and Apache tribes of the region reached a flash point. Kit Carson was ordered by Brigadier General James Carleton to pursue and capture these nomadic people, and Carson led a relentless campaign of harassment and armed conflict. The Indians were finally forced from their homelands, marched to a reservation called Bosque Redondo on the Pecos River, and told to become farmers.

A fort was built here to oversee them, and while the 9,000 or so

Indians worked diligently on digging irrigation ditches, building adobe homes, and planting their fields, weather, insect infestations, lack of firewood, and alkaline water conspired against them. Roughly one-third of them died of starvation and diseases, and in 1868 the federal government admitted failure and allowed the Indians to return to ancestral lands in New Mexico and Arizona.

Today Fort Sumner State Monument marks this dark chapter in Southwestern history. A small visitors center set on a bluff overlooking the Pecos River contains relics of and interpretive information on the fort (which is entirely gone) and its garrison of 600 or so soldiers, and the Apache and Navajo people forced to live here. Living history demonstrations of the arms and equipage of the frontier soldiers are periodically held in summer; a more elaborate memorial to the Indians is being planned.

Details: Head east from Fort Sumner on U.S. 60/84 for 3 miles; turn south on Billy the Kid Road and proceed 3 miles to the monument entrance (next to the Billy the Kid Museum); 505/355-2573. Picnic tables but no overnight camping. Open daily 8:30–5. $1 adults, under age 17 free. (2 hours)

★★★ **Salinas Pueblo Missions National Monument**—Another monument of failed inhabitation, this monument protects the physical remnants of an early Pueblo Indian culture. The root word of *salinas* is *sal*, Spanish for "salt." For thousands of years before the arrival of the Spanish in 1540, Indians resided near a handful of saline lakes and ponds southeast of present-day Albuquerque. They collected and traded salt from these waters and became quite prosperous as traders between the Rio Grande Valley and the Great Plains.

In the 1600s, Spanish priests established mission churches in several of these pueblos, but Apache and other nomadic tribes found the isolated pueblos easy pickings, and repeated raids—combined with Spanish-borne epidemics and natural droughts—led to their abandonment by 1670.

Today the most visible remnants of these pueblos, ironically, are the massive stone mission churches found at **Abo**, **Gran Quivira**, and **Quarai**, but portions of the pueblos have also been restored.

Details: Mountainair Visitor Center, 505/847-2585, provides an overview of each site. Each ruin also has its own self-guiding trails and inter-pretive materials. Abo is located just off U.S. 60 on NM 513 some 9 miles west of Mountainair. Quarai is just off NM 55 about 9 miles north of Mountainair. Gran Quivira, the largest of the ruins, is found 26 miles or so southeast of Mountainair on NM 55. Picnicking, but no camping, permitted.

The visitors center and sites are open in summer daily 9–6, rest of year 9–5. Free. (1 hour per site)

★★ **Norman Petty Studio**—In a span of 13 months in the 1950s, early rock-and-roller Buddy Holly cut 15 hit songs in a tiny recording studio in the obscure town of Clovis. The songs put Holly on the map, and Clovis as well. Today, says the studio's caretaker, Kenneth Broad, busloads of visitors and musicians from here and abroad occasionally show up to tour this remarkable place. Never remodeled, it looks as if its owner—producer and musician Norman Petty—Holly, and the Crickets (Holly's band) have just stepped out for a cup of coffee and will be back any second. Original microphones, recording equipment, and musical instruments—including a custom-made Celeste keyboard—rest as if just put down. Copies of many of the records recorded here are found on the walls, including Holly's "Wake Up, Little Susie," "Peggy Sue," "That'll Be the Day," and "Maybe Baby," as well as "Sugar Shack" by The Fireballs, Petty's "Mood Indigo," and works by Roy Orbison, Buddy Knox, and Jimmy Gilmer.
   Details: 1313 W. Seventh, Clovis; 505/356-6422. Open year-round by appointment. Admission by donation. (30 minutes–1 hour)

★ **Blackwater Draw**—Some of America's oldest archaeological artifacts were found near Portales in 1932 in an area called Blackwater Draw. Studies revealed the site was once on the edge of a large pond in the late Pleistocene era, some 11,000 years ago. Here humankind's ancestors gathered to hunt wooly mammoth and bison and to be hunted by saber-toothed tigers and dire wolves. The site, located six miles north of Portales just off NM 467, is on the National Register of Historic Places, and public admission is limited to summer hours. However, artifacts from the site are on display at a museum.
   Details: Museum 7 miles northeast of Portales on U.S. 70; 505/ 562-2202. Generally open year-round Mon–Sat 10–5, Sun 12–5. $2 adults, $1 seniors and ages 6–15. (1 hour)

★ **Puerto de Luna**—The "Gateway to the Moon" village on the Pecos River was named, say locals, by Coronado in 1541 when he noticed the way the moon rises through a gap in the canyon walls during certain times of the month. It was first settled in 1863 and is far off the beaten track today. There is a pretty stone church and an old stone courthouse. The drive to and from the village is quite beautiful.

Details: To get there from the south, travel north from Fort Sumner on U.S. 84. Keep an eye peeled for the Guadalupe County line, then proceed another 10 miles to Guadalupe County Road 2P. Turn west (left) onto this dirt road (suitable for normal vehicles except in wet weather) and proceed 5 miles west into the Pecos River Valley. Here you'll find the village and paved NM 91. Head north on it 10 miles or so to Santa Rosa, where it becomes Third Ave. Coming from Santa Rosa, reverse these directions. (1 hour drive time Santa Rosa to U.S. 84)

✵ **Route 66**—The "Main Street of America," as it's been called, crawled across the east-central plains of New Mexico on its run from Chicago to Los Angeles, leaving the flats and monotony of the Texas panhandle on a slow but gradual rise toward the highlands bordering the Rio Grande Valley. Original major stops along the route on this leg included **Tucumcari** and **Santa Rosa**, and along a later alignment, **Moriarty** as well. Original motels, gas stations, and restaurants still dot the edges of the old roadway in these towns, as well as at more isolated points in between. Tucumcari hosts an annual summer festival dedicated to "the Mother Road."

Details: For more information on Route 66, contact the chambers of commerce in the towns noted above. (1 hour minimum)

✵ **Tucumcari Historical Museum**—This is a town museum with odd and interesting displays, including a schoolroom, sheriff's office, trade tools, Indian artifacts, rocks, barb wire, and chuck wagon.

Details: 416 S. Adams St., Tucumcari; 505/461-4201. Open year-round, but hours and days vary widely. Small admission fee. (1 hour)

✵ **Windmill Collection**—The nation's largest collection of windmills—some 78 vane and vaneless wooden and steel models—is located on the private property of Bill Dalley of Portales. The windmills can be viewed for free across a field from Kilgore Avenue.

Details: Drive .75 mile south of Third St. on Kilgore Ave. at Portales' east end. (30 minutes)

FITNESS AND RECREATION

Santa Rosa is chock full of natural spring-fed ponds and manmade lakes, so offers terrific swimming, fishing, and boating. One spring—the 80-foot-deep **Blue Hole** that stays a constant 64 degrees and flows at 3,000 gallons a minute—is the state's prime locale for scuba diving certification programs. Permits ($10), available from the police station, are required. **Santa Rosa State Park**, 505/472-3110, located about five miles north of town via the Louis Page Highway (NM 91), covers 3,800 surface acres and is large enough for water skiing.

Three other large manmade reservoirs are nearby, each with a state park. **Conchas Lake**, 505/868-2270, located 31 miles northwest of Tucumcari via NM 104, is 25 miles long and covers 4,200 surface acres. Rental boats are available. **Ute Lake**, 505/487-2284, located 22 miles northeast of Tucumcari via U.S. 54, covers 8,200 surface acres. It is the state's second-largest water body. Rental boats are available, as well as trails for off-road vehicles, hiking, and biking. **Sumner Lake**, 505/355-2541, located 16 miles northwest of Fort Sumner on the Pecos River via U.S. 84 and NM 203, covers 4,500 surface acres. It also has tennis courts, a nature trail, playground, and a restaurant in operation May to September. Day use fees are charged. There are also some private facilities, including a lodge, marina, bait and tackle shop, and restaurant at Conchas.

There is not much mountainous terrain in this area. Along the far western fringe are the Manzano Mountains, home to **Manzano Mountains State Park**, 505/847-2820, reached via NM 55 from Tijeras, to the north, or Mountainair, to the south. The park has excellent birding, cross-country skiing in wet winters, hiking trails, picnic tables, a small lake for fishing and swimming, and one of the nation's oldest apple orchards (*manzano* means "apple").

Also in the area is a notable birding locale centered on a playa lake—a shallow natural body of water found on the High Plains. The 700-acre **Ladd S. Gordon Wildlife Area**, 505/445-2311, is located on Tucumcari Lake and features outstanding shorebirds from October to March, as well as geese, teals, ducks, raptors, and songbirds in fall and spring. It is located on the northeast edge of Tucumcari. To get there take the gravel road north of the Motel 6. Entry is free.

Quay County is also considered by many to have the best blue-quail hunting in the nation, and the rimrock country also is a haven for deer, mountain lion, antelope, and other game. For details, contact local chambers of commerce or the state Game and Fish Department, 505/841-8881.

Caprock Creek Ranch Adventures, 10 miles south of San Jon,

888/GIDDY-UP, offers mule-drawn rides, ropin', hikin', horseshoe pitchin', and chuck wagon dinner meals.

If more sedate recreation is your preference, check out the **Tucumcari Municipal Golf Course**, 505/461-1849, open daily except Mondays year-round and offers rental clubs and carts. There are also golf courses at Conchas Lake, in Santa Rosa, Fort Sumner, and Portales.

Clovis' **Hillcrest Park & Zoo**, 10th at Sycamore, 505/769-7871, has tennis courts, a pool and a golf course, as well as a zoo (505/769-7873) with some 500 animals. Facilities are open from nine to six daily, except Monday. Admission is one dollar.

FOOD

This is still the frontier when it comes to fine dining. One of the more unusual and entertaining places I discovered is Clovis' **Foxy Drive-in**, 720 W. 7th, 505/763-3995. Opened over four decades ago, it features its original layout and furnishings. Inside are four chrome stools and a handful of small tables; most diners order from their cars. For breakfast, two eggs with meat, hash browns, coffee, and toast will set ya back just $2.50. The cheeseburgers, steak fingers, milkshakes, and sundaes are incredibly inexpensive, too.

In Santa Rosa, **Joseph's Restaurant and Cantina**, 865 Will Rogers, 505/472-3361, has long been a popular spot for New Mexican and American fare. The **Rt. 66**, 1819 Will Rogers, 505/472-3162, serves sandwiches, burgers, and breakfast options. East of town at the intersection of I-40 and U.S. 84 is Truckstops of America's **Country Pride**, 505/472-3432, with about everything under the sun for travelers.

There are some 20 restaurants in Portales, but at night almost every one open is some kind of chain eatery. Locally owned joints include the **Wagon Wheel Café**, 521 W. 17th, 505/356-5036, with its Friday special of delicious all-you-can-eat fried catfish; **Juanito's**, 813 S. Ave. C Pl., 505/359-1860, with New Mexican food; and **Pizza Mill**, 300 N. Chicago, 505/356-8762.

Pleasant Mountainair has several places to eat. **Ancient Cities Café**, on U.S. 60, 505/847-2368, is open for three meals daily, as is the Shaffer Hotel's **Pueblo Café**, 103 E. Main, 505/847-2888. **Carol and Company**, at Main and Grand, 505/847-0631, serves breakfast and lunch.

SANTA ROSA

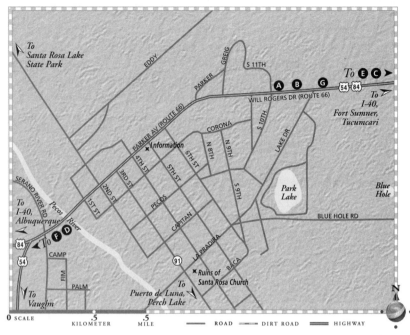

Food

Ⓐ Joseph's Restaurant and Cantina

Ⓑ Rt. 66

Lodging

Ⓒ Best Western Adobe Inn

Ⓓ Budget 10

Ⓔ Holiday Inn Express

Ⓕ Holiday Santa Rosa Motel

Camping

Ⓖ Santa Rosa KOA

LODGING

There are lots of motels in Santa Rosa, though the town can fill up on summer nights. Among the options are the **Best Western Adobe Inn**, Will Rogers Drive (old Route 66) at Exit 275, 505/472-3446, with rooms for $55; the **Holiday Inn Express**, 3300 Will Rogers Dr., 505/472-5411, with a pool, café, and $60 doubles with queen beds. The **Holiday Santa Rosa Motel**, Will Rogers Drive at Exit 277, 505/472-5414, has a pool, café, and laundry, with doubles for $32. One of the nicer, cheaper places is the **Budget 10**, 120 U.S. 54, 505/472-3454, with a swimming pool and double rooms for $25.

Portales has a handful of chain motels. The **Super 8**, 1805 W. Second, 505/356-8518, is nice, with a Jacuzzi that was on the fritz when I was last there. Local calls are free, as are HBO movies and continental breakfasts, and rates are $40.

In Fort Sumner, lodging is available at the **Oasis Motel**, 1704 E. Fort Sumner Ave., 505/355-7414, and the **Coronado Motel**, 309 W. Fort Sumner Ave., 505/355-2466; both are around $35 for two. There is a B&B in Portales, the **Morning Star Inn**, 620 W. Second St., 505/356-2994, with in-room phones; rooms go for $45.

"Motel row" in Clovis is found on Mabry Drive on the east side of town where U.S. 64, 84, and 70 converge. Lodgings include a **Motel 6**, 2620 Mabry, 505/762-2995, with rooms for $32. In Tucumcari, motels stretched along old Route 66 include the **Blue Swallow Motel**, 815 E. Tucumcari Blvd., 505/461-9849, with rooms as cheap as $20, and the **Best Western Aruba**, 1700 E. Tucumcari Blvd., 505/461-3335, with pool, laundry, and decent restaurant; doubles go for $46.

Tiny Mountainair has some pleasant surprises, in particular the **Shaffer Hotel**, 103 E. Main, 505/847-2888, which was built in 1923. Its facade is decorated with Navajo symbols, including the reverse-swastika. Today it operates as a B&B. Rooms with a shared bath are $36; suites with private baths are $56. The Pueblo Café in the hotel serves breakfast, lunch, and dinner.

CAMPING

Area state parks all have camping facilities (see Fitness and Recreation, above). **Santa Rosa State Park** has 50 sheltered sites, including 15 with RV hookups, and solar-heated showers. **Conchas Lake State**

Park has sites for $7 or $11 for RV hookups. **Ute Lake State Park** has two public campgrounds with tent and RV sites for the same cost. **Manzano Mountains State Park** has 48 picnic, tent, and RV sites, including six with hookups and one wheelchair-accessible site. There is also dispersed, primitive camping in the **Cibola National Forest**, 505/847-2990, of the Manzano Mountains.

The **Santa Rosa KOA**, 2136 Will Rogers Dr., 505/472-3126, has 96 sites. The **Clovis KOA**, four miles west of town on U.S. 60/84, 505/762-2971, has a laundry and showers, and RV hookups for $18. The **Tucumcari KOA**, a quarter mile east of Exit 355, 505/461-1841, is a shady spot with pool, laundry, and showers; RV hookups are $18 and tent sites $14.

NIGHTLIFE

Every July the town of Clovis hosts a music festival, sometimes with tie-ins to Buddy Holly and the other west Texas/New Mexico musicians of the past. Downtown is a wonderful old theater-turned-music-hall, the **State Theater**, 402 Main (no phone), where live shows are held regularly year-round. Across the street is the **Lyceum Theater**, 411 Main, 505/763-6085, which was considered one of the best stages west of Kansas City during its heyday in the 1920s. In the 1980s it was rebuilt and today hosts a wide variety of events.

Caprock Amphitheater and Park, 10 miles south of San Jon (on I-40 near the Texas border), just off NM 469, 505/461-1694, presents evening melodramas and musicals in a natural stone amphitheater from late June through late August. Most popular is *The Real Billy the Kid*. Barbeque dinners, beginning at 6:30, are available prior to the 8 p.m. shows. Dinner is $6 for adults and $4.50 for kids; show tickets are $8 for adults and $2.50 for kids.

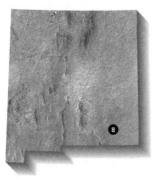

8

SOUTHEAST CORNER—
LITTLE TEXAS

While the northern half of the state suffers in spring through terminal mud and snow, southeastern New Mexico, sitting at the fringe of the Chihuahuan Desert, enjoys terrific weather with temperatures in the 70s and even 80s. Fall is another wonderful season here. Summer is the most popular time to visit this region—most tourists then are families intent on seeing world-famous Carlsbad Caverns. However, though the caverns are cool in July and August, the 100-plus daily highs on the surface wilt other possible activities. And there are lots of things to do and see in the area beyond the typical tour of the caverns.

In addition to Roswell's famed UFOs, documented in a quirky museum, the Roswell Museum and Art Center has a surprisingly fine collection of Southwestern and contemporary art. And, though the region does not have the wealth of historical and cultural draws found in the northern part of the state, it has a slew of outstanding natural attractions, friendly residents, and a pleasant, easygoing pace. Just say "howdy" in this cornerland, which is socially and geographically more akin to west Texas than the rest of New Mexico.

A PERFECT DAY IN LITTLE TEXAS

The perfect day in this area has to include time spent underground, in the world-famous Carlsbad Caverns. Begin the day here with a

ROSWELL

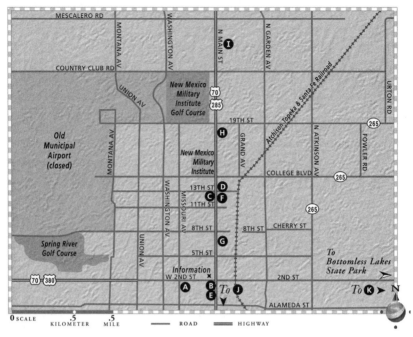

Sights

A Historical Center for Southeastern New Mexico

B International UFO Museum and Research Center

C Roswell Museum and Art Center

Food

D The Claim

E El Toro Bravo

F Keuken Dutch Restaurant

G Pecos Rose Tearoom

H Roswell Inn

Lodging

I Frontier

H Roswell Inn

Camping

J Town and Country Mobile Estates

K Trailer Village Campgrounds

walk through the Big Room, most easily reached via the elevator. Afterwards, walk to see the cavern's incredible mouth, then drive back to the park entrance through Walnut Canyon. Eat lunch at the visitors center before leaving, or head to nearby Rattlesnake Springs for a late picnic lunch. If the wind is blowing, spend the late afternoon at Living Desert State Park. Have dinner at the Flume Room or Lucy's.

SIGHTSEEING HIGHLIGHTS

★★★ **Carlsbad Caverns National Park**—This magnificent limestone labyrinth is the area's major draw. I first visited it when I was eight years old and was impressed. As an adult, I've returned several times and found that, if anything, I am even more amazed by it now. My own kids have turned into real cavern cravers—they want to go every spring. But on their first outing, at ages one-and-a-half and three-and-a-half years old, they were not ecstatic about the idea. In truth, we had to coax them into it, but once underground they were totally caught up in the realm known by cavers as "the Dark Zone."

The easiest and fastest excursion finds one riding an elevator down to the bottom of the caverns and taking the one-mile, one-and-a-half-hour walk through the **Big Room**, which contains many of the cavern's highlights. Stepping off the elevator, you are 750 feet beneath the surface. Immediately you notice the chill—be sure to wear a light sweater, even if it's 110 degrees in the parking lot!—and humidity. There are pools of water down here, as you will see, and the steady tap, tap of falling droplets echoes the building and carving process that sculpted these remarkable caves. Sprawling over 14 acres, the Big Room's ceiling soars some 225 feet overhead. Its floor is punctured by pits and shafts more than 140 feet deep. You'll see drapery formations that look like flowing taffy, delicate crystal "whiskers" and "soda straws," "cave pearls" and "lily pads," massive stalagmites growing from the floor, and jagged stalactites hanging from the ceiling.

If you have more time and energy, you can opt for a hike through the cavern's awesome natural entrance and along a three-mile trail to the Big Room, where you ride the elevator back to the surface. This outing takes three to five hours, depending on your speed. Another popular and interesting sight is the flight of the bats out of the cavern mouth every evening at dusk, from May to October, when some 400,000 Mexican freetail bats take to the air during a half-hour to two-hour period on their run to their insect feeding grounds. It is said that the emergence of this black cloud first drew cowboys to the cavern.

The national park, established in 1923, also protects some 80 known caves besides Carlsbad Caverns. A few are open to the public on a limited basis, others only to seasoned spelunkers. On our last trip to the area, my family visited **Slaughter Canyon Cave** (also known as New Cave) on a ranger-guided "primitive caving" tour into the unlit chambers. The cave was once "mined" for its bat guano, and relics of this era are still found. The mildly strenuous, one-and-a-half-mile, two-hour walk (my six-year-old daughter, Isabel, had no difficulty completing it) on the unpaved trail brought us to fantastic chambers with dazzling formations. But perhaps the most unusual aspect of the cave was the absolute darkness that prevailed and the beauty and brilliance of the daylight filtering through the cave mouth as we approached the end of the tour.

Details: About 38 miles southwest of Carlsbad. Take U.S. 180/62 south to Whites City, turn right onto NM 7 and follow the signs; 505/785-2232. Visitors center has excellent displays on the caverns, as well as books, photos, posters, and souvenirs. Also on site are a kennel, a surface restaurant, a bizarre underground cafeteria, and a daycare center. Park open daily, except Christmas; $6 adults, $3 children ages 6–15. Primitive cave tours available, often running four hours; $7–$20 adults, $3.50–$10 ages 6–15 (children under 6 not permitted); reservations recommended. The Slaughter Canyon Cave tour, available only with advance reservations made through the park service, 800/967-2283, held daily in summer, weekends rest of year; $15 adults, $7.50 children. Bring one flashlight per person. (3–6 hours on site)

★★★ **Living Desert State Park**—This outstanding park focuses on the animal and plant life of the surrounding Chihuahuan Desert. Like its world-famous cousin, the Living Desert Sonoran Museum near Tucson, it proves deserts are actually full of beautiful and hardy life.

The park has both impressive indoor exhibitions and a 1.3-mile paved trail that winds across the Ocotillo Hills overlooking Carlsbad. The trail brings you to a series of naturalistic (if small) animal habitats, where you'll see cougars, bobcats, quail, hawks, badgers, bear, wolves, elk, javelina, fox, buffalo, waterfowl, snakes, lizards, and many other creatures. You'll also encounter some of the loveliest flowering cactus you'll ever lay eyes on (they bloom from early through late spring), as well as desert trees, bushes, flowers, and shrubs. And don't miss the **Cactus Greenhouse**, which shelters a great collection of cactus from around the world. Every May the Mescalero Apache people carry out a traditional mescal cactus roast and Spirit Dance in the park.

Details: *Located just off U.S. 285 on the north edge of Carlsbad on a well-marked road; 505/887-5516. Open daily, except Christmas, 8–8 in summer, 9–5 in winter, spring, and fall (last entry 1.5 hours prior to closing). $3 adults, $1 children over age 6. (2–4 hours)*

★★★ **Sitting Bull Falls**—In this special spot, you'll find a spring-fed waterfall and stream in the middle of a serious desert in the Guadalupe Mountain foothills. Water drips off a cliff at least 100 feet tall into a series of pools cupped in rock shelves. Lovely sycamore trees arch over the pools, which are filled with some type of minnow. Various forms of cactus grow only feet from the cool waters and thick grass mats clog the stream bed as it drops down a steep canyon below the falls. When I last visited on an April afternoon, the sun was out and we toasted on the rocks like iguanas, listening to the tinkling of water and the breeze rustling the new green leaves. I even took a brief, cool dip. There are a few campsites, picnic tables, drinking water, toilets, fire pits, and a nice shelter built from on-site stone.

Details: *32 miles west of Carlsbad on Lincoln National Forest land. Head north on U.S. 285 for 12.5 miles (measured from the center of town) to NM 137, a gravel road. Turn left and head west onto NM 276 (follow signs at forks). Open 6 a.m.–10 p.m. daily. Free. (1–2 hours on site)*

★★ **International UFO Museum and Research Center**—In July 1947, the U.S. Army Air Corps of Roswell issued a press release stating it had recovered a "crashed disc" that had fallen in the area. A day later it issued a retraction, saying the odd materials were the remnants of a weather balloon. Thus was born one of the most enduring mysteries of the space age, the so-called "Roswell Incident."

In recent years Roswell has cashed in on the public's growing interest in UFO phenomena. The International UFO Museum and Research Center is dedicated to all manner of UFO-ism, from local lore to worldwide reportings. It is stuffed with an odd assortment of blurry photos, handwritten accounts of alien abductions, illustrations of the 50 or so most common spaceship shapes and types, UFO movie posters, and other materials.

The museum also has continuous screenings of UFO videos and a macabre but undeniably interesting scene of the alien autopsy from the movie *Roswell*. It also conducts guided tours of the supposed UFO

CARLSBAD

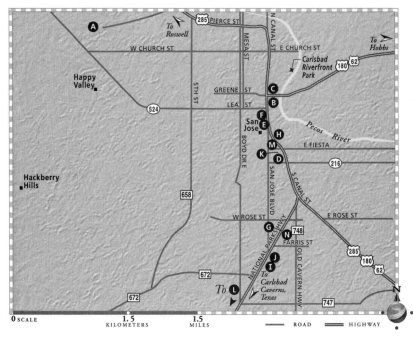

Sights

Ⓐ Living Desert State Park

Food

Ⓑ Cortez Café

Ⓒ Deluxe Café

Ⓓ Flume Room

Ⓔ Lucy's

Ⓕ Ventana's Restaurant

Lodging

Ⓓ Best Western Motel Stevens

Ⓖ El Rey

Lodging *(continued)*

Ⓕ Holiday Inn

Ⓗ La Fonda

Ⓘ Motel 6

Ⓙ Quality Inn

Ⓚ Stagecoach Inn

Camping

Ⓛ Carlsbad RV

Ⓜ Midcity Trailer Park

Ⓝ Windmill Grocery & RV Park

Note: Items with the same letter are located in the same place.

crash sites. For refreshments, beam into its Alien Caffeine Expresso Bar. The gift shop has a huge selection of UFO products, books, key chains, videos, and the like.

Details: Located in a former movie theater, 114 N. Main St.; 505/625-9495. Open daily 11–5. Free. (1–2 hours)

☆☆ **Roswell Museum and Art Center**—One doesn't associate fine art with Roswell, but this is actually one of the better small art and science museums in the state, if not the country. It naturally concentrates its holdings on Southwestern artists and has a particularly strong collection of the work of Roswell-raised Peter Hurd. Other regional artists shown here include Georgia O'Keeffe, Marsden Hartley, Henriette Wyeth, Howard Cook, John Sloan, Victor Higgins, and John Martin—many associated with the world-famous art scene of northern New Mexico that flourished in the early to mid-1900s.

Also found here is a surprisingly strong body of contemporary art—including work by Luis Jimenez and Elmer Schooley—as well as wonderful American Indian and Hispanic arts, crafts, and antiquities. In addition to these holdings, the museum has a wing devoted to the life and work of Robert H. Goddard, who successfully tested the world's first liquid-fueled rocket in Roswell in 1926. The **Goddard Planetarium** offers shows one week a month. The museum has a library and a gift shop.

Details: Corner of Main and 11th Sts.; 505/624-6744. Open Mon–Sat 9–5, Sun and some holidays 1–5. Free. (1–2 hours)

☆ **Guadalupe National Park**—This major regional destination—with very beautiful high mountains, huge canyons, desert lands, historic sites, and recreational opportunities—is located in Texas, some 55 miles south of Carlsbad, out of the scope of this book. There are two developed campgrounds in the park, 80 miles of trails, and several four-wheel drive excursion roads.

Details: For additional information, contact Guadalupe Mountains National Park, HC 60, Box 400, Salt Flat, TX 79847-9400; 915/828-3251. (3 hours minimum)

KIDS' STUFF

For some corny but fun entertainment where hissing at the bad guys is encouraged, take in a melodrama at **Granny's Opera House** in Whites City on most summer nights. Kids love the **Presidents Park**

Amusement Village, 711 Muscatel Ave., 505/887-0512, accessible from Riverfront Park via a footbridge. Its attractions include carnival rides and a narrow-gauge train. Days and hours of operation vary. Kids and adults will also enjoy taking in a movie at Carlsbad's three-screen **Fiesta Drive-in Theater,** San Jose Boulevard and Fiesta Street, 505/885-4126. Also in Carlsbad is a go-cart track and baseball batting cages at the south end of town on U.S. 62/180 next to the Motel 6. My kids still talk about the carts years after our last go-round.

FITNESS AND RECREATION

The grasslands, marshes, and ponds of **Bitter Lakes National Wildlife Refuge,** located in the Pecos River Valley some 11 miles east of Roswell, are a magnet for feathered critters—some 285 species regularly visit or live here. From October through March there are clouds of waterfowl and shorebirds, and migratory bird species in the spring and fall, yet the 23,000-acre refuge receives few human visitors. One can drive around the refuge on an 8.5-mile self-guided tour or get out and hike on some trails. To get there, head east on NM 380 (Main Street) in Roswell. Drive three miles to NM 265 (Red Bridge Road), turn left (north), and continue for four miles to East Pine Lodge Road. Turn right and continue four miles. Overnight camping is not permitted. Visiting hours are from one hour before sunrise to one hour after sunset. Admission is free. A visitors center provides additional information, 505/622-6755.

    Rattlesnake Springs is another haven for birders, but this spot of greenery in the rough desert south of Carlsbad is also a fabulous place for a pleasant picnic or walk. Small ponds and the spring, bubbling up beneath large overhanging trees, attract lots of wildlife while a network of small ditches conveys water around the site. On a hot day, there are few things as refreshing as putting one's feet into crystal clear, cold water. You'll find a nice picnic area carpeted in grass and shaded by massive cottonwoods. To get here from Carlsbad, take U.S. 62/180 south about 26 miles past Whites City and the Caverns turnoff. Turn right onto County Road 418 and follow signs three miles to the site. The site is open to the public during daylight. Admission is free. Call 505/785-2232 for more information.

    Carlsbad Caverns National Park also includes some 30,000 acres of seldom-trod backcountry wilderness and 50 miles of foot trails open to hikers and backpacking campers. A free backcountry permit is required, available at the visitors center. Experienced spelunkers enjoy primitive caving outside of Carlsbad National Park in the Guadalupe Ranger District of the **Lincoln National Forest**, 505/885-4181.

Roswell's **Spring River Park and Zoo**, 1306 E. College, 505/624-6720, is a real find, even though the zoo is quite small. Spacious lawns and numerous shade trees provide a nice place to picnic or stretch your legs on 5.5 miles of walking and biking trails. In warm weather a scaled-down passenger train chugs about the park, providing a real thrill for kids. The facility is open daily 10 to 8.

Bottomless Lakes State Park, outside Roswell, 505/624-6058, offers some lovely waters for fishing and summer swimming. New Mexico's oldest state park, opened in 1933, includes seven sinkhole lakes, which actually range in depth from 17 to 90 feet. Off-season there is surprisingly good birding here, particularly around Lazy Lagoon—beware of its treacherous, stinky mudflats! The park has a visitors center, self-guiding nature trails, and in summer, concession stands, a shower/changing house, and rental paddle boats at the only lake open to swimming, Lea. The lakes are located 12 miles from Roswell. To get here drive east from town on U.S. 380, then south on NM 409. There is a three-dollar day use fee.

There are also numerous golf courses in the area, including the 18-hole **Spring River Golf Course** in Roswell, 1612 W. 8th St, 505/622-9506; the 18-hole **NM Military Institute Golf Course** in Roswell, 201 W. 19th, 505/622-6033; the **Ocotillo Golf Course** in Hobbs, NM 18 next to McAdams State Park, 505/397-9297; and 18-hole **Lake Carlsbad Golf Course**, 901 N. Muscatel, 505/885-5444.

The **Carlsbad Riverfront Park** also has a nice area for free swimming right in town on the Pecos River along Park Drive. There are large lawns, picnic areas, playgrounds, and a swimming area with slides and diving boards. You can also rent paddle boats.

FOOD

Most guidebooks list **Lucy's**, 701 Canal, next to the Holiday Inn, 505/887-7714, as *the* place to eat in Carlsbad, and as a result the place is generally packed. The menu of predominately New Mexican fare is immense, the margaritas are fountain-sized, prices are moderate, service is fast, and Lucy is gregarious and charming, but the food is only so-so. It's open for lunch and breakfast; closed Sunday.

Other Carlsbad options include the **Cortez Café**, 508 S. Canal, 505/885-4747, which opened in 1937—it's funky but the food is pretty good and the price is right. The **Flume Room** in the Motel Stevens, 1829 S. Canal, 505/887-2851, features steaks, prime rib, and a large salad bar. The **Deluxe Café**, 224 S. Canal, 505/887-1304, is anything but deluxe—but the food is fine and cheap, and the place has a well-worn and warm ambiance. Probably the fanciest restaurant in town is **Ventana's Restaurant**, in the Holiday Inn, 505/885-8500, with linen tablecloths and a menu of steaks and seafood.

In Roswell, locals head to the **Roswell Inn**, 1815 N. Main, 505/623-4920, for the best breakfast in town; to the **Pecos Rose Tearoom**, 709 N. Main, 505/625-9256, in an 1885 building, for lunch; and to **The Claim**, 1310 N. Main, 505/623-6042, for dinner cocktails, steaks, and seafood—reservations recommended on week-ends. **El Toro Bravo**, 102 N. Main, 505/622-9208, features Mexican food while **Keuken Dutch Restaurant**, 1208 N. Main, 505/624-2040—for breakfast, lunch, and dinner—is noted for its Dutch-inspired dishes.

Artesia has some drive-ins and fast-food franchises, but for a good New Mexican meal drop into **La Fonda**, corner of Main and Second Streets, 505/746-9411, open daily for lunch and dinner.

LODGING

This is the land of the motel—hotels and B&Bs are almost nonexistent. In Carlsbad my young kids and I have enjoyed staying at the **Stagecoach Inn**, 1819 S. Canal St., 505/887-1148. It has a small pool shaded by Siberian elm trees, an old playground, and a cheerful restaurant with booths. Rooms with queen and king beds go for $40 and up. Among the nicer motels are the **Holiday Inn**, 601 S. Canal St., 505/885-8500 or 800/742-9586, with a larger pool and hot tub, large rooms with queen beds ($75 for a double), a coffee shop, and upscale restaurant; the **Best Western Motel Stevens**, 1829 S. Canal St., 505/887-2851, with a pool and doubles for $58; and the **Quality Inn**, 3706 National Parks Highway (U.S. 62/180), 505/887-2861, with lovely grounds, a coffee shop, lounge, and laundry. Doubles run $58 and up in summer.

Just outside the entrance to Carlsbad Caverns National Park, in Whites City, are two Best Westerns: the **Cavern Inn** and the **Guadalupe Inn**, both at 505/785-2291 or 800-228-3767, with pools, hot tubs, and large rooms for $78. A restaurant and saloon are next door. Cheaper accommodations include the **El Rey**, 3515 National Parks Hwy., 505/887-5331, with rooms from $23; the **La Fonda**, 1522 S. Canal St.,

SOUTHEAST NEW MEXICO

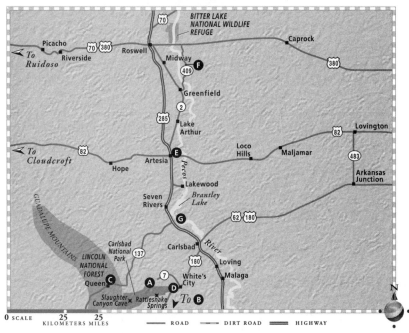

Sights

A Carlsbad Caverns National Park

B Guadalupe National Park

C Sitting Bull Falls

Lodging

D Cavern Inn

D Guadalupe Inn

E Heritage Inn

Camping

F Bottomless Lakes State Park

G Brantley Lake State Park

D Park Entrance RV

Note: Items with the same letter are located in the same town or area.

505/885-6242, with a pool and rooms from $30; and the **Motel 6**, 3824 National Parks Hwy., 505/885-0011, with doubles for $40.

Roswell has more than 20 motels, including the **Frontier**, 3010 N. Main St., 505/622-1400 or 800-678-1401, with a pool, queen beds, and doubles for $38; and the **Roswell Inn**, 1815 N. Main St., 505/623-4920 or 800-426-3052, with a pool, large rooms with queen or king beds and doubles for $65. Artesia, of all places, has one of the area's few B&Bs—the **Heritage Inn**, 209 W. Main, 505/748-2552. The Victorian-styled lodging is located above a shop, with rooms for $55.

CAMPING

Bottomless Lakes State Park (see Fitness and Recreation, above) outside Roswell has hot showers, restrooms, tent sites for $7, and RV sites with partial hookups for $11. **Brantley Lake State Park** (see Fitness and Recreation) outside Carlsbad offers the same facilities.

There is also dispersed, primitive camping in the **Lincoln National Forest** of the Guadalupe Mountains west of Carlsbad. Call 505/885-4181 for details.

RVers have many options, though not in Carlsbad Caverns National Park. In Roswell, there's **Trailer Village Campgrounds**, 1614 E. 2nd St., 505/623-6040, with hookups for $15; and **Town and Country Mobile Estates**, 333 W. Brasher Rd., 505/624-1833, with hookups for $17 and tent sites for $12. In and near Carlsbad, check out **Carlsbad RV**, 4301 National Parks Hwy., 505/885-6333, with pool, showers, laundry, and playground and tent sites for $12 and hookups for $17; **Midcity Trailer Park**, 1701 S. Canal St., 505/887-6220; or the **Windmill Grocery & RV Park**, 3624 National Parks Hwy., 505/885-9761. Whites City also has RV facilities, at **Park Entrance RV**, 505/785-2291 or 800/CAVERNS, with tent sites or RV hookups for $17.

NIGHTLIFE

Carlsbad has a lively bar, the **My Way Lounge**, 223 S. Canal St., 505/887-0212, with pool tables and country and rock bands most nights. The **Roswell Symphony Orchestra**, 3201 N. Main St., 505/623-5882, has been presenting full concerts and chamber music since 1960; the prime season is October through April. The **Roswell Community Little Theater**, 1101 N. Virginia Ave., 505/622-1982, presents dramas from September through June.

9

RUIDOSO AREA

This mountainous parcel in south-central New Mexico has a lot packed into it. As the closest mountain region to the Lone Star state, it's a big playground for Texans. Tequila in wine *botas* on the ski slopes? Yep, with their sliders on. But the *Tejanos* do give the area a happy-go-lucky atmosphere that can be infectious. Bordering the mountain's southern edge are the highlands of the Cloudcroft area, where crystal clear days overlooking the Tularosa Basin far below are as common as breath. Here you'll find all the natural attractions of the Ruidoso area and one of the state's nicest hotels, without crowds.

Aside from the hikin' and skiin' and ridin' and boatin' and swimmin' and dancin', one of the nation's strangest legends unfolded here in the hamlet of Lincoln during the Lincoln County War between chief antagonists Billy the Kid and Sheriff Pat Garrett. Walk the streets of Lincoln on a winter day and you can almost hear the bullets fly and the fires crackling.

Other area attractions include the Hondo Valley, a life-affirming linear path winding eastward out of the mountains onto the edge of the Great Plains. America's premier artistic family, the Wyeth/Hurd clan, settled here among the Hispanic herders and fruit orchards. The Mescalero Apache reservation is also a place of great beauty—vast thick forests dotted with lakes, creeks, and small rivers. The town of Mescalero, on the reservation, has an interesting culture center with historic black-and-white photos, providing a glimpse into a way of life largely gone today.

RUIDOSO AREA

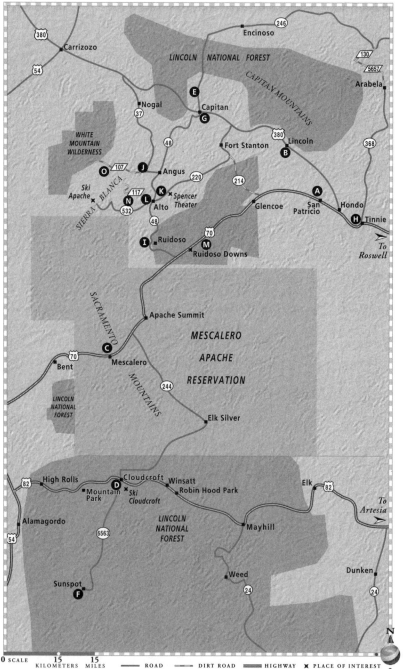

LINCOLN NATIONAL FOREST

Encinoso
246

Carrizozo
380
54

130
5657
Arabela

CAPITAN MOUNTAINS

E
Nogal
37
Capitan
G
48
Fort Stanton
380
Lincoln
B
368

WHITE
MOUNTAIN
WILDERNESS

O
107
J
Angus
220
214
A
San
Patricio
Glencoe
Hondo
H
Tinnie

Ski
Apache
117
K
N L
Alto
532
48
Spencer
Theater

SIERRA BLANCA

70
M

I
Ruidoso
Ruidoso Downs
To
Roswell

SACRAMENTO

Apache Summit

MESCALERO

70
C
Mescalero
APACHE

Bent
244
RESERVATION

MOUNTAINS

LINCOLN
NATIONAL
FOREST

Elk Silver

High Rolls
82
Cloudcroft
Winsatt
Elk
82

D
Mountain
Park
Ski
Cloudcroft
Robin Hood Park
To
Artesia

Alamagordo
6563
LINCOLN
NATIONAL
FOREST
Mayhill

54

Dunken

Weed
24
24

Sunspot
F

N

0 SCALE   15   15
KILOMETERS MILES   ROAD   DIRT ROAD   HIGHWAY   ✕ PLACE OF INTEREST

Sights

- **Ⓐ** Hondo Valley
- **Ⓑ** Lincoln
- **Ⓒ** Mescalero Apache Reservation
- **Ⓓ** Mexican Canyon Trestle
- **Ⓔ** Smokey Bear Historical State Park
- **Ⓕ** Sunspot

Food

- **Ⓓ** Aspen Restaurant
- **Ⓑ** Eatery
- **Ⓖ** Hotel Chango
- **Ⓓ** Rebecca's
- **Ⓗ** Silver Dollar
- **Ⓑ** Wortley Hotel

Lodging

- **Ⓑ** Casa de Patron B&B
- **Ⓑ** Ellis Store & Co. B&B
- **Ⓘ** Inn of the Mountain Gods
- **Ⓓ** The Lodge
- **Ⓙ** Monjeau Shadows
- **Ⓚ** Sierra Mesa Lodge
- **Ⓑ** Wortley Hotel

Camping

- **Ⓓ** 16 Springs Canyon RV Park
- **Ⓛ** Bonita Hollow Campground
- **Ⓜ** Circle B Campground
- **Ⓓ** Lincoln National Forest Campgrounds
- **Ⓝ** Skyline Campground
- **Ⓞ** South Fork Campground

Note: Items with the same letter are located in the same town or area.

A PERFECT DAY IN THE RUIDOSO AREA

You'll have no trouble filling a day in this area. In winter spend the morning skiing at Ski Apache and the afternoon touring Lincoln. In summer visit Lincoln before it gets hot and spend the afternoon picnicking, hiking, and/or fishing in the mountains or visiting the Museum of the Horse. If you're in the Cloudcroft area, drive to Sunspot in the morning and go for a horseback ride or a hike in the afternoon. Then splurge a little and spend a night at The Lodge at Cloudcroft, one of the state's premier hotels. If you're overnighting in Ruidoso or Lincoln and there's a performance at the Spencer Theater, go! The facility alone is the worth the visit.

SIGHTSEEING HIGHLIGHTS

★★★ **Lincoln**—In July 1878, this sleepy four-block town in the gentle valley of Bonito ("Pretty") Creek was the focus of a five-day gun battle that culminated in a house being set afire and the owner shot down when he emerged to surrender. That man was Alexander McSween, one of the principal characters in the so-called Lincoln County War.

Another leading figure in the conflict was named William Bonney, otherwise known as Henry McCarty, or Billy the Kid. Billy, then 19, was the employee and some say protegé of an Englishman named John Tunstall. Tunstall and McSween, you see, opened a mercantile store in direct competition with one Lawrence Murphy. Tunstall also began to bid for and win lucrative contracts for the sale of cattle to local military posts and Indian reservations—a market Murphy had monopolized until then. One afternoon Tunstall was intercepted in the countryside by a band of men, shot, and killed. Billy vowed to avenge his death and emerged as the leader of a group of men called the Regulators. Before long the entire county—then the largest in the nation—was divided into the Murphy or McSween camps.

Today you can walk through the very streets, homes, shops, courthouse, and jail where much of this story played out. For a great overview of the Lincoln County War, first visit the **Lincoln County Heritage Trust Historical Center**, which houses exhibits about the war and the Kid, as well as some very informative displays on the local Mescalero Apache people, the so-called Buffalo Soldiers (the all–African American army units who served in the area), and the Hispanic settlers who first established the town in 1849 as Las Placitas del Rio Bonito. One of their round, multi-story stone defensive *torreons* (towers) still stands prominently on Main Street.

Also visit the **Tunstall/McSween Store**, with its shelves full of original stock, and the **Old Courthouse**, just a few blocks down the street from the historical center. It looks much as it did the year Billy made his deadly escape. On the first full weekend in August, the town really comes to life with its Old Lincoln Days festival.

Details: Lincoln is on U.S. 380, 12 miles east of Capitan, 10 miles west of Hondo and 35 miles northeast of Ruidoso. Historical Center is on the east side of town; 505/653-4025. Open daily 9–6. $4.50 adults, free to children under age 17. For additional information, call the Lincoln State Monument, 505/653-4372 or 800/434-6320. (1–3 hours)

★★ **Hondo Valley**—The land and people of this lovely river valley were immortalized by the masterful landscapes and portraits of one of America's more underappreciated major artists, Peter Hurd. Hurd and his equally talented artist-wife, Henriette Wyeth, lived in the village of San Patricio for decades. His artistic focus centered on his immediate surroundings. In his pictures of watering tanks and windmills on a dry plain, you can feel the heat of a summer afternoon; sense the beauty of a late afternoon as the sun slants down the Hondo valley, softening the already rounded hills; and grasp a life of small but appreciated rewards etched in the faces of the local herders and farmers.

The Wyeth/Hurd clan maintains homes (some for rent—see Lodging, below) and the **Hurd–La Rinconada Gallery** in San Patricio. Also here is **Fort Meigs**, which is not really a fort but the home, shop, gallery, and gardens of John Meigs, a Renaissance man, artist, and collector whose house is stuffed with an impressive array of art, furniture, books, and Asian artifacts—all for sale.

Details: San Patricio is located on U.S. 70 some 20 miles east of Ruidoso. Riconada Gallery, just south of U.S. 70 (follow the signs); 505/ 653-4331 or 800-658-6912; open varying hours—call first. Fort Meigs, reached via a gravel road next to the old church, 505/653-4320, is generally open daily 9–5. (1–2 hours on site)

★★ **Mescalero Apache Reservation**—The 460,000-acre Mescalero reservation in south-central New Mexico near Ruidoso actually harbors the descendants of a number of Apache people of common heritage, including the Mescalero, Chiricahua, Warm Springs, and Lipan who formerly roamed southern New Mexico, southeastern Arizona, west Texas, and north-central Mexico.

Today the nearly 4,000-strong Mescalero are one of the nation's more progressive and prosperous Indian tribes. Under the leadership of tribal president Wendell Chino, they have developed a premier destination resort, the **Inn of the Mountain Gods** (see Lodging, below), RV camps, a large ski area (see Fitness and Recreation, below), cattle ranches, timber operations, and retail businesses.

The tribe's primary event open to visitors is the annual **Coming of Age Ceremony** held for young women around July 4. In the village of Mescalero you will find historic **St. Joseph's Church** and the tribal cultural center, with displays of baskets, clothing, and historic photos.

Details: The reservation is located just to the west and south of Ruidoso. The population and administrative center is in the village of Mescalero, 15 miles southwest of Ruidoso on U.S. 70; 505/671-4494. The culture center, 505/671-9254, is open Mon–Fri 8–4:30. (1 hour minimum)

★★ **Museum of the Horse**—A vast array of carriages, buckboards, covered wagons, saddles, tack, and other horse-related materials, as well as the Race Horse Hall of Fame, forms the heart of this outstanding institution opened in 1992 in Ruidoso. Also on view are excellent collections of Southwestern Indian arts and artifacts gathered and donated by Anne C. Stradling, an outstanding gun collection, Western and regional fine arts, and many other interesting displays.

Details: U.S. 70 1 mile east of the Ruidoso Downs racetrack—look for the life-size horse sculptures in front; 505/378-4142 or 800/263-5929. Open daily 10–5. $5 adults, $4 seniors, $3 students ages 5–17. (1–3 hours)

★★ **Sunspot**—Also known as the Sacramento Peak Observatory or the National Solar Observatory, this is one of the only astronomical facilities in the world dedicated exclusively to the study of the closest star to Earth—our sun. Here you'll find four major telescopes—Hilltop House, the Grain Bin Dome, Vacuum Tower, and Evans Solar Facility—with their technological "eyes" trained on the sun. Several of the buildings housing these scopes are open to the public, connected by an asphalt path that provides a pleasant stroll under ponderosas and terrific views of the Tularosa Valley and White Sands more than 6,000 feet below. A good visitors center opened in 1998. At 9,200 feet, it is comfortably cool in summer, but access in winter can be difficult.

Details: 18 miles south of Cloudcroft. Turn off U.S. 82 at the western edge of town onto NM 130 for 2 miles, and then onto Forest Road 6563; the route is well-marked; 505/434-7000 or www.sunspot.noao.edu. Grounds open daily 8–6. Visitors center open Apr 6–Oct daily 10–6, Nov–Apr 5 Fri–Mon 10–4. Admission fee to center. (1–2 hours on site)

★ **Mexican Canyon Trestle**—One of Cloudcroft's most enduring and popular sightseeing stops takes in an impressive railroad trestle built entirely of wooden beams by the Alamogordo and Sacramento Mountain Railway. The rail line is now abandoned, but the tall bridge built at the turn of the century continues to stand. Best light for photographing it is in late afternoon.

Details: 1 mile west of Cloudcroft just off U.S. 82, just east of mile marker 16, where there is parking, a picnic area, and access to the Osha Trail. (15 minutes–1 hour)

☆ **Smokey Bear Historical State Park**—This facility celebrates prob-ably America's most famous bear (after Yogi), Smokey, who was found in the area after a devastating forest fire in 1950. The bear, then a cub, was flown to Washington, D.C., where the media and the U.S. Forest Service pumped him up into an icon for the forest fire suppression mantra then in vogue (today forest fires are recognized as a vital ele-ment in forest ecology). The park includes displays, Smokey's grave, a small botanical garden, a playground, and picnic tables.

Details: The small park and a visitors center are located in the town of Capitan, 20 miles north of Ruidoso, on U.S. 380; 505/354-2748. 25 cents admission. (30 minutes–1 hour)

FITNESS AND RECREATION

The **Sacramento**, **Sierra Blancas**, and **Capitan Mountains** dominate this area, providing outstanding skiing and snow play, as well as fishing, hiking, biking, and hunting.

As the closest high alpine terrain to Texas, you'll find New Mexico's friendly neighbors flocking here in droves to recreate in sum-mer, and in winter to play on their "sliders" at the nation's southern-most major ski area, **Ski Apache**, 505/336-4356, some 16 miles northwest of Ruidoso at the end of NM 532. This resort, owned and operated by the Mescaleros, is an excellent, relatively small ski area, with a pleasing mix of trails on the flanks of the highest mountain in southern New Mexico, 12,003-foot Sierra Blanca Peak.

Also in the area is **Ski Cloudcroft**, 505/682-2333 or 800/333-7542, formerly known as Snow Canyon, where skiing is like skiing was. Three miles east of Cloudcroft on U.S. 82, this family ski hill has a short chair and a few rope tows. It also offers night skiing and adjoining cross-country ski trails. Lincoln National Forest offers ample opportunities for cross-country skiing. For details, contact the **Sacramento Ranger Station** on U.S. 82 in Cloudcroft, 505/682-2551, or Ruidoso's **Smokey Bear Ranger Station**, 901 Mechem Dr., 505/257-4095.

Hundreds of foot trails weave through the mountains of the area. Popular trails near Cloudcroft include **Rim Trail**, which runs 14 miles along the western rim of the Sacramentos through pine, fir, aspen, and meadows with occasional huge views westward across the Tularosa Basin. The **Cloud Climbing Rail Trail** runs on the bed of the old local railroad. It ambles along one mile from the old, newly replicated **Town Depot** to the famous wood trestle. The depot is reached via an access road off U.S. 82 just west of NM 130. Near Ruidoso, a popular hike summits the highest peak in the southern half of the state, Sierra Blanca Peak. Just northwest of Ruidoso is the **White Mountain Wilderness Area**, and just northeast of Capitan the seldom-visited **Capitan Mountain Wilderness Area**. Call 505/257-4095 for details.

The best fishing is found on the Mescalero reservation or in the national forest lands near Ruidoso, including the **Rio Bonito** and **Rio Bonito Lake, Mescalero Lake, Grindstone Lake, Rio Ruidoso, Timberon Lake**, and **Alto Lake**. For details contact the **Smokey Bear Ranger Station** in Ruidoso, 505/257-4095, or the **Mescalero Tribal Game & Fish Office**, 505/671-4427.

Trophy deer and elk—as well as bear, turkey, and other game—are often taken on the Mescalero reservation. A tribal permit is required. Contact the **Mescalero Tribal Game & Fish Office**, 505/671-4427.

Golfers also enjoy the area, partly because the altitude carries their drives farther than normal. One of the two nicest courses, among the oldest in the nation, is found at **The Lodge**, 505/682-2566. Located at the sky-scraping altitude of 9,200 feet, it is open mid-April to mid-November. The original six-hole course (now nine-hole) was opened in 1899, fewer than 12 years after the game was first introduced to America. Additional options include perhaps New Mexico's most remote course, in **Timberon**, 505/987-2260; the 18-hole, Jim Corbett–designed **Links at Sierra Blanca**, 505/258-2330, in Ruidoso; and **Cree Meadows**, 505/257-5815, in Ruidoso.

Finally, for horseback riding, try **Grindstone Stables**, 505/257-2241, and **Buddie's Stables**, 505/258-4027, both of Ruidoso; and **Chippeway Riding Stables** 550/682-2565 or 800/471-2384. The world's richest quarter-horse race—the $2-million All American Futurity—is held every Labor Day at **Ruidoso Downs**, 505/378-4140, as the highlight of its May through September season. General admission is free. Post time is usually 1 p.m.

FOOD

It isn't much to look at from the outside, and it's in a town whose claim to fame is Smokey the Bear, but the **Hotel Chango**, intersection of U.S. 380 and NM 48 in Capitan, 505/354-4213, is one of New Mexico's better restaurants. Creativity is key here, with reasonably priced dishes like poached salmon with smoked chiles, and fine wines. It's open Wednesday through Saturday for dinner.

RUIDOSO

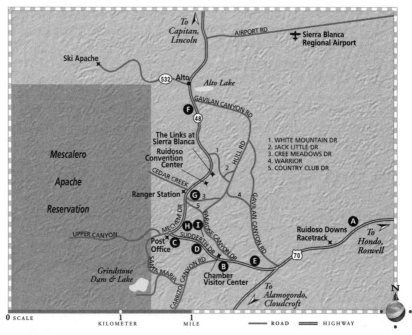

To Capitan, Lincoln

AIRPORT RD

Sierra Blanca Regional Airport

Ski Apache

532 Alto

Alto Lake

GAVILAN CANYON RD

48

The Links at Sierra Blanca
Ruidoso Convention Center

HULL RD

1. WHITE MOUNTAIN DR
2. JACK LITTLE DR
3. CREE MEADOWS DR
4. WARRIOR
5. COUNTRY CLUB DR

Mescalero

Apache

Reservation

CEDAR CREEK

Ranger Station

UPPER CANYON

MECHEM DR

SUDDERTH DR

PARADISE CANYON DR

GAVILAN CANYON RD

Ruidoso Downs Racetrack

To Hondo, Roswell

70

Post Office

SANTA MARIA

CARRIZO CANYON RD

Chamber Visitor Center

To Alamogordo, Cloudcroft

Grindstone Dam & Lake

N

0 SCALE   1   1
        KILOMETER   MILE   ROAD   HIGHWAY

Sights

A Museum of the Horse

Food

B Cattle Baron

C Che Bella

D La Lorrraine

Lodging

E Apache Motel

F Best Western Swiss Chalet

G Innsbrook Village

Camping

H Blue Spruce RV Park

I Tall Pines RV Park

Another real find is **Rebecca's**, in the Lodge at Cloudcroft, 505/682-2566 or 800/842-4216. I had a mouth-watering baked sea bass last time I was there. The room—in dark woods, mirrors, and crystal chandeliers—is also quite impressive. A pianist often plays at dinner. Its breakfasts—other than an outstanding Sunday brunch—are more ordinary, but choices expand again at lunch. It is open daily year-round. Another Cloudcroft option is the **Aspen Restaurant**, on U.S. 82, 505/682-2526, with surprisingly good German fare at lunch and dinner.

Ruidoso also has a few fine places to eat mixed in amongst a horde of fast-food and chain eateries. Among the nicest and most expensive is **La Lorrraine**, 2523 Sudderth Dr., 505/257-2954, with French cuisine; its outdoor patio is pleasant in summer. It is open for lunch and dinner daily, except Monday. In a town of many steak houses, the **Cattle Baron**, 657 Sudderth Dr., 505/257-9355, is perhaps the best. In a setting both elegant and relaxed, it also serves excellent seafood and has a rousing bar. Among several Italian restaurants, I like **Che Bella**, corner of Sudderth and Mechem, 505/257-7540, with its fine northern-style dining and extensive beer and wine selection; it's closed Tuesday.

Lincoln has a few choices: the dining room of the historic **Wortley Hotel**, on Main Street, 505/653-4676, and the **Eatery**, also on Main Street, which serves snacks and light fare daily. In Tinnie, some 12 miles southeast of Lincoln and six miles from San Patricio, is another of the more distinguished restaurants in southern New Mexico: the **Silver Dollar**, on U.S. 70/380, 505/653-4425, with succulent ribeye steaks and seafood at dinner, and simpler but appealing weekend lunches. It has a wonderful Brunswick bar, veranda for summer seating, and a mercantile. It's open Wednesday through Sunday.

LODGING

One of the state's finest places to spend a night is found in tiny Cloudcroft at **The Lodge**, located just off U.S. 82 on at the west edge of town (turn on Curlew, the first street east of NM 130), 505/682-2566 or 800/842-4216. First opened in 1899, then rebuilt in 1911, it sports a front facade dominated by a four-story tower capped by a copper dome. Its guests have run from Pancho Villa to Judy Garland, Clark Gable, Mexican and U.S. governors, astronauts, and military leaders. Conrad Hilton ran the property in 1933. A large stone fireplace greets arriving guests; the elegant but fun bar was once in the home of Al Capone and is tended today by my favorite barperson anywhere, Nosie Crosby. A warm-season outdoor pool, sauna, massage services, 37-channel TV, golf course, mercantile, excellent restaurant, exceptionally friendly and help-ful staff, and finely appointed rooms almost guarantee an outstanding stay. Doubles run from $79 to $125, suites from $129 to $205.

One of the most interesting and relaxing B&Bs you'll ever encounter is found in Lincoln. The **Ellis Store & Co. B&B**, on Main Street, 505/653-4610 or 800/653-6460, is an 1850s-era adobe with shady portals, period furnishings, and historical associations to Billy the Kid. I was intrigued by the proprietor David Vigil's ghost stories and over-whelmed by the delicious breakfast prepared by Jinny. Rooms—all with fireplaces or stoves, fine linens, and handmade quilts—run $69 to $89.

Just down Main Street is **Casa de Patron B&B**, 505/653-4676, another historic adobe with nice New Mexican decor and rooms run-ning $80 to $110. Yet another outstanding place is the **Wortley Hotel**, also on Main Street, 505/653-4300, once owned by Pat Garrett. Sit a spell on a rocker on the front porch. Rooms run $60 to $65.

Ruidoso is home to many motels and hotels, as well as condomini-ums and cabins. It can totally fill up, however, on horseracing week-ends and holidays. The **Inn of the Mountain Gods**, 505/257-5141 or 800/545-9011, owned and operated by the Mescalero tribe, has a superb location overlooking a lake and distant Sierra Blanca. Its facilities include restaurants, a bar, and a casino (see Nightlife, below). It also offers a renowned 18-hole golf course, pool, tennis courts, riding, fish-ing, hunting, and other activities. However, it is quite sprawling and can seem rather cold despite its amenities. Doubles start around $100.

Ruidoso area B&Bs are limited but include the exceptional four-star **Sierra Mesa Lodge**, located two miles east of Alto on Fort Stanton Road, 505/336-4515. Its contemporary design includes a glass-enclosed hot tub and rooms with private baths beginning at $90. The **Monjeau Shadows**, 16 miles from Ruidoso on Bonito Road near Angus, 505/336-4191, is a Victorian-style B&B with a 10-acre garden, game room, library, and rooms beginning at $78.

Other Ruidoso options include the **Innsbrook Village**, Mechem Drive (just north of Furr's), 800/284-0294, with lovely grounds, trout pond, outdoor heated pool, tennis courts, and restaurant/bar, rooms at $90, and condos beginning at $125. **Best Western Swiss Chalet**, 1451 Mechem Dr., 505/258-3333 or 800/47-SWISS, has a restaurant/lounge, small indoor pool, sauna, and rooms beginning at $68. The **Apache Motel**, 344 Sudderth Dr., 505/257-2986 or 800/426-0616, rents rooms for $34 and up.

CAMPING

There is dispersed backpack camping in local wilderness areas (see Fitness and Recreation, above). Near Ruidoso there are four Lincoln National Forest campgrounds operated seasonally by the **Smokey Bear Ranger District**, 901 Mechem Dr., 505/257-4095. **South Fork Campground** is near Bonito Lake (take NM 48 11 miles north of Ruidoso and turn left onto Forest Road 107 for five miles), with fishing, hiking trails, drinking water, and sites for six dollars. **Skyline Campground**, on Forest Road 117 four miles off the ski area access road, has a playground, flush toilets, showers, RV hookups for $10, and tent sites for $6.

Near Cloudcroft, there is a slew of campgrounds in the Lincoln National Forest (details at Sacramento Ranger Station, U.S. 82 in Cloudcroft, 505/682-2551). Just to the south are **Sleepy Grass, Deer Head**, and **Slide**; just to the north are **Pine, Apache, Silver Lake**, and **Saddle**.

Commercial campgrounds in and near Ruidoso include the **Circle B Campground**, 2.5 miles northeast of Ruidoso Downs on U.S. 70, 505/378-4990, with showers, tent sites, and RV hookups for $16; **Blue Spruce RV Park**, 302 Mechem Dr., 505/257-7993, with showers and hookups for $16; and the quiet **Tall Pines RV Park**, 1800 Sudderth Dr., 505/257-5233. **Bonita Hollow Campground**, in Alto, 505/336-4325, has showers, tent sites for $10, and RV hookups for $14. In Cloudcroft, the **16 Springs Canyon RV Park**, 571 16 Springs Canyon Rd., 505/687-3129, has 20 hookup sites, showers, and laundry.

NIGHTLIFE

For live music in Ruidoso, generally C&W with a Texas slant, drop into **Win, Place & Show**, 2516 Sudderth Dr., 505/257-9982, or the **Winner's Circle**, 2535 Sudderth Dr., 505/257-9535. In Cloudcroft, the **Western Bar**, on the boardwalk, 505/682-2445, is popular. For poker and blackjack, slots, craps, and Bingo, drop into the **Ina Da Room** and **Casino Apache** (associated with the Inn of the Mountain Gods, 505/257-7507). Near Ruidoso is the state-of-the-art **Spencer Theater**, 505/336-4800, which hosts major events.

10
ALAMOGORDO AND THE TULAROSA BASIN

Not far from the Dark Mountains (Oscuras) and within the harsh desert valley known as the Journey of Death (Jornada del Muerto), mankind first released the awesome power of atomic weaponry. The date was July 16, 1945, and the place was a site now found within White Sands Missile Range northwest of Alamogordo. The range is just one of the military's major facilities in the Tularosa Basin, the bottom of a huge lake bed that long ago evaporated. Over it today fly the black triangular Stealth aircraft from Holloman Air Force Base.

Juxtaposed with this contemporary environment, however, is a landscape of amazing beauty and character. In March 1998 I was walking at White Sands National Monument over a sea of pure white sand. Ahead on the horizon rose Sierra Blanca Peak, more than 7,000 feet higher than my bare feet, with deep canyons snaking out of its western face and snow ringing some 3,000 thousand feet of its summit. No wonder the Apaches fought so desperately to hold onto this place.

Dog Canyon is one of the state's prettiest spots, with an illuminating history. Aguirre Springs has lovely fat old oak trees, their bark like alligator skin, scads of birds, and tiny streams. At Valley of Fires you'll find one of the nation's freshest lava flows. And don't overlook the small, oldest settlements of the valley, La Luz and Tularosa, with roots sunken deep into this southern soil.

TULAROSA BASIN

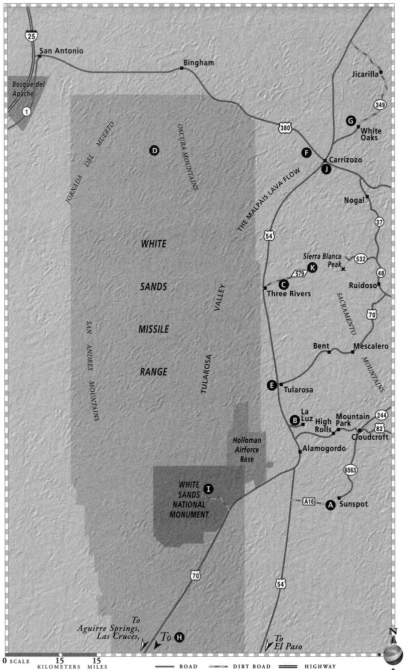

Sights

Ⓐ Dog Canyon/Oliver Lee State Park

Ⓑ La Luz

Ⓒ Three Rivers Petroglyphs National Recreation Area

Ⓓ Trinity Site

Ⓔ Tularosa

Ⓕ Valley of Fires National Recreation Area

Ⓖ White Oaks

Ⓗ White Sands Missile Range Museum

Ⓘ White Sands National Monument

Food

Ⓙ Four Winds Restaurant and Lounge

Ⓙ Outpost

Lodging

Ⓔ Pecan Tree

Camping

Ⓔ Mountain Meadows RV Park

Ⓐ Oliver Lee State Park

Ⓚ Three Rivers

Ⓕ Valley of Fires Recreation Area

Note: Items with the same letter are located in the same town or area.

A PERFECT DAY IN THE TULAROSA BASIN

Here are two options: Spend the morning at Oliver Lee State Park, have a picnic in Dog Canyon, then return to town in the early afternoon for a visit to the International Space Hall of Fame. Catch sunset on the dunes at White Sands National Monument. Or visit the dunes early in the morning, then head north through Tularosa, have lunch at The Outpost in Carrizozo, and then visit Valley of Fires National Recreation Area, the ghost town of White Oaks, or the petroglyphs at Three Rivers.

SIGHTSEEING HIGHLIGHTS

✵✵✵ **Dog Canyon/Oliver Lee State Park**—This narrow slot canyon that emerges from the Sacramento Mountains south of Alamogordo is another hidden New Mexico gem. At its base, the site of Olive Lee Memorial State Park, the terrain is full-on desert: rocky, dotted with ocotillo and cactus, brown, and somewhat barren. The canyon, however, begins more than 2,000 feet higher, where there is considerably more moisture. Fed by rain, snowmelt, springs, and seeps, the perennial water flow in Dog Canyon supports a great diversity of plant and animal life. Cottonwoods and ash crowd the narrow canyon floor at the lower elevations, with delicate maidenhair ferns and orchids clinging to moist rock walls. Mountain lions and ringtail cats patrol the slopes alongside the canyon, as well as mule deer and lots of other fauna.

This wonder of water, naturally, also proved irresistible to people over the eons. Archaeological evidence reveals that humanity has been using Dog Canyon as a refuge for more than 4,000 years. In historical times, it was a hideaway of the Apache, including the great chief Nana. They would raid in the Rio Grande Valley, retreat across the Tularosa Basin, and then seemingly vanish. Actually they would slide up Dog Canyon. Eventually the cavalry found the canyon, but even then they were unsuccessful for many years in pursuing the Apache up it. The canyon's switchback trail, today a National Recreation Trail, was easily defended.

Later the canyon mouth was settled by several parties, including rancher Oliver Milton Lee. His ranch house has been completely restored and provides an interesting glimpse into the life of an influential "pioneer" figure of New Mexico. The park also has a nice visitors center and interpretive trails.

Details: *From Alamogordo, head south on U.S. 54 for 9 miles. Turn left and continue 4 miles to the park boundary; 505/437-8284. Open year-round. Day use $3 per vehicle. (1 hour minimum on site)*

★★★ **White Sands National Monument**—As with my first visit to the Grand Canyon, White Sands surpassed my expectations; I'd seen lots of photographs and even movie footage shot here, so I figured I had it figured out. Wrong.

No visual reproduction can prepare you for the *feel* of the sand itself. It is almost silky, so fine are its grains of ground-up gypsum. And the pictures don't even capture the almost blinding brilliance of this scene when the sun is upon it. On our first stop along the eight-mile-long road that rolls through the monument, I was also surprised to find there is a fair amount of vegetation that lives on some sections of the dunes. I had to admire these plants' tenacity: As the dunes shift, the plants' roots are slowly exposed—many living plants are suspended several feet above the sand! It was late afternoon and a thunderstorm was dumping some rain between us and the San Andres Mountains to the west. Sunlight pierced the blue-gray clouds, backlighting the rain in bursts of golden sheets. The sound of a gentle breeze mixed with the gleeful laughter of children rolling down the steep dunes.

A visitors center has a museum, bookstore, gift shop, and refreshments. Summer middays are very hot.

Details: From Alamogordo, head west on U.S. 72/80 15 miles to the visitor's center; 505/479-6124 or www.nps.gov/whsa. Ranger-guided tours held year-round; lectures, including summer stargazing sessions, summers only. Limited backpack camping allowed; no camping facilities but covered picnic tables available. Day use fee $3 for adults, $1.50 for kids. Park hours 7 a.m.–9 p.m. in summer, 7 a.m.–sunset otherwise; the visitors center opens at 8 a.m. (2 hours minimum on site)

★★ **International Space Hall of Fame**—This remarkably comprehensive, interesting, and entertaining facility is dedicated to humankind's exploration of supersonic flight and outer space, in which New Mexico institutions and individuals have played a surprisingly major role.

The prominent main building—a reflective, golden-hued, four-story cube—houses many displays of actual rocket and satellite hardware, as well as models, photos, and other descriptive and historical materials, including moon rocks.

Within the center is the **Clyde Tombaugh Planetarium and Omnimax Theater**, named after the New Mexican who discovered the planet Pluto. The theater's 2,700-square-foot screen wraps overhead and behind you for memorable visual flights of fancy.

Outdoors is the **John Stapp Air & Space Park**, with numerous full-scale rockets on display, and the **Astronaut Memorial Garden**, dedicated to the *Challenger* shuttle crew. The center also has a space-oriented gift shop.

Details: Located on the town's northeast edge, on Scenic Dr. near Indian Wells Rd.; 505/437-2840 or 800/545-4021. Museum open summer daily 9–6, winter daily 9–5. The planetarium occasionally hosts summer-night star and planet viewing with telescopes. Theater films change periodically and run summer daily every hour 10–4, winter every other hour 10–4 on weekdays and hourly on weekends. $2.50 adults, $2 kids to the museum; $5.50 adults, $4.50 kids to the theater. (1–3 hours)

★★ **Three Rivers Petroglyphs National Recreation Area**—One of the better collections of Indian petroglyphs on public land is found at this isolated site on the northwestern slope of Sierra Blanca. The 21,000 or so drawings pecked into basalt boulders were created primarily by the inhabitants of nearby Jornada Mogollon villages, which were inhabited circa A.D. 900 to 1400. One village has been partially excavated.

A half-mile trail winds through the rock art panels, and another shorter trail leads to the village. There is also a small shaded picnic area with six tables, and restrooms. The site, set in a black volcanic boulder field, gets very hot in summer—visit early or late in the day. Camping is not allowed (see Camping, below, for nearby possibilities).

Details: The park is located between Carrizozo and Tularosa. Head north from Tularosa on U.S. 54 some 17 miles (28 miles south of Carrizozo), turn right (east) onto gravel County Road B30, and proceed 5 miles to the site; 505/354-2231. Open daily. Small admission fee. (1–3 hours)

★★ **Valley of Fires National Recreation Area**—Some 1,500 to 2,000 years ago—just a blink in geologic time—the earth turned itself inside out here, expelling huge sheets of molten lava that flowed 44 miles or so down a gentle valley like a river of fire. At points the lava collected into pockets more than 700 feet thick, and at other places surrounded higher ground, leaving sandstone promontories exposed like islands. Over time, wind deposited dirt and sand, and within these pockets flourishing stands of grasses, bushes, cactus, and other plant life secured a toehold. Wildlife—including mule deer, badger, skunk, coyote, bobcat, ringtail cat, numerous reptiles (including rattlers!), and all kinds of birds and raptors—followed.

This Bureau of Land Management holding also contains rare petroglyphs and bits of pottery and other artifacts left by the Jornada people (a branch of the Mogollon culture). The area features a paved .75-mile nature trail loop running through a small portion of the rugged lava flows, campgrounds, restrooms, picnic tables, and a visitors center with book and gift store.

Details: Located 4 miles west of Carrizozo just off U.S. 380; 505/648-2241. Open daily. Day use $3 per vehicle. (1–3 hours)

★★ **White Oaks**—If you like ghost towns, this is your spot. Once among the state's largest towns, with some 4,000 inhabitants, it is almost entirely deserted today. Many of its original buildings have disappeared, but enough remain—including the **White Oaks Schoolhouse & Museum** and some mansions—for an interesting visit. In addition to an old cemetery on the south side of town, there are a number of artists' studios and a saddlemaker here. Directions to their places are posted at the corner of Pine Street and White Oaks Avenue. In summer, the **Birdsong Crafty Cage**, a restaurant and gift shop, is open daily nine to five. If you're lucky the **White Oaks Bar** will be open (its hours are erratic). Don't be put off by its front sign stating "No Scum Allowed." One day each summer, local residents and neighbors collect to relive the good ole times during the Lincoln–White Oaks Pony Express Race.

Details: Located northeast of Carrizozo. Head north out of town on U.S. 54 for 3 miles and turn right onto NM 349 for 9 miles. (1–2 hours)

★ **Trinity Site**—This was where the world's first atomic bomb was detonated, in a test some of its makers believed could set off a chain reaction that would burn off the world's atmosphere. Fortunately, that didn't happen, but "the gadget," as it was euphemistically named, did erupt in an explosion of then undreamed-of destructive force. The blast, at 5:29 a.m. on July 16, 1945, was noted as far away as Arizona and the Texas panhandle, and observed by its creators' wives, who gathered on mountainsides near Los Alamos, where the bomb had been conceived and built. A blinding flash followed by a fireball estimated at its center to be four times hotter than the sun, a roar that rolled and echoed across the twilight landscape, and a sucking wind that lifted tons of desert soil as it rushed toward ground zero ushered in the nuclear age.

The spot where the bomb was detonated—a flat plain devoid of vegetation at the northern end of the Tularosa Basin—was too radioactive to be casually visited until 1953. Sand, which had fused into a new form of greenish glass called Trinitite, was scraped off and trucked away, and today the site is open to visitation twice a year.

Details: White Sands Missile Range; 505/678-1134. Generally off-limits to the public. Open first Sat of Apr and Oct. Visitors can reach the site in two ways: by escorted caravan sponsored by the Alamogordo Chamber of Commerce, which forms at the Otero County Fairgrounds at 7:30 a.m., or through the Stallion Range Center gate, located 12 miles east of San Antonio on U.S. 380 on a paved and marked road. No gasoline available on missile range. Free. (5-hour tour)

★ **Tularosa and La Luz**—The oldest communities in the Tularosa Basin were founded by Hispanic settlers who permanently occupied the area in the early 1860s, dug irrigation ditches to the Rio Peñasco, and planted orchards and fields. The first recorded settlement was at La Luz, as early as 1719. There are many historic and pretty homes here of both adobe and Victorian styles, and most of the original ditches still carry water in the summer, creating a shady oasis. In Tularosa, on U.S. 70, is **St. Francis de Paula**, the best example of massive adobe church architecture in the southern part of the state; on Christmas Eve it is covered with *farolitos*—brown paper bags filled with sand and illuminated by candles. **La Luz Plaza** is also worthy of a look at its gazebo, massive agave cactus, and flowers. Speaking of flowers, Tularosa (named after a local reed) is known as "the City of Roses," has many wonderful flower gardens, and hosts the annual **Rose Festival** on the first weekend in May.

Details: Both communities are located north of Alamogordo. Tularosa is substantially larger. To get to La Luz, travel about 2 miles north of the intersection of U.S. 82 and U.S. 54/70 to NM 545 and turn right (east) and proceed just over 2 miles to the center of the village. To get to Tularosa, travel 9 miles north of the intersection of U.S. 82 and U.S. 54/70. (30 minutes–1 hour per town)

★ **White Sands Missile Range Museum**—People interested in space exploration, aerospace engineering, or U.S. military history will enjoy this facility. Exhibitions include materials on Dr. Werner von Braun, Dr. Clyde Tombaugh, and the origins of America's missile, high-tech weaponry, and space programs. The outdoor **Missile Park** has samples of many rockets developed during the Cold War and Operation Desert Storm.

Details: White Sands Missile Range administrative and housing center; 505/678-2250. Enter base at gate on U.S. 70 some 34 miles west of Alamogordo, and proceed 4 miles south; or go through the gate at Orogrande, some 35 miles south of Alamogordo on U.S. 54. Museum open Mon–Fri 8–4:30; Missile Park open daily. (1–2 hours on site)

KIDS' STUFF

More than 1,200 feet of model railroad and 2.2. miles of outdoor miniature railroad thrill both kids and adults at Alamogordo's **Toy Train Depot**, 1991 N. White Sands Blvd., at the north end of Alameda Park, 505/437-2855. Hundreds of model trains are on display in the 90-year-old train depot, with some usually in operation. I'll never forget the ear-to-ear grins on my kids' faces when they took a spin around the park. It's open Wednesday through Monday noon to five. There is a small fee for riding the rails.

Alamogordo's **Alameda Park Zoo**, 1321 N. White Sands Blvd. (U.S. 54/70), 505/439-4290 or 800/545-4021, is a small but well-run and shady seven-acre enclave. It is home to more than 90 species and 300 animals, including the endangered *lobo*, or Mexican wolf. Opened in 1898, it is New Mexico's oldest zoo. There are nice picnic grounds and a playground. It is open daily from nine to five. Admission is two dollars for adults, one dollar for seniors and kids ages 2 to 11.

FITNESS AND RECREATION

One of the primary outdoor recreation possibilities in the area is hiking—at **White Sands National Monument, Valley of Fires Recreation Area**, or in **Dog Canyon** at **Oliver Lee State Park** (see Sightseeing Highlights, above). Mountain biking is restricted at these sites.

Another outstanding hiking option is **Aguirre Springs**, 505/525-4300, located in national forest lands of the **Organ Mountains**, which border the Tularosa Basin's southwestern edge. There is a delightful 4.5-mile trail here with a 1,180-foot elevation gain that loops from the campgrounds up along the bases of the prominent spires forming the mountain's spine—passing through thickets of oak, massive and ancient alligator juniper trees, and tall pines—and then down through a succulent valley watered by a tinkling creek. To get here, take U.S. 70 west from Alamogordo some 48 miles to the access road, which runs three miles south to the entrance. There is a three-dollar day use fee; camping is available. Gates are open from eight to eight April through September, eight to six October through March.

Of special interest to birders is **Holloman Lakes**, 505/525-4300, which includes perennial Lake Holloman and shallow seasonal playa ponds. Expect to see snowy plovers, avocets, sandpipers, yellowlegs, ibis, gulls, terns, and many other wading and shorebirds. To get here, drive west from Alamogordo on U.S. 70 for seven miles to the western edge of Holloman Air Force Base, and turn right (north) onto the signed access road.

Alamogordo's **Desert Foothills Park** has a one-mile trail for biking, hiking, and skating, as well as access to other trails. Alamogordo also is home to the 18-hole **Desert Lakes Municipal Golf Course**, 2351 Hamilton Rd. (off U.S. 54 south of town), 505/437-0290, with restaurant/bar, lighted driving range, and pro shop. About two hours away is **Ski Apache**; some 45 minutes away is **Ski Cloudcroft** and the myriad hiking, biking, riding, fishing, and other mountain recreation opportunities of the Sacramento Mountains (see previous chapter). The main office of the **Lincoln National Forest** is located in Alamogordo, 11th Street and New York Avenue, 505/434-7200.

FOOD

One of my favorite roughstock bar/restaurants in New Mexico is in Carrizozo, the **Outpost**, 415 Central, 505/648-9994, with its walls plastered with mounted game, posters, photos of friends, and so forth. You can shoot pool, play the jukebox, and chow down on excellent green-chile cheeseburgers—the menu is very basic. Also in Carrizozo, I've often eaten the basic highway fare of the **Four Winds Restaurant and Lounge**, at the intersection of U.S. 380 and U.S. 54, 505/648-2964.

For some tasty New Mexican fare in Alamogordo, try **Margo's**, 501 E. First St., 505/434-0689, serving lunch and dinner daily. Other Alamogordo eateries include the casual **Angelina's**, 415 S. White Sands Blvd., 505/434-1166, for good pasta and pizza; the town's best Oriental restaurant, **Chinese Dragon**, 606 E. First St., 505/434-2494, open daily for lunch and dinner; **Cattleman's Steak House**, 2904 N. White Sands Blvd., 505/434-5252; **Country Rose Brewpub**, 2203 E. First St., 505/434-9633, with simple but good food and numerous tap beers; and **Keg's**, 817 Scenic Dr., 505/437-9564, which serves sandwiches, burgers, and steaks; its bar has pool tables and weekend dancing to a DJ. There is also a **Denny's**, 930 S. White Sands Blvd., 505/437-6106, open 24 hours daily.

LODGING

There's nothing fancy here, but Alamogordo offers a decent range of motels. The **Holiday Inn**, 1401 S. White Sands Blvd., has a swimming pool with a child's wading area, laundry, restaurant, and lounge, with doubles beginning at $80. The **Best Western Desert Aire**, 2110 S. White Sands Blvd., 505/437-2110, also has a pool, as well as a sauna, laundry, and café, with doubles for $54 (includes breakfast). The **Satellite Inn**, 2224 N. White Sands Blvd., 505/437-2224 or 800/221-7690, has a pool, with doubles for $35. At the low end, the **Alamo Inn**, 1400 N. White Sands Blvd., 505/437-1000, has a pool and doubles for $28.

ALAMOGORDO

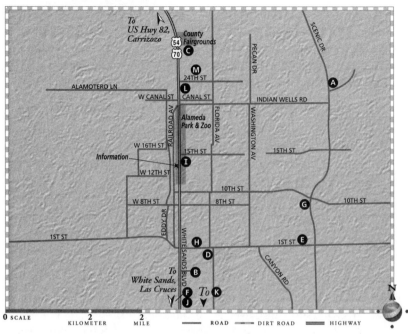

Sights

Ⓐ International Space Hall of Fame

Food

Ⓑ Angelina's

Ⓒ Cattleman's Steak House

Ⓓ Chinese Dragon

Ⓔ Country Rose Brewpub

Ⓕ Denny's

Ⓖ Keg's

Ⓗ Margo's

Lodging

Ⓘ Alamo Inn

Ⓙ Best Western Desert Aire

Ⓚ Holiday Inn

Ⓛ Satellite Inn

Camping

Ⓜ KOA Alamogordo

There is at least one area B&B, Tularosa's **Pecan Tree**, 802 Old Mescalero Rd. (Higuera Street), 505/585-2238, set among nine acres of flower beds and roses, pecan orchards, cypress, walnut, apple, pomegranate, and quince trees. The two-story Illinois-style home dates to 1912. The three double rooms run $50 to $60.

CAMPING

While there is no camping at **Three Rivers** Petroglyph Site (see Sightseeing Highlights, above), there is a public campground with a spring and trees just eight miles further up the dirt access road from U.S. 54. Camping is available at **Valley of Fires Recreation Area** (see Sightseeing Highlights), with 14 RV hookup sites and additional tent sites. **Oliver Lee State Park** (see Sightseeing Highlights) has 50 sites with hot showers, shelters, and great views of the Tularosa Basin and the Sacramento Mountains; in spring thousands of ocotillo and other cacti put on quite a show. Developed campsites and free, primitive camping are also available in the nearby **Lincoln National Forest** (the office is at 11th Street and New York Avenue, Alamogordo, 505/434-7200).

The BLM-managed **Aguirre Springs National Recreation Area**, 505/525-4300, is located about 20 miles northeast of Las Cruces and 51 miles from Alamagordo. Its windy five-mile access road (not recommended for trailers over 22 feet) begins on U.S. 70 some two miles east of San Augustine Pass. The area provides camping with incredible views of the Tularosa Basin, strenuous hiking along trails at the foot of the Organ Mountain spires, and good birding. It has pit toilets but no drinking water. Day use is free; camping costs three dollars.

There are also a few commercial camping facilities in and around Alamogordo. **KOA Alamogordo** is on 24th Street, one block east of U.S. 54/70, with lots of nice shade trees, RV hookups for $18, and tent sites for $16. Tularosa's **Mountain Meadows RV Park** is at 240 Mt. Meadows Rd., 505/585-4979.

11

LAS CRUCES AND THE LOWER RIO GRANDE VALLEY

Travelers once passed as quickly as possible through this area: Its desert lands and incessant Apache raids gave rise to its name as the place of The Crosses (Las Cruces). But today the Lower Rio Grande Valley between El Paso, Texas, and Hatch, New Mexico, is anything but a graveyard. In fact, in a recent 10-year period, Dona Ana County experienced a 24 percent growth rate. Las Cruces, the county seat, is popular with retirees, who enjoy its mild winters. It has become the state's second-largest city, with 78,000 people (twice that number in the county) and the state's agricultural university.

As is so often the history in New Mexico, human habitation of the area winds back to farmers tapping into the waters of the Rio Grande. People whose image of New Mexico revolves around the many-armed saguaro cactus (which don't in fact exist in New Mexico) won't believe the thousands of acres of farms north and south of Cruces.

Here too is one of the Southwest's most intriguing small towns: Old Mesilla, or La Mesilla, the oldest Hispanic town in southern New Mexico. Its chile fields, winding acequias, tall cottonwoods, and adobe homes remind me strongly of my childhood in the North Valley of Albuquerque—up the Rio Grande some 230 miles.

Old cavalry posts, the spires of the Organ Mountains in a sunset glow, water trickling out of a black boulder in a desert canyon, mariachi music—these are a few of the things visitors here will recall.

LOWER RIO GRANDE VALLEY

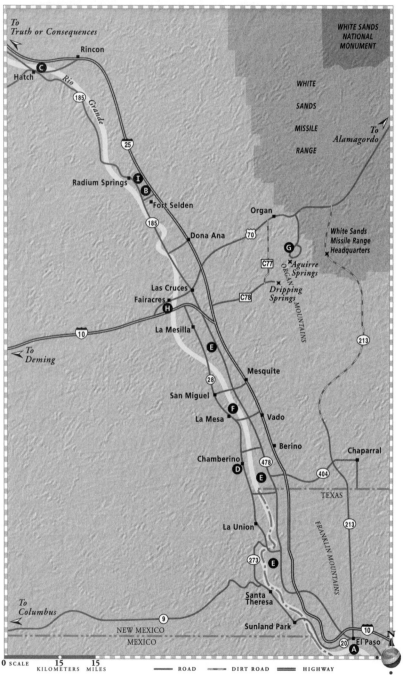

To Truth or Consequences

Rincon

Hatch

Rio Grande

185

25

Radium Springs

Fort Selden

Dona Ana

Las Cruces

Fairacres

La Mesilla

10

To Deming

Mesquite

28

San Miguel

La Mesa

Vado

Berino

Chamberino

478

La Union

273

Santa Theresa

Sunland Park

To Columbus

9

NEW MEXICO
MEXICO

WHITE SANDS NATIONAL MONUMENT

WHITE

SANDS

MISSILE

RANGE

To Alamagordo

White Sands Missile Range Headquarters

Organ

70

C77

Aguirre Springs

C78

Dripping Springs

ORGAN MOUNTAINS

213

Chaparral

404

TEXAS

213

FRANKLIN MOUNTAINS

10

20 El Paso

N

0 SCALE 15 15
KILOMETERS MILES

ROAD   DIRT ROAD   HIGHWAY

Sights

Ⓐ El Paso and Juarez

Ⓑ Fort Selden State Monument

Ⓒ Hatch

Ⓓ La Vina Winery

Ⓔ Mesilla Valley

Food

Ⓕ Chope's

Camping

Ⓖ Aguirre Campground

Ⓗ Best View RV Park

Ⓘ Leasburg Dam State Park

A PERFECT DAY IN LAS CRUCES AND THE LOWER RIO GRANDE VALLEY

After breakfast at Nabes in Cruces, head out to Dripping Springs for a walk, then into Mesilla for a stroll, perhaps some shopping, and lunch at Double Eagle. In the afternoon take a drive down the lush Mesilla Valley and into Juarez for dinner, or return to town and drop into the Farm and Ranch Museum.

SIGHTSEEING HIGHLIGHTS

★★★ **Mesilla**—First settled in 1850 by Mexicans from Las Cruces who left it to avoid losing their Mexican citizenship (Cruces was then in the U.S., Mesilla in Mexico), it still retains much of its early character. The town clusters around its historic plaza, surrounded by fields and orchards watered by acequias from the nearby Rio Grande, and Spanish is still heard. While fairly quiet and easygoing today, Mesilla was once rip-roaring, the leading community of southern New Mexico, and a major stop on the Butterfield Stage Line. In 1853, the Gadsden Treaty—which ceded parts of southern Arizona and New Mexico, including Mesilla, from Mexico to the United States—was signed here. From 1860 to 1861, it served, oddly, as the capital of the Confederates' vast Arizona Territory.

The narrow plaza area—dotted with one-of-a-kind shops, galleries, a handful of restaurants, and modest but historic houses—is quite charming and makes for a pleasant stroll. The shady plaza is capped by a small white gazebo and sprinkled with wrought-iron benches. On its north side is **San Albino**, a pretty brick church built in 1850. For local history visit the **Gadsden Museum**, just a few hundred yards east of the plaza, run by Mary Alexander—the great-granddaughter of the once-prominent southern New Mexican, Colonel Fountain.

Details: Mesilla, also known as La Mesilla and Old Mesilla, is 3 miles southwest of Las Cruces. Take Avenida de Mesilla (NM 28) from Main St. or I-10; or University Blvd. from I-25; 505/524-8521 or 800/343-7827. San Albino still holds regular Masses but is open to the public on a limited basis. Gadsden Museum, Barker Rd. just off NM 28; 505/526-6293; open Mon–Sat 9–11 and 1–5, Sun 1–5; $2 adults, $1 children ages 6 and up. (1–3 hours)

★★ **Fort Selden State Monument**—Another of the string of forts established across southern New Mexico in the mid-1800s in response to Apache raids on miners, ranchers, and homesteaders of the region, this fort north of Las Cruces on the Rio Grande was once home to units of the Buffalo soldiers (African American soldiers), and to a young Douglas MacArthur of World War II and Korean War fame. His father commanded this post in the 1880s.

Only remnants of its adobe walls remain, but there is a signed foot trail through the ruins, as well as an interesting museum and visitors center here. On summer weekends from 11 a.m. to 3 p.m. people in period clothing present living history enactments and activities.

Details: 15 miles north of Las Cruces, just west of I-25 off Exit 19 at Radium Springs; 505/526-8911. Open daily 8:30–5. $2 adults. (1–2 hours)

★★ **Mesilla Valley**—One of New Mexico's prime farming areas lies along the Rio Grande south of Las Cruces in the Mesilla Valley. While there are no outstanding landmarks, a series of small farming towns— including **San Miguel, Mesquite, La Mesa, Chamberino, Anthony,** and **La Union Vieja**—and a patchwork of huge farms, fields, and orchards make for a nice drive. Along the way you'll pass through **Stahmann Farm**, said to be the largest pecan orchards in the world. You can visit their all-pecan gift shop and take a free tour.

Details: I would suggest a drive southward on the west side of the river on NM 28 and a return north on the east side of the valley on TX 20/NM 478. Several bridges link the roads, providing for tours of varying time frames. Stahmann Farm about 6 miles south of Mesilla on NM 28; 505/525-3470 or 800/654-6887. (1–4 hours)

★★ **Mesquite and Alameda Historic Districts**—Travelers on their way from the outpost of El Paseo del Norte to the Hispanic colonies of north-central New Mexico were frequently attacked by Apaches in southern New Mexico. One place favored for ambushes became known as La Placita de las Cruces (The Place of the Crosses). With U.S. occupation in 1846, the deadly ground was slowly reborn as a trail stop and, with the arrival of the railroad in 1881, a trading center.

While it is difficult to find any center to the burgeoning "Cruces,"as it's called by locals, two historic districts do break up its strip-development pattern. The **Mesquite Historic District**, part of the original 1849 townsite, is sprinkled with graceful old adobe homes painted in a variety of pastel hues. The **Alameda Depot Historical District** dates to the 1880s and features Victorian-era architecture, including Hip Box and Queen Anne, as well as Bungalow.

Details: *Mesquite District east of Main St. between Picacho and Lohman. Alameda District west of Main St. between Picacho and Lohman. Maps of both districts available from Convention and Visitors Bureau, 311 N. Downtown Mall; 505/524-2444. (1 hour)*

★★ **New Mexico Farm and Ranch Heritage Museum**—Farming and ranching have played a major role in the state's history. While diminishing today in overall economic importance, much of New Mexico's character continues to be shaded by its ranching and farming heritage. Thus this museum, which opened in 1997, is long overdue.

It features displays on farming history, agricultural sciences, and animal husbandry, as well as hands-on exhibits and demonstrations of farming and ranching skills—from blacksmithing to plowing.

Details: *4100 Dripping Springs Rd.; 505/522-4100. Open Wed–Sun 9–6. $2 adults. (1–2 hours)*

★ **Branigan Cultural Center**—This Las Cruces facility features changing art and local history exhibits, as well as special cultural events and creative art programs. The center also oversees the **Log Cabin Museum**, Lucero and Main Streets, 505/524-1422, a hand-hewn mining cabin moved from Grafton, New Mexico, that is furnished with 1850- to 1900-era artifacts.

Details: 500 N. Water St., in the downtown mall; 505/527-8471. Open Mon–Fri 10–4:30, Sat 9–3, Sun 1–5. Free. (1 hour)

✩ **El Paso and Juarez**—Though not part of New Mexico today, El Paso was founded by New Mexican refugees following the Pueblo Revolt of 1680, and is culturally, historically, linguistically, gastronomically, and socially more aligned with its parent than its latter-day Texan usurpers. It is 47 miles south of Las Cruces via I-25/I-10.

Just across the Mexican border is the booming city of Juarez, with more than 2.5 million people. A visa is not required for U.S. citizens visiting Juarez. A piece of advice: Leave your car in a parking lot on the U.S. side and take a taxi or the El Paso–Juarez Trolley (800/259-6284) into Juarez. Its streets are crowded and getting your vehicle through U.S. customs can take hours.

Details: For further information on sights, dining, shopping, or accommodations in El Paso, call 800/351-6024. For details on Juarez, call 800/406-3491. (4 hours minimum)

✩ **Hatch**—Here chile rules. More green chile—particularly mild to hot varieties grown for the frozen and canned markets—is grown in New Mexico than any other place in the world, and most of that chile farming occurs around Hatch. So, whether you are a neophyte or professor of the pod, this should be a primary pilgrimage point. The **Hatch Chile Festival**, held annually on Labor Day weekend, includes cooking contests, live music and dancing, and crowning of a Red Chile Queen and a Green Chile Queen.

Details: 40 miles north of Las Cruces. An interesting and pretty route between the two towns is along the Rio Grande Valley floor through farm country on NM 185. (1 hour)

✩ **La Vina Winery**—Come sample Red Zinfandels and Chardonnays bottled here at the state's oldest contemporary winery. Tours, a gift shop, and festivals every April and October draw visitors.

Details: 18 miles south of Mesilla just off NM 28; 505/882-7632. Open Sat and Sun 12–5, other days by appointment. (2 hours)

✩ **Las Cruces Museum of Natural History**—Live animals and plants of the Chihuahuan Desert are the prime attractions here, along with hands-on science stations for kids and natural history exhibitions.

Details: Southwest corner of the Mesilla Valley Mall, 700 Telshor;

505/522-3120. Open Mon–Thu 12–5, Fri 12–9, Sat 10–6, Sun 12–6. Free. (1–2 hours)

☆ **New Mexico State University Art Gallery**—This facility houses the largest collection of contemporary art in southern New Mexico, as well as more than 1,800 Mexican retablos of the nineteenth century. Each year some 10 different shows are hung.

    Details: *Kent Hall, corner of Solano Dr. and University Blvd.; 505/646-2545. Open Mon–Fri 10–4, Thu evening 7–9, Sun 1–4. Free. (1 hour)*

FITNESS AND RECREATION

What a difference some water makes. While most of the landscape around Las Cruces is desolate, tucked into the foothills of the nearby sawtoothed **Organ Mountains**—a popular spot for highly technical rock climbing—are a handful of springs and ephemeral streams that give life to a flourishing variety of flora and fauna.

    Dripping Springs National Recreation Area is a prime destination for taking a lovely walk or checking out bountiful birdlife. It also shelters five endangered endemic (found only here) plants and some interesting historical ruins. Its **A.B. Cox Visitors Center**, 505/522-1219, includes interpretive displays, drinking water, picnic tables, and restrooms. A half-mile from the visitors center is the **La Cueva Picnic Area**. A short trail leads to the mouth of a large cave that was inhabited as far back as 500 B.C.

    The trail to the springs is about 1.5 miles long (one way). Don't expect a gusher—"dripping" is the operative word—but the trickle of water does support dense mats of ferns, flowers, and a canopy of trees. Close by the spring you'll find the remnants of a former health resort first opened in 1870—Van Patten's Mountain Camp—which included residents' quarters, a dining hall, and large ballroom. The area is open daily year-round. The entrance gate is open from eight in the morning to sunset, the visitors center from nine to five, and Dripping Springs Trail from eight to three April to October and eight to three October through March. It is managed by the Nature Conservancy and the Bureau of Land Management. There is a three-dollar day use fee. To reach it, take University Boulevard east from I-25 across Telshor Boulevard and past Tortugas Mountain with its cross-topped summit to the visitors center. Most of the 10-mile route is on an all-weather gravel road.

    Las Cruces is also home to numerous public pools and tennis

courts run by the Parks and Recreation Department, 505/526-0688, and the **New Mexico State Golf Course**, 505/646-3219, at Telshor and University Boulevards.

Leasburg Dam State Park, one mile north of Fort Selden on the Rio Grande and some 15 miles north of Las Cruces (take Exit 19 off I-25), has a small lake with swimming, boating, and fishing, as well as picnic grounds and a playground. Day use fee is three dollars per vehicle.

SPECTATOR SPORTS

Sunland Park, located in Sunland Park, New Mexico, some 40 miles south of Las Cruces via I-25/I-10, 505/589-1131, presents quarter horse and thoroughbred horseracing from November through early May on Wednesdays, Fridays, and weekends. Post time is 12:40 p.m. Cruces also is the home court of the **New Mexico State Aggies**, and its immense **Pan American Center**, 505/646-4413, just off I-25 at University Boulevard, is often packed to the rafters for games.

FOOD

I always enjoy a meal at the **Double Eagle**, 505/523-6700, which fronts the plaza in Mesilla. The historic building is quite charming and nicely decorated, and has a very pretty patio where meals are served in good weather. It serves fine, and somewhat pricey, Continental fare for lunch and dinner daily, as well as a Sunday brunch. Sharing its patio is **Peppers**, 505/523-4999, with less expensive items such as spit-roasted chicken, seafood chimichangas, and Mexican wontons.

Another option popular with tourists on the Mesilla Plaza (its southeast corner) is **La Posta**, 505/524-3524. Located in the former Butterfield Stage Line station house, it serves moderately priced, so-so steaks and New Mexican dishes. Another more promising possibility is **Meson de Mesilla**, 1803 Avenida de Mesilla, 505/525-9212, a B&B that has a bar and a public dining room serving delicacies like quail.

A surprising find is **Tatsu**, 930 El Paso Rd., 505/526-7144, which prepares excellent Japanese food at reasonable prices. For breakfast, locals head to **Nellie's**, 1226 W. Hadley, 505/524-9982, a traditional diner that also serves lunch and dinner with a New Mexican slant. Also popular for breakfast is **Nabes**, 2001 E. Lohman, 505/523-9339, which has fine coffees and espresso, pastries, full breakfasts, and a wide assortment of newspapers. For a great selection of sandwiches, try the **Brown Bag Deli**, 300 El Molino, 505/524-2857.

One of the area's most unique and consistently good places to eat is **Chope's**, located 16 miles south of town on NM 28 in the village of La Mesa, 505/233-3420. Open daily for lunch and dinner, it specializes in inexpensive and incendiary New Mexican food.

LODGING

The Las Cruces area has a few B&Bs. Among them is the unusually large **Meson de Mesilla**, located in the pretty village of Mesilla at 1803 Avenida de Mesilla (NM 28), 505/525-9212, with 15 rooms ranging from $45 to $135. Each room has a private bath, TV, and overhead fan. A licensed bar and kiva fireplace make for lively social gatherings in winter while the lovely pool (open April through October) takes the edge off summer heat. It also has a full dining room.

In Cruces' historic Alameda district is **T.R.H. Smith Mansion B&B**, 909 N. Alameda, 505/525-2525 or 800/526-1914. The attractive Hip Box, two-story home was built in 1914 by Henry Trost, and features a marble fireplace, stained-glass windows, a glassed sunporch, a recreation room with pool tables and TV, and choice of four air-conditioned rooms ranging from $60 to $80.

A third choice is **Lundeen Inn of the Arts**, 618 S. Alameda, 505/526-3327, a B&B and art gallery located in a historic adobe. Its 20 rooms—each with queen beds, private bath, and some with fireplaces and kitchenettes—run $50 to $75.

Perhaps the most attractive **Holiday Inn** you'll ever run across is found in Cruces, 201 E. University Blvd., 505/526-4411 or 800/HOLI-DAY, with its emphasis on Mexican decor and ambiance. It has an indoor pool, laundry, room service, the Territorial Dining Room, and the Pancho Villa Cantina and Cafe. Rooms run $70 to $80. The **Las Cruces Hilton**, 705 Telshor Blvd., 505/522-4300, has a restaurant, bar, outdoor heated pool, exercise room, and 203 rooms running $80 to $110.

On a more mundane level is a wide assortment of motels. These include the **Economy Inn**, 2160 W. Picacho, 505/524-8627, with a pool and doubles for $25; the **Desert Lodge**, 1900 Picacho, 505/524-1925, with doubles at $25; the **Motel 6**, 235 La Posada Lane, 505/525-1010, with a pool, coin laundry, and doubles for $37; and **Days Inn**, 2600 S. Valley Dr., 505/526-4441, with an indoor pool, sauna, laundry, bar, restaurant, and rooms for $45 to $55.

LAS CRUCES AND MESILLA

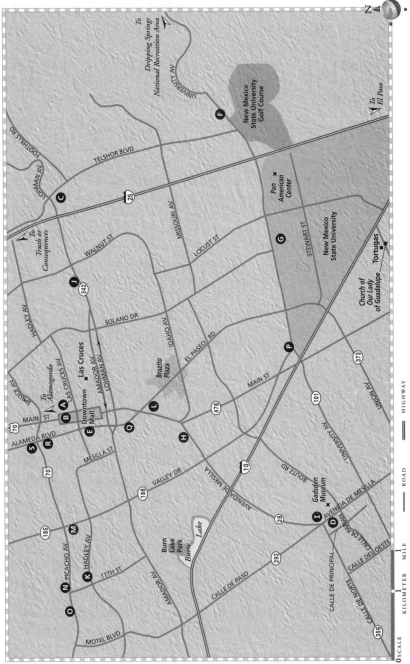

N

To
Dripping Spring
National Recreation Area

New Mexico
State University
Golf Course

To
El Paso

UNIVERSITY AV

TELSHOR BLVD

FOOTHILLS RD

LOHMAN AV

25

F

C

MISSOURI AV

Pan
American
Center

To
Truth or
Consequences

WALNUT ST

LOCUST ST

STEWART ST

New Mexico
State University

G

342

J

SOLANO DR

IDAHO AV

EL PASO RD

Church of
Our Lady
of Guadalupe

Tortugas

HADLEY AV

Brazito
Plaza

P

373

Las Cruces

AMADOR AV

LOHMAN AV

MAIN ST

SPRUCE AV

To
Alamogordo

LAS CRUCES AV

A

Downtown
Mall

L

478

101

UNION AV

MAIN ST

B

Q

UNIVERSITY AV

70

E

H

70

R

S

ALAMEDA BLVD

MESILLA ST

10

BOUTZ RD

AVENIDA DE MESILLA

VALLEY DR

188

28

Gadsden
Museum

I

AVENIDA DE MESILLA

D

185

M

Burn
Lake
Park

Burn
Lake

292

CALLE DE PARRAL

CALLE DEL OESTE

K

HADLEY AV

17TH ST

N

PICACHO AV

AMADOR AV

CALLE DE PASO

CALLE DE NORTE

359

O

MOTEL BLVD

SCALE

0

KILOMETER

1

MILE

1

HIGHWAY

ROAD

Sights

Ⓐ Alameda Historic District

Ⓑ Branigan Cultural Center

Ⓒ Las Cruces Museum of Natural History

Ⓓ Mesilla

Ⓔ Mesquite Historic District

Ⓕ New Mexico Farm and Ranch Heritage Museum

Ⓖ New Mexico State University Art Gallery

Food

Ⓗ Brown Bag Deli

Ⓓ Double Eagle

Ⓓ La Posta

Ⓘ Meson de Mesilla

Ⓙ Nabes

Ⓚ Nellie's

Ⓛ Peppers

Ⓜ Tatsu

Lodging

Ⓝ Days Inn

Ⓞ Desert Lodge

Ⓞ Economy Inn

Ⓟ Holiday Inn

Ⓒ Las Cruces Hilton

Ⓠ Lundeen Inn of the Arts

Ⓘ Meson de Mesilla

Ⓟ Motel 6

Ⓡ T.R.H. Smith Mansion B&B

Camping

Ⓝ Dalmont's Trailer Corral RV Park

Ⓢ RV Dock

Ⓢ Siesta RV Camp

Note: Items with the same letter are located in the same town or area.

CAMPING

One mile north of Fort Selden, some 15 miles north of Las Cruces, is **Leasburg Dam State Park** (see Fitness and Recreation, above), which has 45 campsites (almost none with natural shade), showers, and drinking water; tent sites cost $7 and RV hookups $11. The closest other public camping, some 20 miles from Cruces, is at **Aguirre Campground** (see previous chapter).

Other options are all commercial campgrounds. **Best View RV Park** (a former KOA), 814 Weinrich Rd. along Picacho Avenue and U.S.

70 some five miles west of Las Cruces, 505/526-9030, has a pool, laundry, playground, grocery, great views, and full hookups for $17 and tent sites for $15. **Dalmont's Trailer Corral RV Park**, 2224 S. Valley Dr., 505/523-2992, offers 34 hookups for $15 per night. **Siesta RV Camp**, 1551 Avenida de Mesilla, 505/523-6816, has showers, laundry, and 55 hookups at $17 and slightly less for a few tent sites. **RV Dock**, 1475 Avenida de Mesilla, 505/526-8401, has 60 pull-through sites at $18.

NIGHTLIFE

Among the more popular nighttime spots for country-western dancin' is **Cowboy's**, 2205 Main St., 505/525-9050, especially on weekends. **Victoria's**, 2395 N. Solano, 505/523-0440, presents mariachi and Latin bands on weekends. If you like waitresses dressed in Old West dancehall garb, check out **Billy the Kid Saloon**, at the Holiday Inn, 201 University, 505/526-4411, with live music daily except Sundays. On the Mesilla plaza is **El Patio**, 505/524-0982, a good restaurant and bar that features live jazz midweek and blues or rock on weekends. For beer and the college set, visit **Old West Brew Pub**, 1720 Avenida de Mesilla, 505/524-2408, or **High Desert Brewing Co.**, 1201 W. Hadley, 505/525-6752, with live music Thursday and Saturday.

Also in town is the **American Southwest Theater Company**, which plays mostly at the **Hershel Zohn Theater**, 505/646-4515, on the university campus; the **Las Cruces Symphony**, 505/646-3709, which performs at the Pan American Center; and the **Las Cruces Community Theater**, 505/523-1200.

12

BORDERLANDS

This is a place to visit when you've seen everything else New Mexico has to offer. It is the last *frontera* (frontier), the odd no-man's land of sorts far from the state capital of Santa Fe and the Mexican state capital of Chihuahua. Under a broiling-hot sun in the summer and choked by dust storms in the spring, it can be brutal here—yet the area also harbors intriguing secrets.

At the intersection of Sonoran Desert influences from the southwest, Sierra Madrean factors from the south, and Chihuahuan Desert ecology from the east, many species of animals and plants converge here, creating some of the most diverse flora and fauna communities of the state. Mountain ranges puncture the desert floors, some hiding small waterways. Here is a state park that you are encouraged to haul away rock by rock, and another where massive boulders rear up, forming streetlike canyons.

Also a cultural crossroads, one finds a hardy people, descendants of miners, ranchers, and early mercantile traders, Hispanic, Anglo, and Indians. The mixing has not been without violence; in Columbus one can walk the grounds where the only foreign invasion of U.S. soil in this century occurred, when Pancho Villa's raiders slipped over the border and crushed the town in a predawn attack in 1916. From Columbus you can slip back the other way today, heading south into the little-visited territory of northern Mexico—as wild a land as you will find in North America. Or you can slide over the border into Palomas, down a frosty Mexican beer, and search for keep sakes. *Que viva La Frontera!*

BORDERLANDS

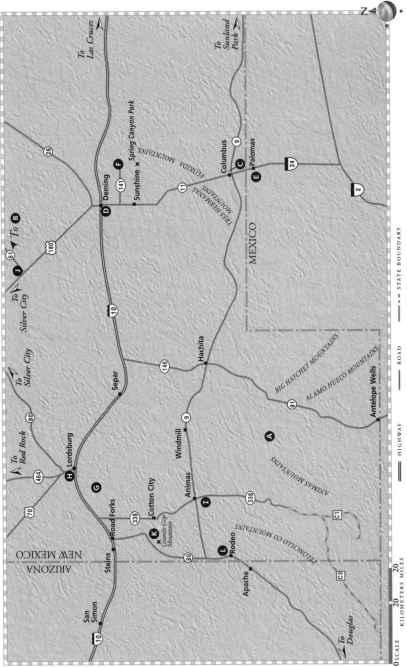

Sights

- **A** The Boot Heel
- **B** City of Rocks State Park
- **C** Columbus
- **C** Columbus Historical Museum
- **D** Deming
- **D** Deming Luna Mimbres Museum
- **E** Palomas, Mexico
- **F** Rockhound State Park
- **G** Shakespeare

Food

- **D** Cactus Café
- **H** El Charro
- **C** Grannie's Corner
- **C** La Casita
- **D** Si Señor
- **H** Soda Shoppe
- **I** Willie Upshaw's Nightmare Café

Lodging

- **D** Belshore Motel
- **H** Best Western American Motor Inn

Lodging (continued)

- **H** Best Western Skies Inn
- **D** Grand Motor Inn
- **C** Martha's House
- **D** Motel 6
- **D** Holiday Inn
- **C** Suncrest Inn

Camping

- **B** City of Rocks State Park
- **D** Dreamcatcher RV Park
- **J** Faywood Hot Springs
- **K** Granite Gap
- **C** La Frontera RV Park
- **D** Little Vineyard RV Park
- **H** Lordsburg KOA
- **C** Pancho Villa State Park
- **D** Roadrunner RV Park
- **F** Rockhound State Park
- **L** Rodeo RV Park
- **D** Sunrise RV Park
- **D** Wagon Wheel RV Park

Note: Items with the same letter are located in the same town or area.

A PERFECT DAY ON THE BORDERLANDS

Camp overnight at or begin the day with a visit to City of Rocks State Park. For lunch head into Deming and a stop at the Luna Mimbres Museum, then push on south to the border. Spend a few hours at Pancho Villa State Park, check into Martha's House B&B, and have a bath. Before dark, cross over into Mexico and stroll about Palomas, where you can get a cheap and good meal washed down with a frosty Mexican beer.

SIGHTSEEING HIGHLIGHTS

✭✭✭ **City of Rocks State Park**—Great stone monoliths rear up out of a flat plain in an odd, natural approximation of those at Stonehenge and Easter Island; they do indeed appear to form street intersections here and there in this "city." You can scamper over low ones and, in the larger formations, marvel at Mother Nature's sculptural hand. From a summit you gaze over a yellow plain, punctuated to the east by mesas and prominent, graceful Cooke's Peak. If you've never watched an old

City of Rocks State Park

windmill at work, one cranks away here as long as a breeze blows—
which is most of the time!

There is also a lovely, small, desert botanical garden, and a parking
observation point overlooking the strange and fascinating rock assemblage. A staffed visitors center opened in 1998 with displays, restrooms,
and information. Camping facilities also are on site, but bring your
own fire wood. As a wry local musician once penned, "There ain't no
wood in the City of Rocks."

Details: *Located southeast of Silver City or north of Deming at mile
marker 3 on NM 61; 505/536-2800. Open year-round. $3 day use fee. (1
hour minimum on site)*

★★★ **Columbus**— Early on the morning of March 9, 1916, General
Francisco "Pancho" Villa's raiders slipped over the Mexican border from
the southwest and passed Camp Furlong to strike the sleeping town of
Columbus, New Mexico—while singing "La Cucaracha" and crying out
"Viva Villa!" So swift, surprising, and effective was the attack that much
of Columbus lay smoldering by sunrise. Eight U.S. soldiers and 10
townsfolk were killed. The Villistas, as they were called, lost 90 men. It
was the only land attack on the continental U.S. this century by a foreign force and, oddly, a result of the Mexican civil war.

Villa, also known as the "Lion of the North," was enraged that
U.S. President Wilson had formally recognized Villa's opponent in
Mexico's internal power struggle, Venustiano Carranza, as President
of Mexico. This was Villa's belly-punch back at Wilson and the
United States.

A prompt response to the attack was organized by the United
States. General John "Black Jack" Pershing was put in command of
10,000 men and the Punitive Expeditionary Force, which pursued
Villa far into north-central Mexico. The chase was the last true cavalry action mounted by the U.S. Army; it also saw the first warfare
use of aircraft and motorized vehicles. The year-long action, which
never succeeded in even seriously engaging the wily Villa, did prepare U.S. forces and Pershing for their upcoming roles in the First
World War.

Several landmarks associated with the battle and the town of
Columbus are open for visitation. Begin by stopping at **Pancho Villa
State Park**. The 49-acre park wraps around a small hill. Camp
Furlong, the U.S. military fort in Columbus during the time of the
attack, had its lookout point on this hill. You can walk up to the top of

Lookout Hill on foot trails. At the east foot of the hill is a tiny, desiccated adobe that is protected from the elements by a taller metal roof, and from vandals by a chain-link fence. The structure was **General Pershing's HQ**. Nearby are the original cement ramps used for servicing the army's mechanized units. These elevated "grease racks" were another first for the time.

A self-guiding walking tour of the park's outdoor landmarks takes about a half hour, winding through the extensive cactus and desert flora gardens on the flanks of Lookout Hill, where more than 30 plant species are found. Birds love it too—more than 50 species have been spotted here.

The 1901 **U.S. Customs Service Building** today serves as the park's visitors center, which screens a well-done video on the history of the Villa raid and the U.S. response. Also on display are some black-and-white stills and other relics of the time. Summer is intensely hot here.

Details: *At the intersection of NM 9 and NM 11, 3 miles from the Mexican border and 32 miles south of Deming; 505/531-2711. Visitors center open daily 8–5. $3 day use fee. (1–2 hours)*

★★ **Deming Luna Mimbres Museum**—One of the more entertaining and substantive small-town museums I've run across, this Deming institution includes large displays of hand bells (some 2,500 models!), dolls and doll houses, gems and minerals, quilts, clothing, local historic photos, fine housewares, and materials about the area's cattlemen, Hispanic settlers, and farmers.

What really elevates its stature, however, is its Mimbres pottery and artifacts collection. The Mimbres culture reached its zenith around 1130, with 13 major villages located just north of Deming in the Mimbres River Valley. Its pottery often was decorated with wonderfully stylized, whimsical animal figures.

The museum, located in the town's original 1916 massive red-brick National Guard Armory, also houses a gift shop. Right across the street is the historic **Custom House Annex**, with fine arts and transportation displays.

Details: *301 S. Silver; 505/546-2382. Open Mon–Sat 9–4, Sun 1:30–4. Admission by donation. (1–2 hours)*

★★ **Rockhound State Park**—If you've ever had fantasies about finding jewels on the ground, this is your spot! It is perhaps the only public park in the nation that encourages you to take its terrain home with you. That's right, haul off all the rock you can carry—actually 15 to 20 pounds per person per visit. If you're lucky, you could actually stumble across white-pink opals, blue agates, quartz crystals, chalcedony, thundereggs, or geodes. The best shot at finding anything in the 250-acre park is off the 1.1-mile loop trail that circles the hillside above the camping and picnic sites.

Deming hosts the **Rockhound Round-up** in early spring, with buyers' market, auctions, field trips, displays, and other related activities. For details contact the Deming Gem & Mineral Society, 505/546-9281.

Details: Head south of Deming 5 miles, turn east (left) onto a gravel road, and proceed 9 miles to the park entrance; 505/546-6182. Open daily year-round; the gate closes at 7:30 p.m. $3 per vehicle day use fee. (1 hour minimum on site)

✸ **The Boot Heel**—Take a look at a New Mexico state map. In the far southwestern corner you'll notice a square of land that juts southward into Mexico. Known as "the Boot Heel," it is perhaps the most isolated sector of the state, with vast grasslands and occasional cotton fields rolling away to distant desert mountain chains that jut jaggedly over the horizon like seagoing battleships. The area—particularly the Peloncillo Mountains and the private Gray Ranch—is a safe haven for many endemic, endangered, and rare plants and animals. People are few and far between, concentrated in **Animas**, **Rodeo**, **Hachita**, and the Mexican border-crossing town of **Antelope Wells**.

Details: NM 338, 81, and 9 provide paved access to the area. Numerous gravel and dirt roads can get you even further off the beaten track. (3 hours)

✸ **Columbus Historical Museum**—Housed in the former Southern Pacific railroad depot, this attractive structure today houses collections of military materials related to the Columbus raid and Punitive Expedition, as well as local artifacts and antiques.

Details: Corner of NM 11 and NM 9; 505/531-2620. Open Mon–Thu 10–1, Fri–Sun 10–4. Free. (30 minutes–1 hour)

✸ **Deming**—Though not particularly old by New Mexico standards—having been founded at the end of the nineteenth century on the site of the silver spike that completed the the nation's second transcontinental railroad in 1881—a handful of Deming's historic buildings still stand, including four on the National Register of Historic Places. These include many structures along Silver and Gold Avenues, among them the dignified red brick **Luna County Courthouse**, at 700 Silver. Some 30 of the Villistas captured in the Columbus raid (see Columbus entry, above) were tried, convicted, and hanged outside this building.

Details: *Touring maps of historic district available from the Deming Luna County Visitor Center, 800 E. Pine; 800/848-4955. (1 hour)*

★ **Palomas, Mexico**—This is not your typical Mexican tourist town. Last time I passed through, I was the only gringo wandering around the somewhat barren plaza and streets at dusk looking for a place to eat. I ended up at **Barbara's** (on the main drag), where I had a delicious plate of flautas covered with pureed guacamole for $3.25 and a cold Carta Blanca beer for $1. U.S. currency is accepted. The road from Columbus through Palomas continues south to the historic town of Janos, and on to **Casas Grandes**—the most important archaeological site in northern Mexico.

Details: *3 miles south of Columbus on NM 11. U.S. citizens can enter Palomas without a visa, required for car travel beyond Janos. Park on the U.S. side and walk across the border. (1–2 hours)*

★ **Shakespeare**—Once a stop on the Butterfield Trail and a booming mine town of 3,000 inhabitants—with no church, newspaper, or local lawmen—Shakespeare was known as a mysterious and potentially dangerous place to drop into. Now a ghost town owned by a family, it is open for tours or casual browsing. Four times a year it hosts reenactments and other special events.

Details: *2.5 miles southwest of Lordsburg. Take the Main St. Exit off I-10, head south, and follow the signs; 505/542-9034. Open Oct–May, with tours on one or two weekends a month. $3 adults, $2 children ages 6–12. (2 hours for tour)*

FITNESS AND RECREATION

This quiet corner of New Mexico has a surprising abundance of wild game, and hunters come from afar to stalk rare Sonoran whitetail (coues deer) in the Peloncillo Mountains, the wily javelina, trophy mule deer, and both California and Gambel's quail. Much of the public land is controlled by the **Bureau of Land Management**, 505/525-4300, out of Las Cruces.

The New Mexico Department of Game and Fish also oversees a few sites in the area. Its **Red Rock** refuge, 505/542-9760, offers perhaps the public's best chance to spot desert bighorn sheep, the endangered cousins of the Rocky Mountain bighorn sheep. The 1,250-acre site is fenced and entry is forbidden. However, sheep are often spotted on cliffs overlooking the refuge's road. The property includes a length of the Gila River and rocky canyons. It is located north of Lordsburg. To get here travel north from town on U.S. 70 for 2 miles; turn right onto NM 464 and continue 23 miles to the Gila River. Take the first right after crossing the river and continue 4.6 miles to the southern boundary of the sheep enclosure. En route you'll pass another state Game and Fish holding with excellent wetland birding, but do not enter unless prior arrangements have been made. The road is impassable in wet weather. A guided birding company, **El Rincon de Oso Plata**, 505/542-9705, conducts tours here.

Granite Gap, in the foothills of the Peloncillo Mountains, has both public and privately owned sites for hiking, observation of wildlife, and other activities. The public land, managed by the Bureau of Land Management, 505/525-4300, climbs from the Chihuahuan Desert floor through rugged limestone and granite ridges. Many varieties of snake live here, including rattlers and rarely seen Gila monsters—the poisonous orange-and-black lizards. Spring through fall there's good viewing of many birds, including verdin, northern mockingbird, roadrunner, rock wren, hummingbirds, quail, and northern harrier. To get here travel 15 miles west of Lordsburg on I-10 and take Exit 5. Proceed south on U.S. 80 and turn right after 11 miles onto an unmarked dirt track, where you will find a wire gate between two wooden posts; close the gate after entering. Take the first left fork and park near the first rock outcroppings. The road has a sandy section and is impassable in wet weather.

The privately owned Granite Gap property has a self-guided trail meandering through stands of ocotillo, cactus, agave, and seasonal wildflowers. Lizards are common, and there are occasional sightings of wild animals. This site was also once an active mining area and, as at Rockhound State Park, you are allowed to collect rocks here. Donkey tours of several mine shafts are available. It is located near the Arizona border southwest of Lordsburg. To get here, take I-10 west from Lordsburg; turn south on U.S. 80 and proceed 11 miles to mile marker 20. There is no phone. The site is open October through May Wednesday through Sunday nine to five, and June through September by appointment. Day use admission is $10 for adults, $5 for kids. Camping is allowed.

Just to the south of Rockhound State Park (see Sightseeing Highlights, above) rise the rocky fins of the **Florida Mountains** (pronounced flor-EE-da) and **Spring Canyon Park**. Though generally a desert range, they harbor small streams in isolated canyons and diverse wildlife—including exotic Iranian ibex, gray fox, rock squirrels, bats, mountain lion, four kinds of rattlers—and fascinating-looking summit spires. Spring Canyon's access road is passed just before the entrance to Rockhound State Park; it is closed on Mondays and Tuesdays and in winter. Summer temperatures can hit 100 degrees. The two-mile access road includes steep inclines. It has picnic tables, but no overnight camping.

For a relaxing dip, visit **Faywood Hot Springs**, 505/536-9663, where you'll find public and private outdoor soaking pools with waters running 104 to 108 degrees. It is located north of Deming, just off NM 26, two miles east of its intersection with U.S. 180.

Deming's **Rio Mimbres Country Club**, 505/546-3023, has an 18-hole golf course and pro shop located at the east end of town. There is also a municipal pool at 900 W. Spruce, 505/546-4129.

FOOD

There must be some hidden culinary gems in this area, but I've yet to find them. Deming's **Si Señor**, 200 E. Pine, 505/546-3938, has good hot New Mexican food. It's open daily and is modestly priced, as are all the area's restaurants. Also in Deming is the **Cactus Café**, 218 W. Cedar, 505/546-2458, with New Mexican dishes for lunch and dinner. While the standard American breakfasts, New Mexican dishes, and steak and chicken dinners are only so-so, I enjoy Lordsburg's **El Charro**, 3209 Southern Pacific Blvd., 505/542-3400. Open 24 hours daily, it has a lounge and comfy booths, and its cool, dark interior is a blessing on a hot day. Also in Lordsburg is the **Soda Shoppe**, 330 E. Motel Dr., 505/542-9142, an old-style soda fountain dishing up floats, shakes, sundaes, and similar ice cream delights. It's inside Eagle Drug, built in 1889. It's closed on Sundays.

If you make it into the Boot Heel area, sustenance is available at Animas' **Willie Upshaw's Nightmare Café**, right on the main drag, 505/548-2444. Down in Columbus there's **La Casita**, on Hellberg Avenue, 505/531-2371, serving BBQ chicken and New Mexican food.

It's open Monday through Saturday. **Grannie's Corner**, at Lima and
NM 11, 505/531-2129, offers American and Mexican fare daily.

LODGING

Tiny Columbus, believe it or not, has a nice B&B, **Martha's House**, at
Lima and Main just north of NM 9 and east of NM 11, 505/531-2467.
The new white stucco, adobe-style lodging has a pretty entryway with
white tile floor and overhead fans, a breakfast room with four tables,
and five upstairs bedrooms with private baths running $55 for doubles.

Also in Columbus is the **Suncrest Inn**, located on NM 11 just
north of the intersection with NM 9, 505/531-2323. Its rooms are
worn out and reek of cheap aerosols, but there's cable TV, a bed, four
walls, and a roof overhead. For spring entertainment, listen to the wind
shriek at night. Rooms are $32.

Deming has a bunch of motels, but they fill up during the annual
Great American Duck Races, held the fourth weekend in August. One
of the nicer options is the **Grand Motor Inn**, U.S. 70/80 East,
505/546-2631, which has a good restaurant open for breakfast, lunch,
and dinner, lounge, heated outdoor pool, and rooms for $40 to $50.
The **Belshore Motel**, 1210 E. Spruce, 505/546-2717, has a restaurant,
tiny pool, and rooms for $22. There is a **Motel 6**, at Exit 85 off I-10,
505/546-2623, with a pool and doubles for $32, and a **Holiday Inn**, at
Exit 85 off I-10, 505/546-2661, with a pool, Fat Eddie's Restaurant,
and rooms for $40 to $50.

In Lordsburg, motel possibilities include the **Best Western
American Motor Inn**, 944 E. Railroad Ave., 505/542-3591, with a
pool, playground, lounge, restaurant, and doubles for $45 (includes
breakfast), and the **Best Western Skies Inn**, 1303 S. Main, 505/
542-3535, with a pool and doubles running for $50.

CAMPING

In Columbus, **Pancho Villa State Park** (see Sightseeing Highlights,
Columbus entry, above) has more than 60 sites, most with full hookups
and shade shelters, showers, and restrooms. Small trees provide modest
shade. Tent sites are $7, RV hookups are $11. Also in Columbus is **La
Frontera RV Park**, on NM 11, 505/531-2636.

City of Rocks State Park (see Sightseeing Highlights) has 52
sites tucked away in the interesting rock formations. **Rockhound State**

Park (see Sightseeing Highlights) has 29 sites, 22 with RV hookups. Tent sites at both parks go for $7 a night, $11 for RV hookups.

Deming has a slew of RV parks, which fill up with snowbirds in winter. These include the **Little Vineyard RV Park**, 2901 E. Spruce, 505/546-3560, and **Roadrunner RV Park**, 2849 E. Spruce, 505/546-6960. Both feature a pool, spa, rec area, laundry, pool, and a few tent sites. Sites go for $10 to $14. Cheaper options with fewer amenities include the **Wagon Wheel RV Park**, 2801 E. Spruce, 505/546-8650; **Sunrise RV Park**, 2601 E. Spruce, 505/546-8565; and the **Dreamcatcher RV Park**, 4004 E. Spruce, 505/544-4004.

The **Lordsburg KOA**, 1501 Lead St. (off Exit 22 on I-10), 505/542-8003, has a pool, playground, laundry, and RV hookups for $17 and tent sites for $13. In tiny Rodeo is the **Rodeo RV Park**, 505/557-2322, with $7 sites.

There is also tent and RV camping at the private **Granite Gap** property (see Fitness and Recreation, above) with sites at $5, and at **Faywood Hot Springs** (see Fitness and Recreation), with RV sites at $15 and tent sites for $13, including bathing privileges.

Dispersed, primitive camping in the isolated mountain ranges of the borderlands is also possible; for details, call the BLM at 505/525-4341.

NIGHTLIFE

If you want to visit a bar in Palomas, Mexico, poke your head into the **Lucky 7**. It has a pool table and jukebox, and people were friendly when I visited.

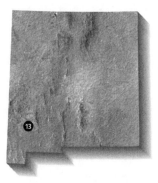

13

GILA COUNTRY

Southwestern New Mexico is largely a land of harsh deserts, but rising from its sandy wastes is a land of cool pine forests, refreshing streams, and lovely valleys transformed by the miracle of water. Known as the Gila (HEE-la) Country, it was the homeland of several Apache tribes—and was largely avoided by New Mexico's Hispanic settlers. It remained a virtual wilderness until the American occupation of New Mexico and the discovery of silver and gold in the mountain foothills.

These strikes led to the creation of Silver City, set at the southern base of the Gila Country, and a handful of mining communities—most of which have since disappeared. Silver, as locals sometimes call it, boomed and then largely went bust, eking out a minimal existence. Today its wealth is measured by its refreshing climate, bountiful natural beauty, and diverse nearby recreation opportunities, and it is growing once again.

Much of the surrounding area, however, remains wild. In fact, the nation's first official wilderness area, named after famed naturalist Aldo Leopold, was established here in 1924. If you seek communion with nature, wildlife, a hike on a lonely summit, or a dip in a hot spring, you'll be well served by a visit here. While its mountains can face prolonged winters, the region's lower elevations are quite mild, making it a great place to visit in almost any season. Birders especially love its prolific neotropical feathered arrivals as the snow melts off the high peaks.

Several good museums, ghost towns, cliff dwellings, and lots of Victorian architecture round out the area's attractions.

GILA COUNTRY

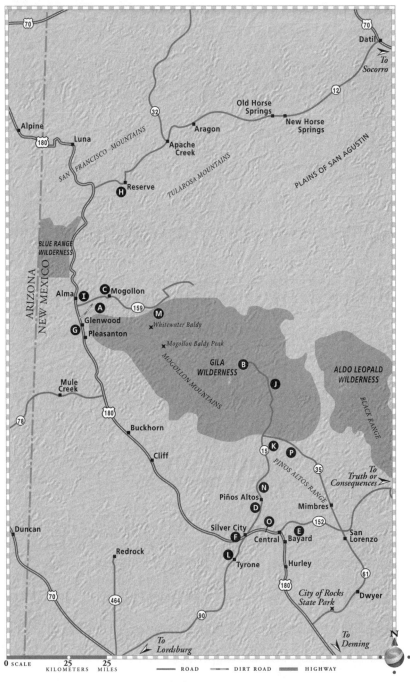

Sights

- **Ⓐ** The Catwalk
- **Ⓑ** Gila Cliff Dwelling National Monument
- **Ⓒ** Mogollon
- **Ⓓ** Piños Altos
- **Ⓔ** Santa Rita/Chino Open Pit Copper Mine
- **Ⓕ** Silver City

Food

- **Ⓖ** Blue Front Bar & Restaurant
- **Ⓓ** Buckhorn Saloon
- **Ⓖ** Ellie's Country Kitchen
- **Ⓗ** Grandma T's
- **Ⓘ** Red Hen Café

Lodging

- **Ⓓ** Bear Creek Motel & Cabins
- **Ⓖ** Crab Apple Cabins
- **Ⓙ** Gila Hotspring Vacation Center
- **Ⓖ** Lariat Motel
- **Ⓖ** Los Olmos Guest Ranch

Food *(continued)*

- **Ⓚ** Sapillo Crossing Guest Ranch
- **Ⓙ** Wilderness Lodge

Camping

- **Ⓛ** Burro Mountain Homestead
- **Ⓜ** Bursum/Ben Lilly/ Willow/Gilita
- **Ⓝ** Cherry Creek/McMillan
- **Ⓞ** Continental Divide RV Park
- **Ⓑ** Gila Cliff Dweller National Monument
- **Ⓙ** Gila Hotsprings Vacation Center
- **Ⓞ** KOA Silver City
- **Ⓟ** Lake Roberts/Mesa Campground/Sapillo
- **Ⓟ** Lake Roberts General Store & Cabins

Note: Items with the same letter are located in the same town or area.

A PERFECT DAY IN GILA COUNTRY

Spend the night at Bear Mountain Guest Ranch or the Carter House B&B. After breakfast, head to the Gila Cliff Dwellings, with a stop en route in Pinos Altos. Picnic at the cliff dwellings, then head back to Silver City on NM 35 through San Lorenzo, stop for a view of the Santa Rita open pit copper mine on NM 152, and spend the late afternoon walking around Silver's historic districts and/or touring the Western New Mexico University Museum. Have dinner at La Familia or the Buckhorn Saloon.

SIGHTSEEING HIGHLIGHTS

★★★ **Gila Cliff Dwellings National Monument**—This 533-acre national monument north of Silver City, which first received federal protection in 1907, guards a collection of cliff dwellings built by the Mimbres Mogollon around A.D. 1270—probably in response to armed incursions. The primary draw is the ruins of **Cliff Dweller Canyon**, a side canyon of the West Fork of the Gila River. They are an eerie sight to come upon. Well hidden in a cleft overlooking a steep, narrow valley, their whitish rock masonry blends with the surrounding rock, and you don't see them until you are almost upon them. Though abandoned around 1300, the presence of the people who occupied the cliff dwelling still seems to linger. Looking at the 40 small rooms where they slept and ate, you have to admire the determination and strength they must have possessed to live in such extreme conditions.

Along NM 35, one of the two roads accessing the monument, in the **Mimbres River Valley**, related people created the enchanting and distinctive black-on-white Mimbres pottery, often featuring stylized but unmistakable animal figures. Examples are seen in the Western New Mexico University Museum (see below) and the Deming Luna Mimbres Museum (see previous chapter).

The visitors center at Cliff Dweller Canyon features audiovisual programs, exhibits, a bookstore, and information. A self-guided one-mile loop trail passes through the main cliff dwelling. Guided tours of the unexcavated **TJ Ruin** can be arranged with advance reservations. There are nice campgrounds here as well.

Details: 44 miles north of Silver City. The most direct route is to head north from Silver City on NM 15. The winding road takes 1.5 hours to traverse one way. It deadends at the monument. Trailers and large vehicles *should take the longer but easier route on NM 35 from San Lorenzo, 17 miles east of Silver City via U.S. 180 and NM 152. Visitors center open summer 8–5, winter 8–4:30; 505/536-9461. Cliff Dweller Canyon is a short drive from the visitors center. Self-guided trail open summer 8–6, rest of the year 8–5. $3 per person over age 8. (2 hours on site minimum)*

★★★ **Piños Altos**—The discovery here of gold in 1860 launched a thriving boom town in the Black Range just north of Silver City. One of its more well-known residents was Roy Bean, who went on to become a famous judge in west Texas. Today it is partly a ghost town, partly a community for artists, retirees, and others dancing to the tune of a different era.

Among its attractions are the **Hearst Church**, the **Buckhorn Saloon & Opera House** (see Food and Nightlife, below), and the **Piños Altos Museum**. The Methodist Hearst Church, an attractive adobe with steeply pitched roof and stained-glasss windows, was built in 1889 with financial assistance from Phoebe Hearst—mother of newspaper publisher William Randolph Hearst. The museum, a tin-roofed log cabin built in 1866, was once the town's schoolhouse.

Details: About 7 miles north of Silver City on NM 15. Museum, 1882 Main St., 505/388-1882 or, for hours, 800/548-9378. The church, on a back street, operates seasonally as the Grant County Art Guild Gallery; call 800/548-9378 for hours. (1–2 hours)

★★★ **Silver City**—This is by far the coolest town in southwestern New Mexico—literally and figuratively. Set at an elevation of 6,000 feet, with the Gila mountain ranges right at its backside, Silver City enjoys a refreshing climate. And with turn-of-the-century architecture still defining its downtown character, a university community, a healthy dose of artists, ranchers who drop into town for supplies, and a modest tourism business, it's a lively place as well. There are galleries clustered around Broadway and Bullard, coffee shops, a decent selection of restaurants, and even a happening bar or two. (Among the interesting galleries in Silver City is **McCray**, WNM University Art Complex off E Street, featuring the talented Dorothy McCray.)

Originally founded by Spanish-speaking New Mexicans and named La Cienega de San Vicente (The Marshes of St. Vincent), the 1870 discovery of gold and silver nearby led to a boom. In its historic downtown core is the **Silver City Museum**, housed in the 1881 brick mansion of miner H.B. Ailman. For a bird's-eye view of town, walk to the top of its

cupola. It houses relics of the Mogollon Indians and the Spanish and
Anglo miners and settlers. It also has a good Southwestern bookstore.

The town also claims a slice of the Billy the Kid legend, who lived
here for a time with his mother and stepfather, working in the **Star
Hotel** (southwest corner of Broadway and Hudson). A Billy the Kid
tour also takes in his mother's grave and a jail where he served time for
robbing a Chinese laundry and from which he reportedly escaped by
climbing up the chimney.

*Details: Museum, 312 W. Broadway; 505/538-5921. Open Tue–Fri
9–4:30, weekends 10–4. Free. Maps for self-guided walking tours available
from the chamber of commerce, 1103 N. Hudson; 505/538-3785. (1–4 hours)*

★★ **The Catwalk**—In the deserts of southern New Mexico, water is
precious, a fact that makes **Whitewater Canyon** all the more enticing.
One of the Gila's largest and longest canyons, deep within its shadowy
course it harbors a good-sized stream called the Whitewater. Along its
banks lush meadows push up tender flowers, sinuous Arizona
sycamores and evergreens sway in the breeze, and a profusion of birds
call out. A mile away, the sun is blazing down on sand and cactus; here
it is cool and humid.

Where the Whitewater emerges from the mountains, the stream is
pinched between hundred-foot-high cliffs and massive boulders clog
roaring, froth-flecked water, creating a series of falls, pools, and plunges.
Clinging directly over the stream, supported by large rods drilled into
the canyon walls, is a series of metal bridges and walkways called the
Catwalk. While the structure was recently rebuilt, it actually follows the
course of a similar framework built in the late 1800s, when the canyon
was the center of a silver and gold mining district.

As a National and Historic Trail, it is one of the more renowned destinations in the area, so expect to see people, especially on weekends and
holidays. The Whitewater Trail is open year round (as far as Redstone
Park in winter), providing access to the high country, but the nicest times
to visit are April and May and September through November.

*Details: Located just outside Glenwood, on the western edge of the Gila
Country. Turn off U.S. 180 in Glenwood onto NM 174 and proceed 5 miles
northeast to the Whitewater Picnic Ground; 505/539-2481. Open year-
round. Free. (1 hour minimum on site)*

★★ **Western New Mexico University Museum**—Southwestern New
Mexico's finest museum sits elegantly atop a high hill overlooking

Silver City. It has outstanding regional paleolithic artifacts; the nation's largest collection of Mimbres pottery and artifacts from the nearby Mimbres River Valley; a rare in-depth look at the important Casas Grandes culture of north-central Mexico; and displays of the town's colorful mining and ranching histories.

Details: *Located on the campus of Western New Mexico University. Turn off Pope St. onto 10th Ave. and head up the hill; the museum is on the right; 505/538-6386. Open Mon–Fri 9–4:30, Sat–Sun 10–4. Closed university holidays. Free. (1–2 hours)*

✯ **Mogollon**—Almost a ghost town today, this community was born around 1879 with the discovery nearby of gold and silver, and once had a population of 2,000. It survived floods, fires, and the 1918 influenza epidemic, but the mines finally played out and only a handful of people hang on here today. A few stores cater to summer visitors, so you can get a drink and a bite to eat. There's also the **Mogollon Museum** and a B&B. The town is plunked down in a skinny, deep valley. The drive on a paved road from U.S. 180 winds sharply over a ridge and down into the valley, offering great views to the north and west. You can continue on up this road, which turns to gravel past Mogollon, into the Gila's high country.

Details: *Head north from Silver City on U.S. 180 for 50 miles through Glenwood. Some 3 miles north of Glenwood, turn east (right) onto NM 159 and proceed 7 miles to the town. The museum is supposed to be open on weekends; 505/539-2016. (1 hour on site)*

✯ **Santa Rita/Chino Open Pit Copper Mine**—Welcome to one of the world's biggest holes. In fact, until you note that the fly-sized trucks crisscrossing the roads inside the hole are actually monster-sized earth-movers you can't grasp its immensity. One mile long by a half a mile wide and 1,800 feet deep, some 300 million pounds of copper are removed from its bowels annually by Phelps-Dodge and Heisei Minerals. Also in the Silver City area is another massive Phelps-Dodge open pit copper mine at **Tyrone**.

Details: *A "scenic" viewpoint of the Santa Rita/Chino mine is on NM 152 some 15 miles east of Silver City—just a mile or so east of Hanover and Turnerville. The viewpoint for the Tyrone mine is 12 miles south of Silver City on U.S. 90 at mile marker 32. Free guided tours of this mine are conducted Mon–Fri at 9 a.m.; 505/538-5331. (15 minutes at viewpoint)*

FITNESS AND RECREATION

There are dozens of wilderness areas in the country, but the very first one was established in the Gila Country in 1924 through the work of one of America's greatest naturalists, Aldo Leopold. The Gila now has three wilderness units protecting 790,000 acres: the **Aldo Leopold Wilderness Area**, the **Gila Wilderness Area**, and the **Blue Range Wilderness Area**.

They, in turn, are part of the larger Gila National Forest, 3.3 million acres of high mountain terrain. Numerous mountain chains, including the rugged **Black Range**, the **Mogollon Mountains**, the **Pinos Altos Range**, the **Elk Mountains**, the **San Franciscos**, and the **Tularosas** receive abundant rain and snow, which feed the headwaters of the **Gila River**, the **San Francisco River**, and the **Mimbres River**. The highest peak in the state's southwestern quadrant is here as well: 10,892-foot **Whitewater Baldy**, located east of Glenwood.

The mountains offer wonderful opportunities for hiking, backpacking, mountain biking, horseback riding, and cross-country skiing on the more than 1,490 miles of trails. Visitors also come for the camping, hot-springs dipping, bird watching, four-wheeling, whitewater recreation, hunting, and fishing. There are more than 186 miles of fishing streams in the Gila Wilderness alone, many harboring populations of the endangered Gila trout. If lake fishing is more to your taste, **Lake Roberts**, **Bill Evans Lake**, **Snow Lake**, and other water bodies beckon.

Birding is big here. With elevations ranging from 4,000 to almost 11,000 feet and many diverse biomes—including desert, grasslands, riparian, and alpine—the Gila supports a great range of bird life: 291 species have been identified to date. Silver City hosts the **Gila Bird and Nature Festival**, 800/548-9378, every April.

As for hot springs, a few bubble up to the surface in the Gila, including **San Francisco Hot Springs**. Because it is situated in a pretty area on a bank of the San Francisco River, you can alternate dips between the hot springs and the cold river water, a practice guaranteed to turn you into a smiling zombie after a few hours. This is strictly a grassroots outing, with the shallow pools maintained by volunteers. Primitive camping is allowed. On weekends it can get crowded and noisy. It is located northwest of Silver City off U.S. 180. To get here, turn west off U.S. 180 onto a dirt road one mile south of Pleasanton (which is three miles south of Glenwood) and follow it to the river.

For horseback riding, try the **Sapillo Crossing Guest Ranch**, 505/536-3206, located at the juncture of NM 15 and NM 35 en route to the Gila monument, which offers rides for novices to experts from one hour ($15) to six hours ($65), or **Gila Hot Springs Vacation Center** (505/536-9551).

There are numerous outdoor recreation outfitters in the Gila Country, many based in Silver City, arranging guided and unguided outings ranging from multi-day goat- or horse-pack excursions to natural history or archaeology tours, cattle drives, and hunting or fishing forays. For details, call 800/548-9378.

For additional details on recreation in the area, contact the **Gila National Forest Supervisor's Office** in Silver City, 2610 N. Silver St., 505/388-8201, or district ranger stations: **Black Range Station**, 2601 Broadway, Truth or Consequences, 505/894-6677; **Luna Ranger Station**, Luna, 505/547-2611; **Glenwood Ranger Station**, Glenwood, 505/539-2481; **Reserve Ranger District**, Reserve, 505/533-6231; or **Wilderness Ranger District**, Silver City, 505/536-9461.

You can also tee up at Silver City's 18-hole **Scott Park Municipal Golf Course** on the southeastern edge of town, 505/538-5041, or take a ride in a hot-air balloon with **Paradise Balloons**, 505/388-3756, at $135 a person for one hour of sunset or sunrise flying.

FOOD

One of New Mexico's more endearing and entertaining places to eat is found on Main Street in Piños Altos, the **Buckhorn Saloon**, 505/538-9911. The 1860s establishment is historic without trying—call it rusting rustic. Its 18-inch adobe walls have soaked up bullets, more than a few whoops of gold-fevered miners, and the tinkling sound of player pianos and bar girls' laughter. Today it is both a restaurant and bar. The food is surprisingly good—from escargot or deep-fried mushroom appetizers to steaks, trout, and pasta at dinner. Dinner is served daily, except Sundays.

I had an excellent bowl of soup and a very good and modestly priced plate of cheese ravioli my last time in Silver City at **La Familia**, 208 W. Yankie, 505/388-8629. The Sicilian-style restaurant serves fancier dishes as well, such as whitefish with marinara on spaghetti, but still at reasonable prices. The atmosphere is elegant but relaxed.

Another of the nicer Silver City restaurants is the **Black Cactus Café**, 107 W. Yankie St., 505/388-5430, with its nouvelle New Mexican focus. It is open for dinner Thursday through Saturday, and Sundays for lunch. Serving up basic but always reliable New Mexican fare is the locally popular **Jalisco Café**, 100 S. Bullard, 505/388-2060. For steaks, the **Red Barn**, 708 Silver Heights Blvd., 505/538-5666, serves up well-prepared beef, as well as seafood and salads. For gourmet coffee and light snacks, visit the **AIR Expresso Bar & Gallery**, 106 W. Yankie St., 505/388-5952. For breakfast in Silver City, the French toast, huevos rancheros, or pancakes at the **Corner Café**, corner of Broadway and Bullard, 505/388-2056, can't be beat. **Kinetics**, on Yankie Street, has an all-organic juice bar, salad bar, and snacks.

Outside of Silver City, there are not many places to get a prepared meal in the Gila Country. In Glenwood is the **Blue Front Bar & Restaurant**, 505/539-2561, which serves New Mexican food and steaks, and BBQ on weekends. **Ellie's Country Kitchen**, also in Glenwood, 505/539-2242, is open daily for breakfast and lunch. In Reserve, at **Grandma T's**, 505/533-6230, I had one of the best plates of fried chicken I've ever munched on, along with homemade mashed potatoes and a big salad. Also highly recommended is the **Red Hen Café**, in tiny Alma on U.S. 180, 505/539-2610.

LODGING

For such an out-of-the-way town, Silver City has a surprisingly good range of places to stay, including some exceptional B&Bs. My first overnight stay here was at the **Bear Mountain Guest Ranch**, 505/538-2538 or 800/880-2538. This B&B is owned and run by the venerable, opinionated, and entertaining Myra McCormick. A knowl-edgeable amateur naturalist, she is full of stories about the area, its his-tory and unusual people. The ranch was built in 1928 on 160 acres of pretty land some three miles northwest of town (take Alabama Street and follow the signs). It has been a B&B since 1959 and is particularly popular with birders. Rooms, all with private baths, start at $70 for doubles, or $100 with all meals.

On my most recent visit I decided to stay in the historic downtown area, and discovered the **Carter House B&B**, 101 N. Cooper St., 505/388-5485. Upstairs in the lovely 1906 Edwardian-style, three-story residence are five rooms (each with private bath), large and finely appointed living and dining rooms, a library, and a relaxing, spacious front porch overlooking town. Doubles begin at $55. In the basement is a certified **international youth hostel** (without age restrictions) that

SILVER CITY

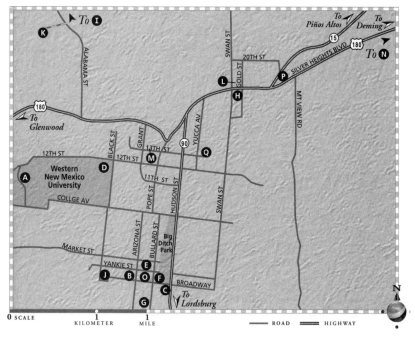

Sights

Ⓐ McCray
Ⓑ Silver City Museum
Ⓒ Star Hotel
Ⓓ Western New Mexico University Museum

Food

Ⓔ AIR Expresso Bar & Gallery
Ⓕ Black Cactus Café
Ⓕ Corner Café
Ⓖ Jalisco Café
Ⓔ Kinetics
Ⓔ La Familia
Ⓗ Red Barn

Lodging

Ⓘ Bear Mountain Guest Ranch
Ⓙ Carter House B&B
Ⓚ The Cottages
Ⓛ Drifter Motel
Ⓜ Guest House
Ⓝ Holiday Motor Hotel
Ⓞ The Palace
Ⓟ Super 8

Camping

Ⓠ Silver City RV Park

Note: Items with the same letter are located in the same area.

is the best bargain accommodation in the whole state that I know of, with a laundry, full kitchen and sunlit dining area, a rec room with television, reading room, male and female dormitories fitted with clean sheets, and segregated bathrooms. Rates are $10 for AYH members; $13 otherwise.

Also in Silver City is the **Guest House**, 1014 W. 13th St., 505/538-3203, with two bedrooms at $50, and **The Cottages**, 505/388-3000 or www.bbhost.com/cottages, formerly owned by the Bromo-Seltzer family on 80 acres at the edge of town. The hot mineral baths are a real treat. The private French-style cottages range from $89 to $199.

Out of town are the **Wilderness Lodge**, in Gila Hot Springs on NM 15 just before the entrance to the Gila National Monument, 505/536-9749, with six doubles running $45 to $55, and **Sapillo Crossing Guest Ranch**, at the juncture of NM 15 and NM 35 en route to the national monument, 505/536-3206. It has RV sites, an okay restaurant that opens at seven in the morning, a gift shop, and 16 rooms; doubles with private bath begin at $50.

Silver City also has a very nice hotel, **The Palace**, 388 W. Broadway, 505/388-1811. Originally built in 1882 as a bank in the heart of the town's historic district, it has been restored as a B&B-style accommodation. Tiny rooms go for $30; suites with queen beds for $55.

Silver City also has lots of motels, though few of the bargain basement variety. The **Holiday Motor Hotel**, outside the old district at 3420 E. U.S. 180, 505/538-3711 or 800/828-8291, has a pool, laundry, restaurant open daily for breakfast, lunch, and dinner, and rooms for $50. The **Drifter Motel**, 711 Silver Heights, 505/538-2916, has doubles beginning at $40. The **Super 8**, at the juncture of U.S. 180 and NM 15, rents doubles for $50.

Outside Silver in Piños Altos, the **Bear Creek Motel & Cabins**, 505/388-4501, has 13 or so cabins, some featuring kitchenettes; rates begin at $42. The **Gila Hotspring Vacation Center** (see Fitness and Recreation) has rooms with kitchenettes for $48, as well as commercial hot springs, laundry, snack bar, gift shop, and doll museum. In Glenwood is the **Lariat Motel**, 505/539-2361, with cable TV, doubles at $37 and kitchenettes at $42; **Crab Apple Cabins**, 505/539-2400, with smoke-free cabins prized by bird watchers beginning at $29; and **Los Olmos Guest Ranch**, with stone cabins clustered around lawns and shade trees, a swimming pool with Jacuzzi, playground, and historic dining room with fireplace. Trail rides, horse shoes, billiards, volleyball, and fishing in a private pond are also available. All rooms have private baths, but no phones or TV; doubles, $62 to $85, include breakfast.

CAMPING

There are about 20 free, developed sites with drinking water at the **Gila Cliff Dwellings National Monument**, 505/536-9461, available on a first-come, first-served basis. Nearby, on NM 15, are both primitive campsites and RV sites at the **Gila Hotsprings Vacation Center**, 505/536-9551. Camping costs $2.50 per adult; RV sites with hookups are $12. The **Lake Roberts General Store & Cabins**, at Lake Roberts on NM 35, 505/536-9929, has RV and tent sites, as well as coin showers, laundry, and some cabins with private bathrooms.

The **Gila National Forest**, 2915 U.S. 180 East, 505/538-2771, maintains both seasonal and year-round campgrounds scattered throughout the area. Two of the closest to Silver City are **Cherry Creek** and **McMillan**, about 12 and 14 miles north of town on NM 15. Neither have water; both are open April to October with 14 free sites. **Lake Roberts**, **Mesa Campground**, and **Sapillo** at Lake Roberts on NM 35, have 42 sites (22-foot trailers maximum, Sapillo is free). Above Mogollon (see Sightseeing Highlights, above) on gravel Forest Road 142 are six campgrounds open April to November, including **Bursum**, **Ben Lilly**, **Willow**, and **Gilita**. All have trailhead access to the Gila Wilderness and are free; some have fishing.

Numerous commercial camping facilities exist, including **KOA Silver City**, 11824 U.S. 180 East, 505/388-3351, located some six miles east of town, with a pool, laundry, playground, RV sites for $18 with hookups, and $14 for tents. Other options are the **Continental Divide RV Park**, in Pinos Altos, 505/388-3005, and the **Silver City RV Park**, Bennett and 13th Street, 505/538-2239. For "boondock" sites, head south out of town on U.S. 90 to the wild **Burro Mountain Homestead**, 665 Tyrone Road in Tyrone, 505/538-2149.

NIGHTLIFE

Lots of Silver City residents and students head up into the hills of Pinos Altos (see Sightseeing Highlights) to the **Buckhorn Saloon**, 505/538-9911, for live music. The bar opens at three in the afternoon. Locals and touring musicians perform here most weekends and many weeknights.

The open-mike sessions are legendary. On occasional weekends at eight in the evening, the **Piños Altos Opera House**, 505/388-3848, adjoining the Buckhorn, stages old-fashioned melodramas.

Silver City's **Buffalo Bar**, 201 N. Bullard, 505/538-3201, is memorable. Owner Sam Trujillo tells me he once thought about changing the crazed red eyes in the buffalo head mounted over the bar but was discouraged by patrons. There are some pool tables; a long, long bar; and a loud crowd of working stiffs, some college kids, and other odds and ends. Adjoining it is a great old dance hall surrounded by a seating balcony, where live music is occasionally presented.

Also in Silver City are performances by touring programs of all kinds and locally staged events organized by the **Mimbres Region Arts Council**, 505/538-2502. Every Memorial Day weekend, the town rocks with the **Silver City Blues Festival**.

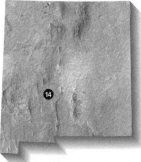

14

MIDDLE RIO GRANDE VALLEY

People speeding up and down I-25 through New Mexico's middle Rio Grande Valley are generally struck by the barrenness of the area—mile after mile of lowland hills and plains dominated by sparse creosote bushes. The highway bypasses Socorro and the oddly-named Truth or Consequences, and until you arrive at either Albuquerque or Las Cruces, little jumps out to grab your attention.

However, this area presents a classic case for the value of getting off the main drag and slowing down. Once off the narrow blacktops, another dimension of the area becomes evident. Although it may appear inconsequential much of the year, the Rio Grande actually creates a series of lakes and marshes throughout New Mexico's linear heartland, attracting clouds of migratory waterfowl. Large reservoirs are a magnet for boaters and anglers while the mountain ranges flanking the valley to the west offer winter sports and, in summer, outstanding and isolated hiking and camping. Here too are found a string of true and near ghost towns, from the slowly reviving Hillsboro to the still-somnolent Chloride.

As attractive as its natural assets are, the area also has notable accommodations, historic properties in pleasant Socorro, some decent places to eat, and an odd but intriguing museum or two. All in all, I'd say the area promises to be another of New Mexico's tourism growth markets. Still a bit rough around the edges, it has a simplicity and authenticity that are quite refreshing as is.

MIDDLE RIO GRANDE VALLEY

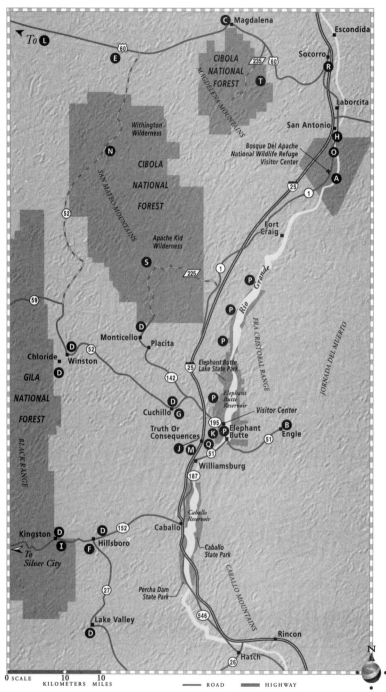

To **L**

Magdalena **C**

Escondida

60 **E**

CIBOLA
NATIONAL
FOREST

235 / 60

Socorro **R**

T

Laborcita

MAGDALENA MOUNTAINS

San Antonio **H**

Bosque Del Apache
National Wildlife Refuge
Visitor Center

O

N

Withington
Wilderness

A

CIBOLA

NATIONAL

FOREST

25

1

SAN MATEO MOUNTAINS

Apache Kid
Wilderness

Fort
Craig

52

S

225

1

P

Rio Grande

59

P

FRA CRISTOBAL RANGE

JORNADA DEL MUERTO

P

D

Monticello

D

Placita

P

Chloride

Winston **D**

52

GILA

NATIONAL

FOREST

142

25

Elephant Butte
Lake State Park

D

Cuchillo **G**

Elephant
Butte
Reservoir

P

Visitor Center

B

Truth Or
Consequences

195

K

P

Elephant
Butte

Engle

51

BLACK RANGE

J **M**

Q

51

Williamsburg

187

Caballo
Reservoir

Kingston **D**

D

152

Caballo

I

Hillsboro **F**

To
Silver City

Caballo
State Park

27

CABALLO MOUNTAINS

Percha Dam
State Park

546

Lake Valley **D**

Rincon

N

26

Hatch

0 SCALE   10   10
        KILOMETERS MILES

ROAD   HIGHWAY

Sights

Ⓐ Bosque del Apache National Wildlife Refuge

Ⓑ El Camino Real

Ⓒ Magdalena

Ⓓ Sierra County Ghost Towns

Ⓔ Very Large Array

Food

Ⓕ Angels Bakery

Ⓖ Cuchillo Café

Ⓒ Evett's

Ⓕ Hillsboro General Store & Country Café

Ⓖ Hillsboro Orchard BBQ

Ⓗ Manny's Buckhorn Bar

Ⓗ Owl Bar & Café

Ⓘ Percha Villa Café

Lodging

Ⓙ Best Western Hot Springs Motor Inn

Ⓘ Black Range Lodge

Ⓗ Casa Blanca B&B

Ⓚ Elephant Butte Resort Inn

Ⓕ Enchanted Villa

Ⓛ Lightning Field

Ⓜ Motel 6

Camping

Ⓝ Beartrap Campground/Hughes Campground

Ⓞ Birdwatchers RV Park

Ⓟ Elephant Butte Lake State Park

Ⓠ Lakeside RV Park & Campground

Ⓡ Socorro RV Park

Ⓢ Springtime Campground/ Luna Park

Ⓣ Water Canyon Campground

Note: Items with the same letter are located in the same town or area.

A PERFECT DAY IN THE MIDDLE RIO GRANDE VALLEY

Arrive in Socorro in the afternoon and walk its historic districts. After a night at the Eaton House, head to Bosque del Apache. Have a picnic here, then proceed south to the ghost towns of Cuchillo, Monticello, and Chloride. Motor into Truth or Consequences at sunset and, after dinner at the Blue Note, bathe at a commercial hot spring.

SIGHTSEEING HIGHLIGHTS

★★★ **Bosque del Apache National Wildlife Refuge**—Each winter tens of thousands of sandhill cranes, snow geese, Canada geese, many species of duck and wading birds, as well as a couple of endangered whooping cranes, migratory songbirds, and raptors settle in at this national wildlife refuge. On my last brief visit, I saw more than a dozen hawks, eagles, and other hunting birds dipping over the shallow ponds, fields, and *bosque* (forests). Don't be surprised if a majestic family of turkeys or colorful pheasants come strutting out of the undergrowth.

While the 329 species of birds found here are the main draw, the refuge also shelters some 50 species of large and small mammals, and 60 kinds of reptiles and amphibians, mule deer, porcupine, and coyote. Straddling the Rio Grande, the 57,000-acre refuge is also a very beautiful place, even absent the wildlife. Large stands of cottonwood trees poke up here and there. Flaming orange willows, ruddy tamarisk, yellow grasses, dried cattails, and other vegetation line the dirt roads that wind through the refuge, offset by the encircling desert hills covered in limegreen creosote, and further off, bluish mountain ranges—their summits topped by winter snow.

One can circle the refuge's bottomlands via the 12-mile, one-way graded **Tour Loop Road** with a two-way cut-off that divides the full tour into a shorter **Marsh Loop** of 7 miles and a **Farm Loop** of 7.5 miles. You can stop anywhere along this road; just pull over to the side.

But for a close-up immersion in the environment I'd suggest a walk. There are several foot trails running 1.5 to 2.5 miles in the wetlands and one up an adjoining scenic desert canyon. Bicyclists can use the loop roads and designated foot trails. Details on these trails are available in free literature at the visitors center.

The prime viewing period for sandhills and waterfowl runs November to February, but there is something to see in each season. Summer brings mosquitos and high daytime temperatures. Winter storms can drop the temperature to 15 degrees. Activities and excitement come to a head every year in late November at the refuge's **Festival of the Cranes**, which attracts an international cast of birding experts and aficionados.

The excellent visitors center includes displays and audiovisual programs on area ecology, geology, and history, a bookstore and gift shop, information, and a viewing window onto a small pond where birds flock to feed stations. Camping is not allowed.

Details: *From Socorro, head south 18 miles on I-25 to Exit 139, continue east 0.25 mile to the flashing signal in San Antonio, then turn south (right) onto NM 1 and proceed 9 miles to visitors center. Visitors center open fall, winter, and spring weekdays 7:30–4, weekends 8–4:30; occasionally closed in summer. Refuge open 1 hour before sunrise–1 hour after sunset. Always available are restrooms and sheltered picnic tables. $3 per vehicle. (1 hour minimum)*

★★★ **Sierra County Ghost Towns**—The mid- to late-1800s saw a slew of boom towns pop up in the mountains of Sierra County due to the gold and silver mining that brought temporary prosperity to the area. Many fine homes, some commercial buildings, and even small hotels were built. Then the veins played out and all of the towns went into decline. Some, however, did not die out completely, and they make for interesting outings. In the northwest are Cuchillo, Monticello, Winston, and Chloride; in the southwest are the better-known Hillsboro, Kingston, and Lake Valley, described below.

Hillsboro, on the mountain route between Silver City and the Rio Grande Valley, produced more than 6 million dollars in gold and silver. More so than the other Sierra County "ghost towns," Hillsboro is maintaining its own. A few antique shops, cafés (see Food, below), a good B&B (see Lodging, below), a few art galleries, and churches exist today on its main street, shaded by great cottonwoods. Here also is the charming **Black Range Museum**, right on NM 52, 505/895-5233 or -5685, which contains local stuff. It's open daily except Tuesday and Wednesday from 11 to 4; closed January and February. Free admission. Hillsboro celebrates its annual **Apple Festival** on Labor Day.

Kingston also is slowly growing. Once the largest of the county's boomers, with more than 7,000 people, it boasted 22 saloons, 14 groceries, gambling halls, a brewery, three newspapers, and an English madam, Sadie Orchard, who had a brothel on Virtue Avenue. There is a B&B (see Lodging), a museum open by appointment, and the nation's oldest active social club—the Spit and Whittle.

Lake Valley is a true ghost town; its last inhabitant left in 1994. One local mine, the Bridal Chamber, produced a silver ore so pure it was shipped unsmelted to the mint. A chapel, several homes, and a school dating to 1904 still stand; the school is open to the public.

Details: *From Truth or Consequences, head south 11 miles on I-25 and exit onto NM 152, then proceed 17 miles west to Hillsboro. Lake Valley is about 12 miles south of Hillsboro on NM 27. Kingston is 9 miles west of*

Hillsboro on NM 152. Note: There are two bridges with only 14.5-foot clearance between Hillsboro and Kingston. A brochure on these "ghost towns" is available from the Sierra County/Truth or Consequences Chamber of Commerce, 800/831-9478. (2–4 hours)

★★★ **Socorro Historic Districts**—Socorro is another New Mexico town that knew glory, then faded into obscurity. Now, with some 6,000 residents, the **New Mexico Institute of Mining and Technology**, nearby Bosque del Apache National Wildlife Refuge (see above), its role as Socorro County capital, and its historic character, it is experiencing modest but steady growth.

Its 60 or so historic properties are clustered around the main plaza and in residential districts to the south and west of the plaza. Much can be seen on foot; a few sites are best reached by car. Specific properties of note include the **J.N. Garcia Opera House**, at Abeyta and California Streets; the **Hilton Block**, on the east side of the plaza, which includes a pharmacy founded by a relative of hotelier Conrad Hilton, who grew up in Socorro and nearby San Antonio; **San Miguel Mission**, 505/835-1620, three blocks north of the plaza on Otero, finished in 1821; the **Socorro County Courthouse**, a 1940 structure at Church and Court Streets; the **Val Verde Hotel**, on Manzanares and Sixth; **Hammel Brewery**, on Sixth Street north of Otero, which was opened in the late 1800s; and many fine homes on Park, Church, and McCutcheon Streets.

Details: *The Socorro Historical Society has a detailed brochure on the town's historic properties. For a copy, contact the chamber of commerce, 103 Francisco de Avondo, 505/835-0424. (1–3 hours)*

★★★ **Very Large Array**—Huge, dazzling metallic dishes cocked skyward, strung out like a string of pearls across the vast Plains of San Agustine, seem utterly incongruous here. Resembling enormous eyeless sockets, they are actually more akin to a series of ears eavesdropping on the Cosmic Babble: the sounds of stars being born, supernova explosions, the machinations of Time itself.

If all this sounds a bit murky, a stop at the VLA's visitors center may shed some light on the subject. Here you'll find eye-dazzling color displays of the work and discoveries carried out at this remote National Science Foundation facility, which has been seen in many major films, including *Contact*.

Details: *From Socorro, head west 50 miles on U.S. 60 through*

Magdalena. Just past mile marker 94 turn south (left) onto NM 52 for 2 miles, then west on a well-marked access road. Park at the visitors center. Open daily 8:30–sunset. Free. (1 hour on site)

⭐⭐ **Truth or Consequences**—Originally known as Palomas Hot Springs, this town—often called "T or C"—took up TV game-show host Ralph Edwards' challenge and switched its name in 1950 in return for Edwards' presence at an annual fair (he hasn't missed one yet!) and tons of free PR on his show. The town grew up around the construction of **Elephant Butte Dam** (see Fitness and Recreation, below) from 1912 to 1916; today it attracts a fair number of snowbirds with its mild winters and relaxing pace. People are also rediscovering its natural hot springs, which range from 98 to 115 degrees. There are several commercial bathhouses, as well as motels with hot-springs baths (see Lodging). Its **Geronimo Springs Museum** is also a very good, small facility, with a film on famed Apache warrior and medicine man Geronimo—who frequented the area's healing hot springs—displays on the area's natural and human history, arts and culture, and Ralph Edwards memorabilia.

Details: Museum, 325 Main St.; 505/894-6600. Open Mon–Sat 9–5, Sun 1–5. $1.50 adults. (1 hour museum)

⭐ **El Camino Real**—While most Americans have at least heard of the Oregon Trail and some even of the Santa Fe Trail, this much older and perhaps ultimately more significant trail has largely gone unknown. It was the main artery of commerce and conquest in the Southwest for over 300 years, running more than 2,000 miles from Mexico City to Santa Fe. However, both the federal and relevant state governments of Mexico and the United States have recently taken steps to formally recognize the trail. Markers are being erected along its path, and a major interpretive center, **El Camino Real International Heritage Center**, is being built between Truth or Consequences and Socorro.

An accessible section of the Camino Real can be found near the village of **Engle**, southeast of Truth or Consequences. There is a trail marker in Engle (as well as a wine and champagne vineyard). Here the track ran through the desolate and often deadly Jornada del Muerto (Journey of Death), where the trail cut across a largely dry basin whose few springs would occasionally give out.

Details: To get to Engle from T or C, head 13 miles east on NM 51, which passes Elephant Butte Dam and then climbs over a pass and descends into the hot and dry Jornada. The interpretive center will be located on Bureau of Land Management property north of T or C and operated by the New Mexico State Monuments Division. No date has been set for its opening.

✯ **Magdalena**—This sleepy town was once a bustling center of mining activity and, as the westernmost railhead of the region, said to be the busiest cattle shipping point in the West, serving ranchers as far away as Arizona. There are several attractions here besides low real estate prices and a quiet atmosphere. Just south of town is **Kelly**, a ghost town and mining district that produced $50 to $60 million in lead, zinc, silver, copper, and gold between 1886 and 1945. In town is the **Boxcar Museum**, located in the turn-of-the-century railroad depot.

Details: Magdalena is located 27 miles west of Socorro via U.S. 60. Kelly is located 3 miles from Magdalena; 505/854-2415. Open summer Fri–Sun 10–4. Museum is on Main St. (Kelly: 1–2 hours; Boxcar Museum: 30 minutes–1 hour)

✯ **Mineral Museum**—This facility of the New Mexico Institute of Mining and Technology displays more than 10,000 regional mineral samples (including glow-in-the-dark varieties), as well as exhibits on local geology, fossil history, flora, and fauna.

Details: School of Mines Rd., in the Workman Center on the Tech campus; 505/835-5420. Open Mon–Fri 8–5. Free. (1 hour)

FITNESS AND RECREATION

New Mexico's most popular state park, by far, is **Elephant Butte Lake State Park**, a 25,000-acre enclave surrounding a 45-mile-long reservoir on the Rio Grande near Truth or Consequences. Water skiers and boaters are particularly drawn here from April through September, but it is also popular with anglers. It has produced enormous black bass and also harbors white bass, catfish, pike, crappie, and, below the dam in public waters, trout. Major fishing tournaments are frequently held on the lake. Numerous guide services can be found in T or C.

From mid- to late summer, temperatures are regularly above 95 degrees in the afternoon, but the heat doesn't deter huge crowds on Memorial Day, July 4, and Labor Day. Summer weekends, when Albuquerqueans arrive in force, can also be busy, particularly around the lake's southeastern shore, where you find the **Elephant Butte Lake State Park Visitor Center**, 505/744-5421, and the **Elephant**

TRUTH OR CONSEQUENCES

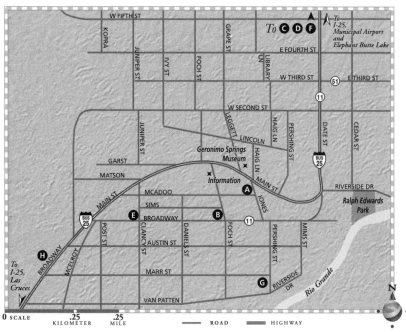

Sights

A Downtown Core

Food

B Blue Note

C Hilltop Café

D Los Arcos

Lodging

E Charles Motel & Bathhouse

F Oasis

Camping

G Artesian Bath House & RV Park

H Cielo Vista RV Park

Butte Marine Resort, 505/744-5486. The latter has a restaurant, launching ramps, boat rentals, camping supplies, and fishing tackle and licenses. There are also boat ramps at **Rock Canyon** and the park's main entrance station. Less frequented are the coves and shoreline along the lake's far northwestern edge, such as **Mitchell Point**. It is reached via I-25, at Exit 92. The dam itself is unusually graceful, even decorative. Good views are available with pullouts along NM 51, which enters Truth or Consequences as Third Street.

The little-known **San Mateo Mountains** contain **Mount Withington Wilderness Area** and the **Apache Kid Wilderness Area**, which offer nearly 80 miles of trails for hiking. Adjacent lands of the **Cibola National Forest** provide an additional 120 miles of trails. Details can be obtained from the **Magdalena Ranger Station** on U.S. 60, 505/854-2281.

The area's varied terrain, many microclimates and environments, and general lack of people also make this an excellent place for wildlife viewing and hunting. A particularly beautiful spot is **Water Canyon**. Between U.S. 60 and the Water Canyon Campground one can often spot pronghorn antelope, ferruginous hawk, and golden eagles year-round. From the campground to higher elevations are found numerous songbirds, from the black-chinned hummingbird to lazuli bunting and white-throated swift, as well as occasional mule deer and turkey. To get here head west out of Socorro on U.S. 60 for 12.5 miles and turn south (left) onto Forest Road 235. Drive 4.5 miles to the campground, where the pavement ends. The road continues upward to **Langmuir Laboratory** (a center for lightning research open in summer, 505/835-5401), near the summit of South Baldy, at 10,783 feet. A high-clearance vehicle is recommended for the unpaved section of road. For information, call 505/854-2281.

There are also a few area golf courses. T or C has the **Municipal Golf Course**, 685 W. Marie, 505/894-2603, and **Oasis Golf and Country Club**, on Stage Coach Road near Elephant Butte Lake, 505/744-5224. **New Mexico Tech Golf Course**, 505/835-5335, in Socorro, has an 18-hole, par 72 layout.

FOOD

While there's lots to see and do in this area, the food options are rather sparse. However, one of the state's most universally known places to eat and drink is in the area: the **Owl Bar & Café**, on U.S.

380 in San Antonio, 505/835-9946, some 11 miles south of Socorro. Its huge, floppy green-chile cheeseburgers are legendary, but can be a bit overwhelming and very messy. You really stop here because of its history and atmosphere. Its massive bar came from a nearby now-defunct boardinghouse run by one Gus Hilton, who was helped in his endeavor by son Conrad—who went on to launch Hilton Hotels. Located at almost the midpoint of New Mexico, the Owl has served as a convenient place for state politicians, business leaders, military personnel from nearby White Sands Missile Range, and other power players to gather for powwows. It is open daily, except Sundays, for breakfast, lunch, and dinner. If it's full, and it often is, walk across the street to **Manny's Buckhorn Bar**, where the food is actually better.

In Socorro, visit the **Val Verde Steakhouse**, 203 E. Manzanares St., 505/835-3380. The moderately priced steaks and seafood are good, but the setting is wonderful, a 1919 Spanish Mission Revival building that once catered to train travelers staying in its hotel (now closed). It's open daily for lunch and dinner. Also here is **Armijo's**, 602 S. U.S. 85, 505/835-1686, and a coffee shop called **Pathfinder**, 300 California SE, 505/838-0034.

Truth or Consequences has a few viable options besides the horde of fast-food spots lining its main drag. **Blue Note**, 407 Broadway, 505/894-6680, has daily specials, sandwiches, homemade soups, and pasta. Locally popular is **Hilltop Café**, 1301 N. Date, 505/894-3407, with inexpensive but well done food served daily. The most expensive place in town is **Los Arcos**, on the north side of town at 1400 Date, 505/894-6200, with a bar, steaks, lobster, and more modestly priced fare including a salad bar. It is open daily for dinner and for Sunday brunch.

In Magdalena, drop into **Evett's**, on the north side of U.S. 60, 505/854-2449, offering a soda fountain and café fare. Hillsboro has two or three seasonal restaurants and at least one open year-round, the **Hillsboro General Store & Country Café** ("since 1879"), right on U.S. 152. With its five tables and short counter, it's not fancy but the staff is nice and the food substantial. It is open for breakfast and lunch daily, and for early dinner on Saturdays. Also in town are the organic **Angels Bakery** and, on the west edge of town, the **Hillsboro Orchard BBQ**, 505/895-5642, with good food but odd hours. The **Percha Villa Café**, in Kingston, serves tasty apple pies and mesquite B&B. Even tiny Cuchillo has a place to get a light bite Friday through Sunday—the **Cuchillo Café**, on NM 52.

SOCORRO

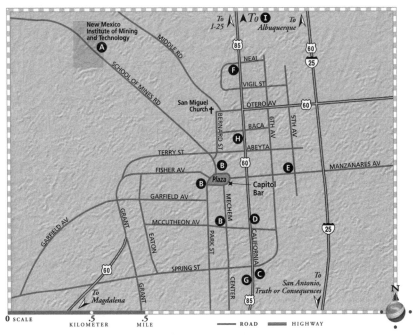

Sights

Ⓐ Mineral Museum
Ⓑ Socorro Historic Districts

Food

Ⓒ Armijo's
Ⓓ Pathfinder
Ⓔ Val Verde Steakhouse

Lodging

Ⓕ Best Western Golden Manor
Ⓖ Motel 6
Ⓗ Sands Motel
Ⓘ Vagabond

LODGING

In addition to a large range of motels in Socorro and Truth or Consequences, the area has a handful of good B&Bs. One of New Mexico's more unusual places to stay is **Lightning Field**, located near Quemado, 505/898-3335, a large-scale environmental art installation created by Walter de Maria. The site consists of 400 steel rods, each 20 feet tall, driven into a level plain over an area measuring a mile by one kilometer. The rods themselves are visually striking, but mix in one of the frequent lightning storms that brew in the area and you have a light show you'll never forget. You can only visit the site on an overnight stay, which runs $85 per person. The accommodations, in a renovated home-steader's cabin, are simple but comfortable and include a small kitchen.

The **Black Range Lodge**, in Kingston, 505/895-5652, is a charming three-story stone and timber historic property serving excellent food. Its seven rooms, each with private bath, run $55 for two people. Hillsboro has an attractive B&B as well, **Enchanted Villa**, right in the town's historic center on NM 152, 505/895-5686. It could use some paint but otherwise looks quite nice. The two-story adobe was built in 1941 for an English nobleman. Rooms run $40 to $65 and include a hot breakfast.

Bird enthusiasts will love **Casa Blanca B&B**, 13 Montoya St., San Antonio, 505/835-3027, only eight miles from Bosque del Apache. Rooms, one with a wood-burning stove, cost $45 to $55. In warm weather guests enjoy sitting on the veranda of this former farmhouse.

Truth or Consequences has a number of motels with on-site hot-springs bathing. The nicest is the **Charles Motel & Bathhouse**, 601 Broadway, 505/894-7154, with one- and two-bed guest rooms with kitchenettes and cable TV. The rooms are clean and large; ditto the private bathtubs, which feature 112 degree, odorless, tasteless waters tapped directly from underlying hot springs. Rooms run $35 to $45. Baths are four dollars; additional spa services are also available. Joe, at Joe's Barbershop next door, executes a fine trim.

Other T or C motel options include **Motel 6**, 805 S. U.S. 85 (at the south end of town at Exit 147 off I-25), 505/835-4300, with a pool and double rooms at $32. The **Oasis**, 819 Date, 505/894-6629 or 800/847-7891, has rooms with queen beds and cable TV for $25 and up. The **Best Western Hot Springs Motor Inn**, 2270 N. Date, 505/894-6665, has a pool and large rooms with queen and king beds running $50. Overlooking the lake, **Elephant Butte Resort Inn**, on

NM 195, 505/744-5431, has golf, a pool, volleyball, tennis, bar, and restaurant. Rooms go for $50 and up.

For Socorro motels, try **Motel 6**, 807 S. U.S. 85, 505/835-4300, with a pool and doubles at $34; the **Vagabond**, 1009 California NW, 505/835-0276, with a bar, restaurant, pool, and rooms for $34; the **Sands Motel**, 205 California NW, 505/835-1130, with rooms for $25; and the **Best Western Golden Manor**, 507 California NW, 505/835-0230, with a pool, café, and doubles for $50 to $55.

CAMPING

Elephant Butte Lake State Park (see Fitness and Recreation, above) has several camping areas, including 56 sites with electricity, showers, and drinking water at **Lyons Point**, and another 47 similar sites at **Ridge Road**. The park also has hundreds of undeveloped sites with portable toilets along its western shore.

Camping in developed or primitive campsites in local national forests is also available. In the Magdalena Mountains west of Socorro is **Water Canyon Campground** (see Fitness and Recreation for directions). It is open April to October and is free. At the north end of the San Mateo Mountains between Socorro and T or C are **Beartrap Campground** and **Hughes Campground**; on the range's south flank are **Springtime Campground** and **Luna Park**. For details, contact the Magdalena Ranger Station on U.S. 60 at 505/854-2281. For details on sites near Kingston or within the Aldo Leopold Wilderness Area south and west of Chloride, contact the **Gila Ranger Station** in Truth or Consequences, 1804 N. Date, 505/894-6677.

There are also numerous commercial RV parks in the area. In Truth or Consequences, **Cielo Vista RV Park**, 501 S. Broadway, 505/894-3738, has a pool, spa, laundry, and hookups for $12. **Artesian Bath House & RV Park**, 312 Marr Ave., T or C, 505/894-2684, offers $10 sites and hot springs bathing. **Lakeside RV Park & Campground**, on Country Club Boulevard in T or C, 505/744-5996, has showers, laundry, and tent and RV sites from $14.

Socorro options include **Socorro RV Park**, on the south frontage road by Exit 147 off I-25, 505/835-2234, with a pool, showers, laundry, and RV hookups for $16. **Birdwatchers RV Park**, on NM 1 between San Antonio and Bosque del Apache, 505/835-1366, has $15 sites.

15

GALLUP AND GRANTS AREA

While Mesa Verde may be more spectacular, the ruins of Keet Seel more beautiful, and the cliff dwellings of Canyon de Chelly more sublime, for me no Anasazi site in the Southwest matches the grandeur and mystifying draw of Chaco Canyon. And while it is the leading attraction in the greater Gallup and Grants area, it is certainly not the only destination worth visiting in the lands flanking I-40 west of Albuquerque.

Though not nearly as popular as the Rio Grande Valley or northern New Mexico, there is much to see and do in this west-central patch of the state. With its mix of Navajo, Zuni, Acoma, and Laguna Indians, Anglo and Hispanic ranchers, miners, small retail businesspeople, artists, and the occasional tourist, it is a down-to-earth slice of the state that represents a slower-paced and unpretentious lifestyle that is disappearing in the West. It's both Main Street U.S.A. and foreign nations within a nation.

Here is a land of great beauty, with starkly contrasting microclimates and landforms: high, snowcapped peaks; sun-blasted deserts; mesas and plateaus; small streams; lava fields; and verdant valleys.

A PERFECT DAY IN THE GALLUP AND GRANTS AREA

Begin the day with an early arrival at Chaco Canyon or, better yet, camp there the night before. Visit the canyon's main sites on the valley floor and have a picnic lunch under the cottonwoods along the Chaco

GALLUP AND GRANTS AREA

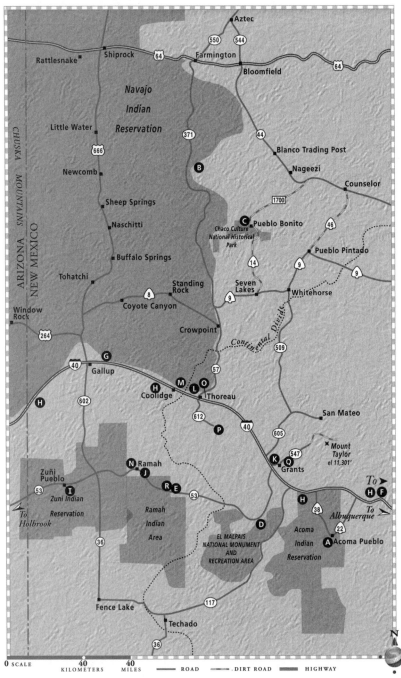

Aztec

550 544

Rattlesnake · Shiprock — 64 — Farmington

Navajo

Bloomfield — 64

Indian

Little Water — 371

Reservation

666

B — Blanco Trading Post

Newcomb · — Nageezi

Counselor

Sheep Springs — 1700

Naschitti — C — Pueblo Bonito — 46

Chaco Culture National Historical Park

· Buffalo Springs — Pueblo Pintado

14 — 9 — 9

Tohatchi · — Standing Rock — Seven Lakes

8 — 9 — Whitehorse

Window Rock — Coyote Canyon — Continental Divide

264 — Crowpoint — 509

G

40 — Gallup — 57

H — M — O

H — Coolidge — L — Thoreau

602 — San Mateo

612

P — 40 — 605

K — Q — Mount Taylor el 11,301'

N — Ramah — 547

J — Grants

Zuñi Pueblo — R — E

53 — I — 53

Zuni Indian — Ramah

To Holbrook — Reservation — Indian Area

H — 38 — To Albuquerque

H — F

36 — EL MALPAIS NATIONAL MONUMENT AND RECREATION AREA — D — Acoma Indian Reservation — 22

A — Acoma Pueblo

Fence Lake — 117

Techado

36

N

0 SCALE — 40 — 40
KILOMETERS — MILES — ■ ROAD — ░ DIRT ROAD — ═ HIGHWAY

CHUSKA MOUNTAINS

ARIZONA NEW MEXICO

Sights

Ⓐ Acoma Pueblo

Ⓑ Bisti Badlands Wilderness Area

Ⓒ Chaco Culture National
Historic Park

Ⓓ El Malpais National Monument
and Conservation Area

Ⓔ El Morro National Monument

Ⓕ Laguna Pueblo

Ⓖ Red Rocks State Park

Ⓗ Route 66

Ⓘ Zuni Pueblo

Food

Ⓙ Blue Corn Restaurant

Ⓚ Grants Station

Ⓚ La Ventana

Ⓐ Sky City Visitor Center

Lodging

Ⓚ Best Western Grants Inn

Ⓚ Econo Lodge

Ⓛ Navajo Lodge

Ⓜ Stauder's Navajo Lodge

Ⓝ Vogt Ranch

Ⓚ Wayside

Ⓞ Zuni Mt. Lodge

Camping

Ⓟ Blue Water Lake State Park

Ⓚ Cibola Sands RV Park

Ⓠ Coal Mine Campground

Ⓔ El Morro National Monument

Ⓡ El Morro RV Park

Ⓒ Gallo Campground

Ⓠ Lobo Canyon Campground

Ⓖ Red Rock State Park

Note: Items with the same letter are located in the same town or area.

River. Then head into Gallup for an afternoon of shopping and exploring the town's history. Or visit El Malpais National Monument, El Morro National Monument, or Acoma Pueblo. If you end up in Gallup for the night, have a drink at El Rancho and dinner at Earl's .

SIGHTSEEING HIGHLIGHTS

☆☆☆ **Acoma Pueblo**—Most of the 19 New Mexico pueblos still in existence feature wonderful settings, but none can beat this one. Set atop a 376-foot-high sandstone butte, it is aptly called Sky City. Accessible only via a rough foot trail until this century, Acoma fiercely resisted acculturation, aided by the impregnability of its mesa. In a three-day battle in January 1599, however, Spanish troops succeeded in mounting the mesa and burned the pueblo. Afterward, all males over 25 years old had a foot chopped off, while the younger males and females were sent to Mexico as slaves. Still, the Acoma clung to their independence and old ways, and even now, Sky City does not have running water or electricity.

Today Acomas welcome visitors to Sky City, as many tribal members earn their living from the sale of their outstanding pottery and, to a lesser degree, jewelry. Tourists must begin at the visitors center, where you purchase a ticket for the van ride up to the mesa top. Before setting off, browse through the gift shop or an interesting display on the pueblo's pottery traditions.

At Sky City, Acoma guides will lead you on an hourlong tour. Highlights include **San Esteban del Rey Church**, one of the most remarkable buildings in the state. Winding through the village's narrow lanes, you can purchase pottery directly from the artisans or perhaps grab a loaf of their wonderful bread baked in the beehive-shaped, wood-fired *hornos* (ovens). End your tour by walking back down the foot trail.

Details: Located between Grants and Albuquerque. Take I-40 Exit 102 and head south 12 miles on Tribal Rd. 38. Park at the visitors center; 505/470-4966 or 800/747-0181. Open daily Apr–Oct 8–7, final tour leaves at 6; daily Nov–Mar 8–4:30. Due to tribal ceremonies, tours are not held on June 24 and 29, July 10–13, July 25, and the first or second weekend of Oct. $7 adults, $6 seniors, $5 children; camera permit $10. (2–3 hours)

★★★ **Chaco Culture National Historic Park**—As all roads once led to Rome, in the Southwest they led to Chaco. For several centuries Chaco was the heart of the Anasazi world, which stretched from Nevada across north-central Arizona and southern Utah into southwestern Colorado and northwestern New Mexico. But where Rome tied its empire together through conquest and brute force, the Anasazi realm was woven together by delicate threads of trade, spiritual association, and cultural community.

Chaco began to flower around A.D. 900. Trade goods from the Pacific coast, tropical Mexico, and the Great Plains flowed into its canyon center. Messengers sped outward on a prehistoric road network while artists and craftspeople created beautiful pottery, turquoise jewelry, and weavings. Farmers built intricate irrigation systems, and villages of finely shaped stone with astronomical observatories and sunken ceremonial chambers emerged out of the wilderness. Complex social, political, religious, and administrative systems were devised to hold it all together. Then, almost overnight, around 1200, the center collapsed and its people dispersed, leaving behind palpable echoes of their once-grand culture.

Chaco remains off the main tourist track, despite the accessibility of its ruins once you're there. Visitors can drive up to half of its 13 primary ruins or step out on short trails that wind through the multi-storied pueblos and earthbound kivas. Or you can enjoy solitude, unexcavated ruins, and the sound of low wind, which seems almost ever-present here, on isolated backcountry trails (see Fitness and Recreation, below).

Your one-way gravel loop road drive on the valley floor should begin with a stop at the visitors center to lay the groundwork for understanding the Anasazi and the specifics of Chaco. Here you can arrange tours guided by rangers (May through September) or pick up self-guiding brochures.

Don't miss **Casa Rinconada**, which harbors Chaco's largest kiva. You can imagine what it must have felt like when it was roofed and you

© John MacLean Photography

Chaco Culture National Historic Park

had to crawl through an entrance tunnel to emerge through a hole in its floor during a ceremony. Flickering firelight would have illuminated singers and drummers, the air scented with incense. At sunset, as the canyon walls turn a golden red, mule deer wander down from the higher slopes, and coyotes announce their presence with eerie calls. Perhaps the people will return tonight.

Details: From the south on I-40, exit at Thoreau (29 miles west of Grants and 33 miles east of Gallup) onto NM 371. About 5 miles north of Crownpoint, turn east (right) onto Navajo Rd. 9 and proceed 13.5 miles to Seven Lakes. Turn north (left) onto NM 57, a washboard dirt road, which runs 20 miles directly into Chaco. From the north, approach on NM 44. Just west of mile marker 112, exit onto the new entrance road, CR 1700. The old road from Nageezi is now closed, despite what your map may indicate. The road heads southwest. Its first portion is paved, but the last 16 miles are washboard dirt roads that are occasionally graded. They have no steep sections and are passable for RVs and ordinary cars in most conditions.

Open year-round; best time to visit is fall. Campground available but no food or lodging. Visitors center, 505/786-7014, open summer 8–6, otherwise 8–5. $4 per vehicle. (3 hours minimum on-site)

★★ **El Malpais National Monument and Conservation Area**—A little more than 1,000 years ago, rivers of molten rock coursed across this landscape in what must have been a fantastic display of volcanic fury. Altogether within the monument's 377,000 acres a mixture of wilderness conservation and national parklands set aside for protection in 1987 are the remnants of 30 volcanoes, 80 vents, sinkholes, lava trenches, older lava flows, land "islands" harboring rare fauna, numerous spatter cones, a 17-mile-long lava tube, and ice caves. Around the edges of the lava flows, which the Spanish explorers labeled *malpais*, or "badlands," are sandstone ridges and cliffs, including New Mexico's most accessible natural arch, petroglyphs, ruins, and the cabins of latter-day homesteaders.

On the east side of the monument, NM 117 passes **Sandstone Bluffs Overlook** about 11 miles south of I-40, where a picnic area offers outstanding views of the lava field. A few miles south on NM 117 is the trailhead for the **Zuni Acoma Trail**, which runs 7.5 miles (one way) across four major lava flows to another paved road, NM 53, on the west side of the monument. Some 17 miles south of I-40 off NM 117 is **La Ventana Arch**, reached via a short hike from the road.

Details: Access from either NM 117 or NM 53 south of Grants. Grants' visitors center, 620 E. Santa Fe Ave.; 505/285-4641; open daily summer 8–5, rest of year 8–4:30. Ranger information center about 10 miles south of I-40 on NM 117; open daily 8:30–5. Backcountry camping allowed with free permit. Monument open year-round. Free. (2–4 hours)

★★ **El Morro National Monument**—Call it America's first scratch pad or the original graffiti corner. For centuries this prominent landmark, with a permanent water source along a natural travel corridor, has served as a type of rock blackboard for people passing by. Some 700 years ago, Indians recorded their journeys and occupation on the mesa top above. The oldest non-Indian marks were left by Don Juan de Oñate, who wrote *paso por aqui*—"passed by here"—in 1605. In 1857 a U.S. Army contingent using camels as pack animals tromped through, leaving some beautiful carved inscriptions. Such work led to the bluff's first name, "Inscription Rock."

Don't, however, try to add *your* name to the rock. In 1906 it became the nation's first national monument and defacing it is a crime. A visitors center provides information on the monument and other associated points of interest. A half-mile asphalt loop trail leads to the inscriptions. If you have an extra hour or two, continue on this trail another 1.5 miles (round-trip) as it turns to dirt and climbs to the top of the 200-foot-high mesa, where you'll find a beautiful landscape of yellow sandstone dotted with junipers, ponderosa pine, and the thirteenth-century ruin of **Atsinna**, once an outlying village of Zuni Pueblo.

Details: Along NM 53, 43 miles southwest of Grants; 505/783-4226. Open summer 8–8, rest of year 8–5. $3 per vehicle. (1–3 hours)

★★ **Gallup**—This town of 22,000 is an interesting place to poke around. It is the focus of the area's vast Indian arts and crafts industry, with an estimated 45,000 people employed at least part time in some facet of this trade. Its pawn shops are renowned for hiding terrific, often old and valuable, jewelry and other goods. (They are carefully regulated, by the way, by federal and state laws.) **Richardsons Trading Co.**, 222 W. Rt. 66, is a notable establishment, with its hardwood floors and pressed-tin ceilings. It's been wheeling and dealing since 1938 and has more than 1,100 saddles in pawn. While not a pawn shop, **City Electric Shoe Shop**, Third and Coal, makes for a great visit: It has almost anything in leather you can think of (except halter tops; visit New York City for those).

Launched as a railroad boom town in 1881 and later a prime stop on fabled **Route 66**, which runs through its heart, Gallup has many fine old brick and stone buildings that echo its history as a travel corridor. Visit the 1922 Mission Pueblo Revival–style **Santa Fe Railroad Depot**, 201 E. Rt. 66, 800/242-4282, today the city's visitors center, where free nightly Indian dances are held in summer.

Gallup also served as home base to many major Hollywood films, including *The Great Divide* (1915), *Red Skin* (with Richard Dix, 1928), *Pursued* (with Robert Mitchum, 1946), *The Bad Man* (with Ronald Reagan), *Sea of Grass* (with Hepburn and Tracy), *Streets of Loredo* (with William Holden), *Rocky Mountain* (with Errol Flynn and Slim Pickens), and *Natural Born Killers* (directed by Oliver Stone, 1993). A great deal of the area's film history can be seen today in the many photos found in the **El Rancho Hotel**, 1000 E. Rt. 66. It was opened in 1937 by the brother of legendary director D. W. Griffith and served as the center of film life in Gallup.

One of the oldest, biggest, and friendliest Indian cultural festivals in the nation, the **Intertribal Indian Ceremonial** is held annually during the second week of August in and around Gallup.

Details: 138 miles west of Albuquerque on I-40; 800/242-4282. (1–4 hours)

★★ **Zuni Pueblo**—Zuni has played a central role in New Mexico's long history. Its current primary village may be only 300 years old, but outlying ruins such as **Hawikuh** and **Taaiyalone** include pit houses dating to A.D. 700. Zuni was the first population center encountered in 1540 on the first Spanish exploration of New Mexico, led by Francisco Coronado. Hoping to find one of the "Seven Cities of Gold," after fighting his way in he discovered instead a basically poor adobe village whose mud walls often glowed a golden hue at sunset.

Today Zuni has the largest population and land base of New Mexico's 19 pueblos. While its residents share many cultural and religious traits with other Pueblo people, it has a completely unique language. Zunis are master jewelers, working with tiny inlaid stones in a style known as needlepoint and petit point. They are also the only New Mexico Pueblo group to produce significant numbers of kachina figures (carved wooden deities), weavings, and tiny carved animal figures called fetishes. These arts can be purchased from many authentic shops on the reservation, the **Zuni Craftsmen Cooperative** on NM 53, or the artists themselves.

Also of note at Zuni is its Spanish mission church, **Our Lady of Guadalupe**, 505/782-4477. On its inner walls is a series of beautiful,

large murals originally painted between 1175 and 1780. They depict
views of the nearby mesas; the four seasons; and figures of mudheads,
Rain Dancers, Father of the Kivas, and the fantastic giant birdlike figure of Shalako, as well as Catholic saints. It is as remarkable a melding
of faiths as you'll find anywhere in the world. The church is open
erratically on weekdays and for Sunday Mass at 10 a.m.

   *Details: Zuni village is 34 miles south of Gallup on NM 53, just west of
its intersection with NM 602. Open year-round, but central plaza may be closed
during occasional ceremonies. For additional information, contact Pueblo of
Zuni, P.O. Box 339, Zuni, NM 87327; 505/782-4481. (1–3 hours)*

★ **Bisti Badlands Wilderness Area**—If you like weird, even
unearthly, desert landscapes, you'll love this place. While at first glance
it seems desolate, if you get out and walk among its wind- and water-
carved earthen formations, small mesas, buttes, hoodoos, mushrooms,
spires, and caps, you may find it fascinating . . . or still simply desolate!

   *Details: 64 miles north of I-40 off NM 371, north of Crownpoint
and south of Farmington. Administered by the BLM in Farmington;
505/599-8900. Open daily year-round. Free. (2–4 hours on site)*

★ **Laguna Pueblo**—This large reservation along I-40 between Grants
and Albuquerque has at least six different villages, but visitors are
generally most interested in Old Laguna, which sits just off the interstate. Most noticeable is the graceful, whitewashed **San Jose de
Laguna Mission Church**, built in 1705 atop a small hill, with an altar
and decorations made by Laguna artisans.

   *Details: Old Laguna is 34 miles east of Grants and 46 miles west of
Albuquerque. Take I-40 Exit 108; 505/552-6654 or 505/243-7616. (1 hour)*

★ **Red Rocks State Park**—This park six miles east of Gallup is the
site of the annual August Intertribal Indian Ceremonial. It also has a
museum of local Indian arts and crafts, and prehistoric Indian artifacts,
plus a gift shop and trading post. Located at the foot of a red-rock
mesa carved into wonderful spires and domes, it offers short trails that
wind back into these formations.

   *Details: Head east out of Gallup on I-40 or Route 66, then north on
NM 566; 505/722-3829. Museum open weekdays 8:30–4:40, with extended
summer hours. (1 hour)*

★ **Route 66**—Several long sections of the original Route 66, the

fabled road of Western adventure and escape, parallel I-40 in western
New Mexico. Crumbling souvenir shops, gas stations, motels, and
towns that modern life blew by lie along its sides, paint peeling, plaster
cracking, signs fading. If you like this sort of thing, you'll be in nostal-
gia nirvana.

Details: *The old roadway begins in the west, just over the Arizona line,
and loops back and forth under I-40, occasionally ending and then resuming
before finally heading past Laguna Pueblo and onto Los Lunas. You can cruise
it all, or short sections, hopping on and off I-40. (3 hours–full day)*

FITNESS AND RECREATION

West-central New Mexico is a land of great physical contrasts, with
opportunities for many diverse outdoor activities.

While most visitors to **Chaco Canyon** stay close to their cars and
the major ruins on the main valley floor, backcountry trails allow you
to experience Chaco as it used to be: silent, touched with a supreme
sense of antiquity and isolation. **Pueblo Alto Trail**, **South Mesa Trail**
(perhaps the most visually striking and isolated of the trails), and
Peñasco Blanco Trail climb out of the canyon, providing awesome
views of the imposing canyon ramparts on all sides as well as expansive
views of the surrounding San Juan Basin and region. From on high, the
vast distances that meet the eye and the forbidding character of the
larger landscape make the Chaco phenomenon all the more impressive.
Wijiji Trail is the park's only backcountry trail open to mountain biking. Hikes can range from a few hours to a full day. Because of the
archaeological ruins, backcountry camping is not allowed at Chaco,
and a backcountry permit (obtain at visitors center) is required even for
day hikes.

Mountain biking is allowed at **El Malpais Monument**, on the
rough roads in the Cerritos de Jaspe area, reached via a primitive
road off NM 53. Biking is also allowed on primitive roads in the
Chain of Craters wilderness study area and in Brazos Canyon. The
monument also has both short and long hiking trails (see Sightseeing
Highlights, above). At the **Bisti Wilderness Area**, hiking is obvi-
ously *the* thing to do.

The **Zuni Mountains**, south of I-40 between Gallup and Grants,
offer stream and lake fishing, as well as water skiing at **Blue Lake**.
The latter, at I-40 Exit 63, then six miles south on NM 412,
505/876-2391, has a 2,350-acre lake, marina, boat rentals, grocery

store, and campground; day use fee is three dollars. Trout-fish at
Zuni Pueblo at **Nutria Lakes**. Call **Zuni Fish and Wildlife**,
505/782-5851, for details.

Just north of Grants, 11,301-foot **Mount Taylor** offers cool
forests for hiking and hunting, and winter cross-country skiing. It is
also the site of the annual **Mount Taylor Quadrathon**, held the second week of February, which combines cycling, running, Nordic skiing, and snowshoeing.

FOOD

Don't look for fine dining, but decent, modestly priced options
abound. In Gallup, one of the fancier places is the dining room of **El
Rancho**, 1000 E. Rt. 66, 505/863-9311. **Panz Alegra**, 1201 E. Rt. 66,
505/722-7229, has somewhat pricey New Mexico food and some
American standards, but it's a popular place, crowded even on weekends. **Earl's**, 1400 E. Rt. 66, 505/863-4201, serves some tasty dishes,
such as green-chile enchiladas. The **Eagle Café**, 200 W. Rt. 66,
505/722-3220, has been serving travelers since 1917, with almost the
exact same interior, owners, and simple but good food. For something
different, try the mutton stew, frybread, and other Indian food at
Shush Yaz Trading Post, 214 W. Aztec; closed Sunday. **Vergie's**,
2720 W. Rt. 66, 505/863-5152, offers fine Mexican food, as well as
steaks, a full bar, and some classic neon outside.

In Grants, I like the atmosphere and food at **La Ventana**, 110½
Geis, 505/287-9393, with worthy New Mexican fare, as well as prime
rib, steak, a fish dish, and salads. It's closed Sunday. A major meal runs
about $15. Cheaper is the locally popular **Grants Station**, 200 W. Santa
Fe. Ave., 505/287-2334, serving American and New Mexican food.

At Acoma Pueblo you can eat in the **Sky City Visitor Center**
restaurant, which has a few Indian-style meals, burgers, and other simple fare. Zuni has a few cafés right on NM 53 in the village center. In
Ramah is the **Blue Corn Restaurant**, NM 53, with excellent New
Mexican food and daily specials. It's open Wednesday through Sunday
for lunch and dinner.

LODGING

The most colorful lodging in Gallup by far is **El Rancho**, 1000 E. Rt.
66, 505/863-9311 or 800/543-6351, built in 1937 by the brother of

GALLUP

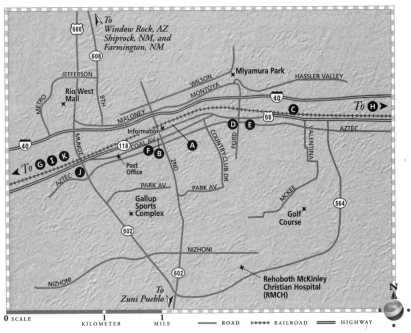

Sights

Ⓐ Santa Fe Railroad Depot

Food

Ⓑ Eagle Café

Ⓒ Earl's

Ⓓ El Rancho

Ⓔ Panz Alegra

Ⓕ Shush Yaz Trading Post

Ⓖ Vergie's

Lodging

Ⓗ Blue Spruce Lodge

Ⓓ El Rancho

Ⓘ Holiday Inn

Ⓙ Motel 6

Camping

Ⓚ KOA

film director D. W. Griffith. The base of operations for many movies shot nearby, it hosted such guests as Humphrey Bogart, Carole Lombard, Clark Gable, Gene Kelly, William Holden, Joan Crawford, Kirk Douglas, and Jean Harlow. Though it fell on hard times, it is now on the rebound. Rates from $32 to $39 include a summer pool, gift shop, restaurant, and the 49er Lounge, which hosts live music on weekends.

Gallup has motel rows on both the east and west entrances to town, where one can find accommodations ranging from upscale chains properties ($75 and up), such as the **Holiday Inn**, 2915 W. Rt. 66, 505/722-2201 or 800/432-2211; to modest ($40) **Motel 6**, 3306 W. Rt. 66, 505/863-4492; and cheap ($25 to $35) **Blue Spruce Lodge**, 1119 East U.S. 66, 505/863-6861.

Grants has more than a dozen motels, including **Econo Lodge**, 1509 E. Santa Fe Ave., 505/287-4426 or 800/434-4777 ($50 rates include a pool), and one of the cheapest joints in the region (under $20), the **Wayside**, 903 E. Santa Fe Ave., 505/287-4268. Perhaps the nicest is the **Best Western Grants Inn**, 1501 E. Santa Fe Ave., 505/287-7901, with indoor pool, hot tub, sauna, game room, room service, and coin and valet laundry, for $70 to $85.

The few B&B choices in the area include **Stauder's Navajo Lodge**, 505/862-7553, 20 miles from Gallup in Coolidge off Exit 44, and **Navajo Lodge**, off I-40 near the Continental Divide, 505/862-7553, providing two cottages with kitchens, living rooms, and bathrooms for $78. The **Vogt Ranch**, one mile west of Ramah, 505/783-4362, was built in 1915 from Anasazi-ruin rocks. It offers two rooms with private baths, for $75 from mid-March through December. Another option is the **Zuni Mt. Lodge** in Thoreau, 505/862-7769.

CAMPING

At Chaco Canyon is the **Gallo Campground**, 505/786-7014, with 68 sites, restrooms, and drinking water (no showers) for eight dollars. Tucked up against the walls of a sandstone cove, this pretty spot is the only camping for more than 60 miles; it's usually full in by early afternoon. It operates on a first-come, first-served basis year-round. **El Morro National Monument** has a nine-site campground that also operates on a first-come, first-served basis. One mile west on NM 53 is **El Morro RV Park**, charging $15 for full hookups, $8 without.

Gallup has several commercial options, including the **KOA**, 2925

W. Rt. 66, 505/863-5021, with $22 RV sites with hookups, laundry, swimming pool, playground, and grocery store; it's open April to mid-October. **Red Rock State Park**, 505/722-3839, six miles from town, is open year-round, with 100 sites, showers, laundry, grocery store, and horse rentals; it charges $12 for hookups, $8 for tents. Grants' **Cibola Sands RV Park**, on NM 53 a half-mile south of I-40 off Exit 81, has store, showers, laundry, and 54 sites at $10 for tents and $14 for RV hookups.

Outside of Grants is the **Lobo Canyon Campground**, 8 miles northeast on Lobo Canyon Road, then 1.5 miles east on unpaved Forest Road 193, with pit toilets. Two miles further up Lobo Canyon is the shady **Coal Mine Campground**, providing drinking water and restrooms. Both facilities are free and open mid-May to late October. **Blue Water Lake State Park** has a campground with laundry and showers; tent sites are $8 and RV hookups, $12. Free dispersed camping and developed campgrounds exist on **Mount Taylor** and in the **Zuni Mountains**, in the Cibola National Forest; call 505/287-8833 for details.

16

NORTHWEST CORNER

Northwestern New Mexico is a fascinating intersection of geography and people. It's the transition zone from the Rio Grande Valley/Southern Rocky Mountains to the great Colorado Plateau that dominates southwestern Colorado, northern Arizona, and southern Utah. The region is also the eastern edge of the immense Navajo reservation and the homeland of the Jicarilla Apache. Most tourists range up and down the Rio Grande Valley from Albuquerque to Taos, leaving the state's northwest corner relatively unexplored. Though it lacks luxury tourist amenities, the northwest compensates with stunning vistas, outstanding outdoor recreation opportunities, and interesting cultural and historical sites.

Train buffs enjoy the steam-powered Cumbres & Toltec Railroad and wandering around the historic railroad district in Chama. If you like Victorian-era architecture, you'll find the downtown core of Aztec entrancing; if Indian Ruins are your thing, you'll be delighted by the majestic Aztec Ruins National Monument.

With high mountains and the immense Navajo Lake, the area also offers ample opportunities for cross-country skiing, hiking, hunting, fishing, and other outdoor sports; the area boasts the state's largest concentration of snowmobiles. And when the late afternoon sun lights up the soaring walls of Shiprock and casts a great shadow across the dry San Juan Basin, one can envision the jagged rock taking flight once again, true to its Navajo name, Tse Bi Dahi, or Rock with Wings.

NORTHWEST NEW MEXICO

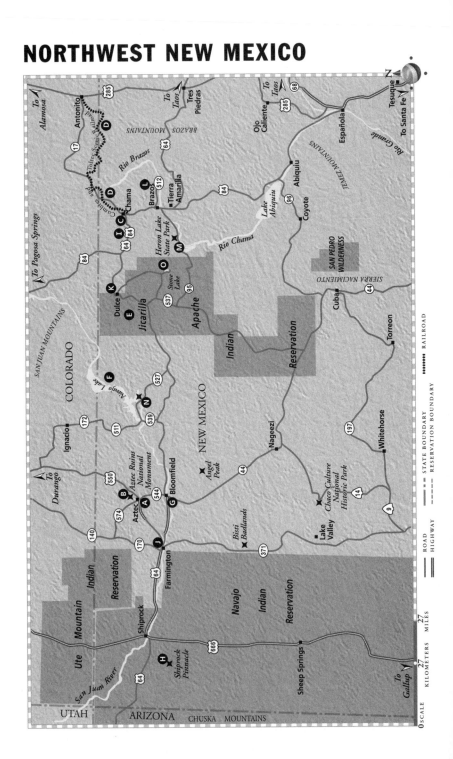

Sights

Ⓐ Aztec

Ⓑ Aztec Ruins National Monument

Ⓒ Chama

Ⓓ Cumbres & Toltec Railroad

Ⓔ Jicarilla Apache Reservation

Ⓕ Navajo Lake

Ⓖ Salmon Ruins

Ⓗ Shiprock

Ⓘ W. A. Humphries State Wildlife Area

Food

Ⓐ Aztec Restaurant

Ⓙ Dad's Diner

Ⓒ Elkhorn Café

Ⓐ Frank's

Ⓐ Hiway Grill

Ⓚ Jicarilla Inn

Ⓙ Three Rivers Eatery & Brewhouse

Ⓒ Viva Vera's Mexican Kitchen

Lodging

Ⓚ Best Western Jicarilla Inn

Ⓙ Bruce Black's Kokopelli Cave

Ⓛ Corkin's Lodge

Ⓒ Elkhorn Lodge

Ⓐ Enchantment Lodge

Ⓒ Foster Hotel

Ⓒ Gandy Dancer B&B

Ⓒ Jones House

Ⓒ Lodge at Chama

Ⓐ Miss Gail's Inn

Ⓐ Step Back Inn

Camping

Ⓐ Aztec Ruins Road RV Park

Ⓜ Heron Lake State Park

Ⓝ Navajo State Park

Ⓒ Rio Chama RV Campground

Ⓐ Riverside Park

Ⓞ Stone Lake

Note: Items with the same letter are located in the same town or area.

A PERFECT DAY IN NORTHWESTERN NEW MEXICO

In this sprawling area, there is no way to take in all the sights in one day. In the Chama region, spend an entire day on the steam-fired railroad or split the time between visiting town and Dulce, the capital of the Jicarilla tribe. Enjoy a day at Navajo Lake or spend the day at Aztec Ruins National Monument and the town of Aztec.

SIGHTSEEING HIGHLIGHTS

★★★ **Aztec Ruins National Monument**—This national park unit provides a rare chance to enter an authentic great kiva, the round, sunken ceremonial chamber of the Anasazi and Pueblo peoples. Almost all Anasazi kiva roofs have long since collapsed, turning them into windswept dirt holes. But in this reconstructed kiva, massive roof beams protect the interior from the elements, providing an inkling of the true kiva experience.

A 400-yard-long trail winds through the surface ruins, which take their name from the early mistaken belief that the site was associated with the great Mexican Indian culture. The pueblo reached its zenith in the twelfth through fourteenth centuries. On Christmas Eve the ruin is decked out in thousands of *farolitos*, brown paper bags filled with sand and illuminated by votive candles. On the grounds are a good visitors center, with displays and interpretive exhibitions, and a picnic ground.

Details: 1.5 miles north of the town of Aztec off NM 550; 505/334-6174. Open daily Memorial Day–Labor Day 8–6; otherwise daily 8–5; closed Christmas–New Year's Day. $1 adults, 50¢ for kids under 16. (2 hours)

★★★ **Cumbres & Toltec Railroad**—Only a handful of coal-fired, steam-powered trains still run in the United States; this is one of the finer ones. The ride traverses a 64-mile route of tunnels, trestles, and great beauty—particularly in the fall, when the high mountain peaks and valleys shimmer in a golden suit of quaking aspen trees. It is the longest and highest (reaching an altitude of 10,015 feet) narrow-gauge rail line in the nation. The train runs day trips in both directions between Chama, New Mexico, and Antonito, Colorado, or can be taken to the midday stop at Osier and back. A snack bar is on board, and lunch can be had at Osier.

Details: 505/756-2151, 719/376-5483, or 888/286-2737. Trains leave both depots daily May–mid-October at 10 a.m. $32 adults, $16 children under 12 for midpoint turnaround excursions; $50 adults, $26 children for full-length trip and bus shuttle. (1 day)

★★★ **Jicarilla Apache Reservation**—The Jicarillas were once a nomadic people of two principal bands—the Hoyero, or "mountain people," and the Ollero, or "plains people." They roamed far and wide across northern New Mexico, southern Colorado, and onto the Great Plains but were restricted to this 742,000-acre central reservation in

1887. Recently they have purchased several major outlying ranches and have derived income from oil and gas wells.

Their lands straddle the Continental Divide and run from dry plains to lush mountains and thick pine forests crisscrossed by streams. Thus it's a popular place for hunters, who have taken many trophy mule deer here. Anglers enjoy perhaps the best trout-lake fishing in the state at **Stone Lake**, as well as **La Jara**, **Mundo**, and **Horse**, while birders head to **Stinking Lake** for waterfowl. Its principal trade and population center is the tribal capital of **Dulce** ("sweet" in Spanish). Tribal members and visitors gather for tribal dances, foot races, a rodeo, and other events during the the annual mid-September **Go-Jii-Ya Feast Day**. The reservation's other major public event is the July **Little Beaver Roundup**. The reservation also has a small, full-spectrum casino, the **Apache Nugget**, 800/294-2234.

Details: Main reservation on U.S. 64 some 35 miles west of Chama. For information on hunting, fishing, camping, or cross-country skiing, call 505/759-3255. For general tourism information, call 505/759-3442. Open year-round. Free. (30 minutes minimum)

✦✦ **Aztec**—This town of 7,000 has done a nice job of preserving its Victorian-era downtown ambiance, and for people who enjoy historic architecture it's a great stop. Aztec also provides convenient access to many of the area's attractions. Also in town is the **Aztec Museum and Pioneer Village**, with excellent Indian and pioneer exhibits, as well as a frontier village with a blacksmith shop, bank, old jail, and other buildings.

Details: 125 Main St.; 505/334-9829. Open May–Labor Day Mon–Sat 9–5, Sunday 1–4; rest of year Mon–Sat 10–4. $1. For additional information on Aztec, call the chamber of commerce, 505/334-9551. (1 hour)

✦✦ **Chama**—Tucked under the Colorado border and beneath one arm of the mighty San Juan Mountains and the Brazos Mountains, Chama is the greenest and wettest locale in New Mexico, receiving substantial winter and spring snows and summer thundershowers; thus it's a great place for outdoor sporting enthusiasts. Besides its outdoor attractions, a block-long section of Chama's old railroad district and the rail depot are still largely intact. Even if you don't ride the train, a half-hour walk around the railyards will make you feel as if you've stepped into a time warp.

Details: Visit the New Mexico Welcome Center, at the intersection of NM 17 and U.S. 84/64; or the chamber of commerce, 499 Main St.; 505/756-2306 or 800/477-0149. (1–2 hours)

Brazos Mountains near Chama

★★ **Navajo Lake**—My pick for the state's most scenic lake, the state's second-largest reservoir backs up many miles into slickrock canyons and around majestic buttes—New Mexico's mini-version of Lake Powell. The lake holds trout, bass, crappie, catfish, and northern pike, and below the dam are the state's world-famous fly-fishing waters of the San Juan River. Located near the dam are Navajo Lake State Park and three developed recreation areas: Pine, San Juan, and Sims Mesa. Motorboat and houseboat rentals are available.

  Details: About 25 miles east of Aztec on the N.M./Colo. border. State park visitors center is at the Pine facility, 505/632-2278. Open year-round. $3 day use. For details on fishing the San Juan River, call 505/632-1770, or the N.M. Dept. of Game and Fish, 505/827-7911. (1 hour minimum)

★ **Salmon Ruins**—This privately owned archaeological site preserves a relatively small Anasazi settlement on the bank of the San Juan River, birthplace of the Anasazi culture. It includes a museum and the **San Juan Archeological Research Center and Library**.

  Details: 2 miles west of Bloomfield, just off U.S. 64; 505/632-2013. Open daily. $1 adults, 50¢ kids. (2 hours)

✯ **Shiprock**—The Navajos call this jagged spire Tse Bi Dahi, Rock with Wings, and it does look like a shattered bird wing rising from the desert floor. This 2,000-foot peak is the remnant core of a volcano; the covering soil has eroded away. It's a prominent Four Corners area landmark. On Navajo land, it is off-limits to climbers today.

Details: Southwest of the town of Shiprock. For a closer view, head south on U.S. 666 some 6 miles to the Red Valley Rd. and turn west (right). Rough dirt roads lead to the formation. (1–3 hours)

✯ **W.A. Humphries State Wildlife Area**—Here's a convenient place to spot some of the abundant wildlife in the region. Some 9,000 acres right on the **Continental Divide** protect elk, bear, cougar, a great variety of birds, and other critters in a setting of beautiful meadows carpeted with flowers and grasses.

Details: 9 miles west of Chama along U.S. 64. Access via either a poorly marked dirt road on the right or just down the main highway on the left (parking lot in front) through the small gate next to the locked vehicle gate; 505/756-2585 or 505/841-8881. Closed periodically. Free. (1 hour–multiple days)

FITNESS AND RECREATION

There are ample chances for a broad range of outdoor activities in the Chama area. There's great trout fishing in the **Rio Brazos** and the **Rio Chama** (which flows right through town), and in many creeks, as well as at the lovely, 6,000-acre **Lake Heron**, 505/588-7470, 23 miles south of town off NM 95. The latter is also popular for sailing. Close to Bloomfield are the world-famous trout waters of the **San Juan River**. The tailwaters of San Juan Dam regularly produce rainbows and occasional Snake River cutthroats averaging 14 to 20 inches, year round. A renowned guide service for the river is **Abe's Motel & Fly Shop**, 505/632-2194.

This area is the snowmobile capital of northern New Mexico—you may run into the auto-racing Unser family on a trail—and its premier cross-country skiing spot. Quite popular is the **Community Trail**, 12.5 miles north of town on NM/CO 17. **Southwest Nordic**, 505/758-4761, runs a series of hut-to-hut yurts (with guided and unguided day to multi-day trips), off Highway 17 on **Cumbres Pass**, where the town also maintains a free trail. The same mountains also boast excellent summer hiking. You can rent horses in Chama at

Western Outdoor Adventures, 800/288-1386, or **Reed Hollo Enterprises**, 505/756-2685.

The **Jicarilla reservation** and **Navajo Lake** also present great outdoor sports opportunities, including hunting, fishing, boating and water skiing (see Sightseeing Highlights, above).

FOOD

My first visit to Chama's **Elkhorn Café** , 505/756-2229, 2663 S. U.S. 84/64, was more than 30 years ago as a kid, when my family dropped in after we bailed out of a soggy, muddy camping trip. The waitress said, "Hon, you look like a wet dog. What do you want to eat?" The food is always satisfying, from burgers to New Mexican plates, and they still call patrons "hon." Another inexpensive in-town option is **Viva Vera's Mexican Kitchen**, 2209 S. U.S. 84/64, 505/756-2557, dishing up New Mexican and American food daily for breakfast, lunch, and dinner.

In Aztec, point yer feet toward the **Aztec Restaurant** for some very reasonably priced and decent New Mexican and American fare. Likewise, **Frank's**, 116 S. Main Ave., 505/334-3882, is easy on the pocketbook, with breakfast for $3 or so. Another choice here is the **Hiway Grill**, with its roadster motif and simple but good grub. In Dulce, on the Jicarilla reservation, the **Jicarilla Inn**'s good dining room and bar serve mid-priced American fare.

Farmington has a recently built but old-styled diner of the Starlite Company, **Dad's Diner**, 4395 Largo, 505/564-2516, with good food. Another option here is **Three Rivers Eatery & Brewhouse**, 101 E. Main, a microbrewery located in a National Historic Register building, with daily lunch specials, sandwiches, salads, and soups.

LODGING

For outdoors lovers with deep pockets, a prime destination for the entire northern half of New Mexico is the **Lodge at Chama**, 505/756-2133. Encompassing 32,000 acres of mountain forests, valleys, rivers, and lakes, it offers premium hunting and fishing year-round. The cost is about $300 per person, including all meals.

Down a major notch in cost but still pricey is another sports-oriented retreat near Chama, **Corkin's Lodge**, 505/588-7261 or

800/548-7680. It features private fishing in the dependable and rugged Brazos River Canyon, some ponds for kids, and a small pool, at $110 for a two-person cabin. Deer wander through. The **Elkhorn Lodge**, on the south edge of town on U.S. 84, 505/756-2105 or 800/532-8874, has doubles for $45 and rooms with kitchenettes for $50 to $70.

Chama also has some nice B&Bs. The **Jones House**, 311 Terrace at Third, 505/756-2908, is a unique Tudor-style adobe built circa 1927 by the town's first banker. You can spot the steam train chugging past from the yard. Rates are $25 to $50. Also in Chama is the **Gandy Dancer B&B**, 505/756-2191, which is set in an antiques-filled Victorian home; each room has a private bath, with rates of $25 to $50.

Bruce Black's Kokopelli Cave, outside Farmington, 505/ or 800/448-1240, is one of the state's odder and most spectacular accommodations. The 1,650-square-foot residence was carved out of 65-million-year-old Ajo Alamo sandstone on the face of a 300-foot cliff overlooking the La Plata River valley. Two-night minimum stays begin at $110.

The brave might try a night at Chama's **Foster Hotel**, opposite the train depot, 505/756-2296, which was grand at its 1881 opening but has seen little change since. Rates are under $25. On the Jicarilla reservation, there's the **Best Western Jicarilla Inn**, on U.S. 64, 505/759-3663 or 800/742-1938, with the Hillcrest Restaurant and the Timber Lake Lounge, at $80 per room.

In Aztec, the **Enchantment Lodge**, 1800 W. Aztec Blvd., 505/334-6143, offers 20 clean, modern rooms, a pool, playground, and laundry for $35 to $45. The **Step Back Inn**, 103 W. Aztec, at the corner of NM 550 and NM 44, 505/334-1200 or 800/334-1255, has a Victorian theme and queen-size beds. Rates are $54 to $68. There's also the 1907 brick **Miss Gail's Inn**, 330 S. Main St., 505/224-3452, a B&B with ten rooms with private baths at $58 per night.

CAMPING

In the Chama area, **Heron Lake State Park**, 23 miles south of Chama via U.S. 64 and NM 95, 505/588-7470, provides sites (some with partial RV hookups) on the shore of this beautiful lake, along with bathrooms and drinking water. At the north end of town, the **Rio Chama RV Campground**, a quarter-mile north of the train depot on NM 17, 505/756-2303, provides tent sites for $8.50 and RV sites with hookups for $14, May through September.

On the **Jicarilla reservation**, there is a tribal campground at
Stone Lake, 505/759-3442, with sites for four dollars; no RV hookups.
Navajo State Park, 505/632-2278, offers the **Sims Mesa, San Juan
River**, and **Pine** units, some with RV hookups. Sims is the least accessible and least crowded. The **Aztec Ruins Road RV Park**, 312 Ruins
Rd., 505/334-3160, has 30 sites at $10 with hookup, $6 without. Pretty
Riverside Park, just west of the center of Aztec on South Light Plant
Road, 505/334-9456, on the shore of the Animas River, has hookups,
picnic tables, and water.

APPENDIX

CALENDAR OF EVENTS

January

Pueblo Indian Dances—Dances held at many pueblos, including Cochiti, Laguna, Picuris, San Ildefonso, Santa Ana, Santo Domingo. (January 1)

Three Kings Day—Dances held at many pueblos, including Cochiti, Laguna, Picuris, Nambe, Sandia, San Felipe, San Ildefonso, San Juan, Santa Clara, Santa Ana, Santo Domingo, Taos, and Zia. (January 3)

February

Chile Classic—Cross-country ski and snowmobile races in Chama. (Early to mid-February)

Mt. Taylor Winter Quadrathon—Held in Grants. (mid-month)

Pecan Festival—Held in Cuchillo. (late month)

March

Columbus Raid Commemoration—This events honors soldiers and civilians killed in 1916 Villa Raid; held in Pancho Villa State Park, Columbus. (March 9)

Rockhound Roundup—Held in Rock Hound State Park and Deming. (early month)

Ernie Blake Birthday Celebration—Held in the Taos Ski Valley. (late month)

April

Gila Bird Festival—Held in Silver City. (early month)
Pilgrimage to El Santuario de Chimayó—Penitentes and others walk for miles to Chimayó's church, famed for its "healing earth." (Lenten week)
Pueblo Dances—Held at most pueblos. (Easter Sunday)
Taos Talking Pictures Festival—Held in Taos. (mid-month)
Dinosaur Days—Held in Clayton. (late month)
New Mexico Old-Time Fiddlers Contest—Held in Truth or Consequences. (late month)

May

Cinco de Mayo—Celebrations held in various cities, including Albuquerque, Raton, Belen, Mesilla, Roswell, and Hobbs. (May 5)
Ralph Edwards Fiesta—Held in Truth or Consequences. (first weekend)
Rose Festival—Held in Tularosa. (first weekend)
Mescal Roast and Mountain Spirit Dances—Held in Living Desert State Park, Carlsbad. (mid-month)
Riverfest—Music, fine arts, food, and foot races in Farmington. (late month)
Blues Festival—Held in Silver City. (Memorial Day weekend)

June

National Soaring Championships—Held in Hobbs. (date varies)
Festival Flamenco—Held at various Albuquerque locations. (first two weeks)
Aztec Fiesta Days—Held in Aztec. (first weekend)
Pioneer Days—Held in Clovis. (first weekend)
San Felipe de Neri Fiestas—Held in Old Town Plaza, Albuquerque. (first weekend)
Spring Festival—Held at El Rancho de las Golindrinas, La Cienega. (first weekend)
Old Fort Days—Races, rodeo, arts and crafts, and bluegrass music in Fort Sumner. (mid-month)
Sandia Mountain Classic Hang Gliding Competition—Held at Sandia Peak, Albuquerque. (mid-month)
High Rolls Cherry Festival—Held in High Rolls. (late month)
New Mexico Arts and Crafts Fair—Held at the State Fairgrounds, Albuquerque. (last weekend)

July

Santa Fe Opera—Several traditional operas and one debut opera performed nightly at the newly renovated opera house just north of Santa Fe. (July through mid-August)

Eastern Navajo Fair—Held in Crownpoint. (date varies)

Wings Over Angel Fire—Hot-air balloons, birds of prey, gliders, and ultralights; held in Angel Fire. (date varies)

Independence Day—Fireworks, parades, and other festivities; held in most major towns and cities. (July 4)

Mescalero Apache Maidens' Puberty Rites—Ceremonial dances and rodeo; held at Mescalero Apache reservation. (July 4)

Little Beaver Rodeo and Fair—Held at Jicarilla Apache Reservation, Dulce. (mid-month)

Eight Northern Indian Pueblos Arts and Crafts Fair—Held at San Juan Pueblo. (third weekend)

Ruidoso Art Festival—Music and visual and performing arts; held in Ruidoso. (late month)

Spanish Market—Held in and around the Santa Fe Plaza. (late month)

August

Old Lincoln Days—Held in Lincoln. (first weekend)

Inter-Tribal Indian Ceremonial—Held in Gallup and Red Rocks State Park. (second weekend)

Route 66 Festival and Craft Fair—Held in Tucumcari. (second weekend)

San Juan County Fair—The state's largest county fair; held in Farmington. (mid-month)

Great American Duck Race—Held in Deming. (third weekend)

Indian Market—The world's largest and most prestigious event of its kind; held on and around the Santa Fe Plaza. (third weekend)

September

New Mexico State Fair—Held in Albuquerque. (three-week run)

Apple Festival—Held in Hillsboro. (Labor Day weekend)

Hatch Chile Festival—The state's famed fruit celebrated in Hatch. (Labor Day weekend)

New Mexico Wine Festival—Held in Bernalillo. (Labor Day weekend)

La Fiesta de Santa Fe—Burning of Zozobra, parades, dances and music, special masses, and other events; held on and around the Santa Fe Plaza. (second weekend)

October

Oktoberfest—Celebrations, often combined with aspen tree viewing tours, in various New Mexico locales, including Rio Rancho, Ruidoso, Los Alamos, Angel Fire, Glenwood, Socorro, and Cloudcroft. (dates vary)

Peanut Festival—Held in Portales. (date varies)

Grecian Festival—Held at the St. George Greek Orthodox Church, Albuquerque. (first weekend)

Northern Navajo Fair—Powwow, rodeo, parade, and arts and crafts; held in Shiprock. (first weekend)

Rio Grande Arts and Crafts Festival—Held in Albuquerque. (first weekend)

The Whole Enchilada Festival—Held in Las Cruces. (first weekend)

Harvest Festival—Held at Rancho de las Golindrinas, La Cienega. (first weekend)

Albuquerque International Balloon Fiesta—The world's largest event of its kind; held at Balloon Fiesta Park, Albuquerque. (first through second weekends)

49er Days—Dances, mining events, parades, fiddling contest, and other events; held in Socorro. (mid-month)

November

Festival of the Cranes—Held at Bosque del Apache National Wildlife Refuge. (mid- to late November)

Festival of the Trees—Held in Raton. (late November)

December

Las Posadas—A reenactment of Mary and Joseph's search for lodging in many cities and towns, including Albuquerque, Santa Fe, Santa Cruz, Espanola, Las Cruces, Ranchos de Taos, and Chama. (dates vary)

Christmas Eve—Luminaria and farolito displays in most cities and towns, particularly the Country Club area of Albuquerque, the Canyon Road area of Santa Fe, and the Mesilla plaza. (December 24)

Christmas Day—Ceremonial dances; held at most pueblos, including Cochiti, Zia, Sandia, Santa Ana, Santo Domingo, and Isleta. (December 25)

NEW MEXICO MILEAGE CHART

	Alamogordo	Albuquerque	Carlsbad	Clovis	Farmington	Gallup	Las Cruces	Las Vegas	Raton	Roswell	Santa Fe	Silver City	Socorro	Taos
Albuquerque	207													
Carlsbad	146	275												
Clovis	227	219	178											
Farmington	389	182	457	401										
Gallup	327	138	413	357	122									
Las Cruces	68	223	208	295	405	339								
Las Vegas	239	123	268	168	263	261	307							
Raton	345	224	374	234	309	362	413	106						
Roswell	117	199	76	110	381	337	185	192	298					
Santa Fe	221	59	268	212	199	197	282	64	165	192				
Silver City	180	238	320	407	378	256	112	361	462	297	297			
Socorro	134	77	241	248	259	193	147	200	301	165	136	162		
Taos	291	129	388	246	214	267	352	78	95	262	70	369	207	
Truth or Consequences	137	149	289	370	318	287	75	273	379	260	209	90	72	279

RESOURCES

State Offices and Miscellaneous Resources

Department of Travel & Tourism: 491 Old Santa Fe Trail, Santa Fe, NM 87501-2753; 505/827-7400, 800/733-6396; www.newmexico.org/

Department of Game and Fish: 408 Galisteo St., Santa Fe, NM 87503; 505/827-7911

Office of Cultural Affairs: 505/827-6364; www.nmmnh-abq.mus.nm.us/oca/oca.html

Navajo Tourism Office: P.O. Box 663, Window Rock, AZ 85615; 520/871-6436/6659; www.atiin.com/navajoland

New Mexico B&B Association: P.O. Box 2925, Santa Fe, 87504-2925 (no phone)

New Mexico Indian Tourism Association: 2401 12th St. NW, Albuquerque, 87104; 505/246-1668

New Mexico Public Lands Information Center: 1474 Rodeo Rd., Santa Fe, NM 87501; 505/438-7542.

Santa Fe National Trail: 1220 S. St. Francis Dr., Santa Fe, NM 87505; 505/988-6888

Ski New Mexico (snow report): 505/984-0606; www.skinewmexico.com

State Parks & Recreation Division: 408 Galisteo, Santa Fe, NM 87503; 505/827-7173

State Welcome Centers:
Anthony, on I-10, 505/882-2419
Chama, on U.S. 64/84, 505/756-2235
Gallup, 710-A E. Montoya Blvd., 505/863-4909
Glenrio, on I-40, 505/576-2424
Lordsburg, on I-10, 505/542-8149
Raton, 100 Clayton Rd., 505/445-2716
Santa Fe, 10 miles south of city on I-25, 505/471-5242
Texico, on U.S. 60/70/84, 505/482-3321

City and Town Chamber of Commerces and Visitor's Bureaus

Alamogordo: P.O. Box 518, Alamogordo, NM 88311-0518; 505/437-6120 or 800/545-4121

Albuquerque: 20 First Plaza, Suite 601, P.O. Box 26866, Albuquerque, NM 87102; 505/842-9918 or 800/754-4620; www. abqcvb.org

Angel Fire: P.O. Box 547, Angel Fire, NM 87710; 505/377-6661 or 800/446-8117; www.angelfirenm.com

Carlsbad: 302 S. Canal St., P.O. Box 910, Carlsbad, NM 88220; 505/887-6516 or 800/221-1224; www.caverns.com/~chamber

Chama: P.O. Box 306, Chama, NM 87520; 505/756-2306 or 800/ 477-0149; www.chamavalley.com

Cimarron: 104 N. Lincoln Ave., Cimarron, NM 87714; 505/376-2417 or 800-700-4298

Cloudcroft: P.O. Box 1290, Cloudcroft, NM 88317; 505/682-2733

Deming Luna County: 800 E. Pine, P.O. Box 8, Deming, NM 88031; 505/546-2674 or 800/848-4955

Española Valley: 417 Big Rock Center, Española, NM 87532; 505/753-2831

Farmington: 203 W. Main, Suite 401, Farmington, NM 87401; 505/326-7602 or 800/448-1240; www.farmingtonnm.org

Gallup: 701 Montoya Blvd., P.O. Box 600, Gallup, NM 87305; 505/863-3841 or 800/242-4282; www.gallupnm.org

Las Cruces: 211 N. Water St., Las Cruces, NM 88001; 505/541-2444 or 800/FIESTAS; www.weblifepro.com/lascruces/

Las Vegas/San Miguel County: P.O. Box 128, Las Vegas, NM 87701; 505/425-8631 or 800/832-5947; www.worldplaces.com.las.vegas .new.mexico

Los Alamos: 1715 Iris St., Los Alamos, NM 87544-0460; 505/662-8105 or 800/444-0707; www.vla.com/chamber

Raton: P.O. Box 1211, Raton, NM 87740; 505/445-3689 or 800/ 638-6161; www.raton.com

Red River: P.O. Box 870, Red River, NM 87558; 505/754-2366 or 800/348-6444; www.taoswebb.com.RedRiverInfo

Roswell: 912 N. Main, Roswell, NM 88201; 505/624-6860 or 888/ ROSWELL; www.roswell-online.com/

Ruidoso Valley: P.O. Box 698, Ruidoso, NM 88355; 505/257-7395 or 800/253-2255; www.ruidoso.net

Santa Fe: Sweeney Center, 201 W. Marcy, P.O. Box 909, Santa Fe, NM 87504-0909; 505/984-6760 or 800/777-2489; www.santafe.org

Silver City/Grant County: 1103 N. Hudson St., Silver City, NM 88061; 505/538-3785 or 800/548-9378

Socorro County: P.O. Box 743, Socorro, NM 87801; 505/835-0424; www.socorro-nm.com

Taos County: P.O. Drawer I, Taos, NM 87571; 505/758-3873 or 800/732-8267; www.taoswebb.com/taos/

Truth or Consequences/Sierra County: P.O. Drawer 31, Truth or Consequences, NM 87901; 505/894-3536 or 800/831-9487

INDEX

Map Index

ABOUT THE AUTHOR

Daniel Gibson was born and raised in Albuquerque's North Valley. After sailing across the Pacific and helping to write a book about the experience, he went on to study journalism at the University of New Mexico. He worked for several years as arts editor and general writer for the former *Albuquerque News* before he took a job as a public information officer at the Office of Indian Affairs in Santa Fe for four years. He has since worked as a writer and editor for numerous local, regional, and national publications. For four years he served as an environmental and natural history columnist for the *Santa Fe Reporter*. Gibson has also contributed to several major guidebooks and is the president of PEN New Mexico.